PECULIAR PLACES

PECULIAR PLACES

A QUEER CRIP HISTORY OF
WHITE RURAL NONCONFORMITY

RYAN LEE CARTWRIGHT

The University of Chicago Press
Chicago and London

The University of Chicago Press, Chicago 60637
The University of Chicago Press, Ltd., London
© 2021 by The University of Chicago
Published 2021
Printed in the United States of America

30 29 28 27 26 25 24 23 22 21   1 2 3 4 5

ISBN-13: 978-0-226-69691-1 (cloth)
ISBN-13: 978-0-226-69688-1 (paper)
ISBN-13: 978-0-226-69707-9 (e-book)
DOI: https://doi.org/10.7208/chicago/9780226697079.001.0001

Library of Congress Cataloging-in-Publication Data

Names: Cartwright, Ryan Lee, author.
Title: Peculiar places : a queer crip history of white rural
    nonconformity / Ryan Lee Cartwright.
Other titles: Queer crip history of white rural nonconformity
Description: Chicago ; London : The University of Chicago
    Press, 2021. | Includes bibliographical references and index.
Identifiers: LCCN 2021004006 | ISBN 9780226696911 (cloth) |
    ISBN 9780226696881 (paperback) | ISBN 9780226697079 (e-book)
Subjects: LCSH: Conformity—United States—History—
    20th century. | Country life—United States—Public opinion. |
    Americans—Attitudes. | Deviant behavior—United States. |
    United States—Civilization—20th century.
Classification: LCC GT3471.U6 C37 2021 |
    DDC 307.72097309/04—dc23
LC record available at https://lccn.loc.gov/2021004006

♾ This paper meets the requirements of ANSI/NISO Z39.48-1992
(Permanence of Paper).

And yet, here at the confluence, river and ocean collide—current rushing head long, waves pushing back—stones tumble, logs roll. Tell me: where in this hiss and froth might I lay myself down?

ELI CLARE, *The Marrow's Telling*

CONTENTS

INTRODUCTION

QueerCrip Historical Analysis and the Rural White Anti-Idyll

This story ends with an *X-Files* "monster of the week" episode, but I am telling it differently, focusing your attention on the quotidian details. For many decades, four white brothers shared a humble home, a single bed, and a small but sanitary dairy barn in rural upstate New York. The brothers' lifestyle was atypical and often difficult, but it was not without solace. The men, all bachelors and all disabled in different ways, relied on each other for social, emotional, and physical support, and protected each other from the threat of involuntary institutionalization. The brothers were economically interdependent, working the farm together and sharing resources, like their home and the tractor they rode into town. Although they were ostracized by many of their neighbors, they were supported by old friends, as well as their mixed-race nieces and nephews. They also enjoyed the intimacy and safety of sharing a bed; when given opportunities to sleep alone, the men opted not to, preferring the familiar company of their brothers, even though doing so elicited gossip that they were "a bunch of queer farmers."[1] Nevertheless, they were occasionally irritated by each other—by how much one brother's cough kept them awake at night, or by how much attention was bestowed on another. They were fearful about how others viewed them and resistant to changing their ways. And the main assets to their meager reputation were deeply, if implicitly, racialized: first, a claim to refusing welfare, in an era when that was particularly stigmatized; and second, the humble farm that had been in their family for generations, almost certainly a result of what Laura Barraclough describes as "state-sponsored and state-coordinated redistribution of land to whites."[2] The brothers' lives were shaped by the property that is whiteness, as well as deep poverty and social stigma; they were also shaped by the mundane interdependencies and material practicalities necessary to make a life on the margins.

Yet this is not how the lives of the Ward brothers entered the public imagination—not in local and national media in 1990, not in the acclaimed documentary film *Brother's Keeper* in 1993, nor as one of the inspirations for a notorious 1995 *X-Files* episode called "Home."[3] In 1990, sixty-four-year-old William (Bill) Ward apparently died in his sleep. Local police, wary of the brothers' "very different lifestyle," charged Bill's brother Adelbert (Delbert) with murder and suspected that Delbert's motive was "sex gone bad."[4] The news reports were sensational, describing the brothers as living in "unimaginable squalor," and speculating on the "gay-sex-turned-violent situation" that evoked the idea of "'Deliverance'-north types."[5] Yet a much different but equally fanciful vision of the brothers also circulated in the same media: an idyllic image of the brothers' community as a homogeneous, white farm town, a "quaint portrait of pioneer life."[6] This was evoked through appeals to whiteness—erasing the people of color who lived in the area and shared intimacy with the brothers—and the transition narratives that elided Indigenous histories and presents in order to make it possible to imagine the town of Munnsville as home-immemorial to quaint white farmers.[7] The tale of perversion, degradation, and violence proliferated most widely, but it drew its potency from the convenient foil of the idealized white small town. The *X-Files* episode based on the Ward brothers highlighted the power of these paired narratives—the seemingly perfect community hiding the darkest possible secret—in a story about a family of murderous, incestuous, and grotesquely "deformed" hillbillies. The episode became so notorious that even oblique references to "that one *X-Files* episode" have become shorthand for the "type of people" it alluded to. But in decades past, there have been many other shorthands used to evoke "people like that": the strum of a country banjo, conjured by the 1972 film *Deliverance*, for example, or the idea of a family called "the Kallikaks," named for a 1912 eugenic family study.

Peculiar Places offers a way of thinking about the complicated and contradictory lives of people like the Ward brothers and the social formations they evince. This book examines deeply troublesome narratives in order to understand the ambiguous social circumstances that exist beyond the myths of both virtuous conformity and monstrous otherness. In doing so, I analyze twentieth-century US histories of disability, queerness, economic estrangement, and race—whiteness, interracial sociality, settler colonialism, and racialized hierarchies of migrant labor—that are too often obscured.

These histories teach us about white vernacular ways of discussing social nonconformity, about the gulf between mythologized tales of small-town racial homogeneity and histories of interracial sociality, intimacy, and economic exchange that exist—if uneasily—even in predominantly white towns. Histories of gender and sexuality are buoyed by attending to fraternal intimacy, caring labor, and white masculinity, and how "families of origin" become perceived as strange when family bonds persist for too long or are expressed in the "wrong" ways. Understandings of rural whiteness are deepened by an examination of racial relations in places that, while predominantly white, must be navigated by community members and visitors of color; interracial sociality that is simultaneously intimate and violent, present and disavowed; and the ways that poor white non-land owners perpetuated and participated in settler colonialism. Disability studies, building on crip, queercrip, and crip of color analysis, benefits from examining interdependency between people with differing disabilities; how disabled lives are "enriched, enabled, and made possible," as Jina Kim contends, through mutual aid and social safety nets among people who are socially stigmatized;[8] people who are amorphously disabled, hobbled by common but unnamed maladies; and ways that lifelong poverty is embodied. Simultaneously, disability studies, queer studies, and crip theory may be challenged by stories of intentional "chosen families" that become sites of violence—or by mutual aid and other poor, crip skills that are used not to further interdependent disability justice but to shore up racial hierarchies and white settler claims to Indigenous land.

Peculiar Places uses anti-idyllic science, art, media, and politics as an "imaginative resource" for thinking about the materiality and the often ambiguous "ingenuity of living" that being disabled, poor, sexually nonconforming, and gender transgressive requires in the rural United States.[9] The *anti-idyll* is a name for a long-standing cultural trope and social optic that produces tales of white rural nonconformity—of rural white folks who were considered to live a "very different lifestyle."[10] As I employ it, the anti-idyll does not refer to social nonconformity itself, but to the estranged ways of looking that produce cultural narratives naming poor rural white communities as sites of perverse sexuality, deformed bodies, deranged minds—narratives that simultaneously, if paradoxically, appeal to white racial superiority and violent settler masculinity. In other words, in the case of the Ward brothers, the anti-idyll does not properly describe the men, nor their hometown of Munnsville, New York, nor an entrenched narrative about them. Instead, it names the approaches taken, lenses used, and stories told by the law enforcement officers, distant neighbors, journalists, and cultural producers who arrived at the Wards' humble home and expected to find rural white degeneracy.

Peculiar Places renders an interdisciplinary historical analysis that draws from a deep well of archival material and is animated by insights from queercrip writing, including crip of color critique and disability justice analysis. The book examines how the anti-idyll has functioned, manifested social difference, and changed over the course of the twentieth century, while reading against the grain of the anti-idyll's sensationalism. In doing so, it considers material circumstances, mundane sociality, and complex personhood in order to grasp what kinds of skills, support, and intimacies were used by poor rural white folks living on the margins—and how racialized, sexualized, ableist violence has been enacted through quotidian encounters and concerns.

Focusing on the mundane rather than the shocking does not eliminate the moral ambiguity, racial complexity, or vexed power dynamics at play in histories of white rural nonconformity. Power functions through the quotidian as much as it does the sensational. As Avery Gordon asserts, "power can be invisible, it can be fantastic, it can be dull and routine."[11] A queercrip focus on everyday interactions allows for an understanding of social structures and power dynamics that are too often obscured by the anti-idyll's focus on that which is rendered aberrational. In "Body Shame, Body Pride," Eli Clare reaches toward what he describes as a "disability politics of transness," a politics that would treat "bodily difference as neither good nor bad, but as profoundly *familiar*." *Familiar* and *ordinary* are not the same as *normal*—far from it. Normal, to Clare, means "comparing ourselves to some external, and largely mythical, standard."[12] Treating bodily difference as *ordinary*, in contrast, allows us to grapple with "ambivalence, grief, and longing," nurturing "the most complex conversations possible."[13] For historical and cultural analysis to treat social difference and bodymind difference as ordinary means "making narratives unfamiliar," in the words of Lisa Marie Cacho: "asking different questions of evidence and situating that evidence within different contexts."[14]

Peculiar Places spans the twentieth century, locating the ordinary in the anti-idyll from the early 1900s, when that trope became a national and nationalizing discourse, to the 1990s, when it began to fracture into discrete sociopolitical identities. As the anti-idyll waxed and waned in popularity, it continued to accrue meaning: the language of gossip from eugenic family studies of the 1910s, a visual vernacular of white poverty from 1930s documentary photography, associations with perverse violence in media coverage of the 1950s Heartland psychopath scare, and the spectacle of Appalachian poverty tours of the 1960s. The elements taken to be representative of rural white "unfitness"—poverty, physical and mental disabilities, nonheteronormative intimacies and domesticities, and gender nonconformity—coalesced in 1970s horror films, but began, unevenly, to fracture along identity lines in documentary films of the 1990s. Many of these representations were not clearly anti-idyllic when they originally appeared, becoming so only in retrospect. (This is true for 1930s documentary photography, for example, as well as the 1950s Heartland psychopath scare.) Since the anti-idyll and idyll work in tandem to negotiate meanings of rural life, they are present in some way in nearly every representation of US rural life. Although *Peculiar Places* offers a genealogy of the anti-idyll, it does not aim to be a comprehensive history. That readers often respond to an explication of the anti-idyll by naming additional instances of it may, I hope, speak to the power and popular resonance of the anti-idyll as a formation.

Returning briefly to the Ward brothers' story illustrates how gossip, a visual vernacular of poor white domesticity, associations with perverse violence, and embodied understandings of poverty coalesced into the white rural anti-idyll. However their story was told, it evoked earlier instances of the anti-idyll: the *New York Times* described the Ward brothers as reminiscent of a Walker Evans photograph,[15] a review of *Brother's Keeper* declared that the brothers' home elicited the title of the "most depressing domicile north of Appalachia," and a review of the *X-Files* episode "Home" described the fictional brothers' home as "so filled with horror it would have sent Norman Bates screaming in terror."[16] When *Brother's Keeper* filmmakers Joe Berlinger and Bruce Sinofsky congratulated themselves for their "courageous" work in reaching out to the Ward brothers—for their bravery in seeking to find the "human beings beneath the squalor and stench"— they echoed the rural "slumming" work of eugenic field investigators of the 1910s.[17] Perhaps most telling is that Berlinger and Sinofsky chose the Ward brothers to be the subject of their first film because it seemed to be "Deliverance II," a possible "gay-sex-turned-violent situation."[18] The optics through which filmmakers, reviewers, and viewers saw the Ward brothers had been in the making for a century. The story felt familiar to outsiders because they had been trained by decades of media to view white rural nonconformity through the optic of the anti-idyll. The story told in *Brother's Keeper* appealed to viewers not because the Wards' story was so singularly compelling, but because it fit into a larger, pre-existing narrative about the "perversity of the simple life."[19]

The anti-idyll is by definition sensational, yet the lives it purports to represent are as mundane, multifaceted, and morally ambiguous as any other. As Gordon asserts, "Even those who live in the most dire circumstances possess a complex and oftentimes contradictory humanity and subjectivity," a "complex personhood" that gets flattened when they are lodged into the static roles of victims or "superhuman agents."[20] Reading for materiality and mundane sociality allows us to think beyond and beneath the sensationalism of the anti-idyll, about *white rural nonconformity*. To do so, I begin by unpacking the centuries-old US myth of white rustic virtue, including its racialized relationship to heteronormativity and ablenormativity.

I then articulate *queercrip historical analysis*, a methodology for reading the anti-idyll otherwise and remaining attentive to the flawed but complex lives rendered through its estranged optics. Finally, I analyze the anti-idyll itself: how it functions as an optic, what happens when gossip travels, and the consequences of acceding to anti-idyllic viewpoints.

OUT OF SORTS; OR, WHITE RURAL NONCONFORMITY AND THE POWERFUL MYTH OF WHITE RUSTIC VIRTUE

In 1919, a pair of researchers from the State School for the Feeble-Minded in Faribault, Minnesota, encountered a white man whom they called Ezra. They locked their anti-idyllic gaze on Ezra's home while researching the sexual nonnormativity, interracial sociality, and mental disabilities that they believed to characterize Ezra's extended family and rural community. As they catalogued Ezra's curious domestic arrangements—his unfriendly male housemate and his friendly horses, his wife who visited only now and again—the researchers remarked on the man's loquaciousness and sharp analysis of his own social conditions. Ezra was a "sort of a philosopher of the soil in his own queer way," they asserted, adopting rural vernacular to describe a man who used that same kind of vernacular for insightful self-reflection. Even so, they shrouded the word "philosopher" in hedges: he was a philosopher only "of the soil," not of the city, and then, too, he was only "sort of" a philosopher of the soil. To be both "a philosopher" and "of the soil" required an uneasy estrangement from each.[21]

We might say that Ezra and his family are "out of sorts," as challenging to early twentieth-century researchers as they are to researchers a century later. The term "queer" offers one place to apprehend these knotted threads of disability and domesticity, family and intimacy, race and settler colonialism. When eugenicists used "queer" in Ezra's story, it was not, of course, a proxy for "lesbian, gay, bisexual, transgender (LGBT)," nor did it name an antinormative politics, as it might a century later.[22] Then again, it is not incomprehensible that it could have evoked the possibility of same-sex sexuality or gender nonconformity in 1919; that was one of many ways that "queer" functioned colloquially, and the researchers noted that Ezra "kept house" with another man.[23] The fact that Ezra's homemaking partner was considered "feeble-minded" could mean that the researchers found it odd for Ezra to make a home with a disabled man, whether or not they imagined them to be sexually intimate; or, "queer" might name their unease with the fact that Ezra's male domestic partner was his cousin. Perhaps it referred to Ezra's acceptance of his wife's independence—his resignation that she came and went on her own terms. More broadly, "queer" could, as

Siobhan Somerville's work indicates, name how Ezra's family both crossed and adhered to the Black/white color line: Belle Marie, one of Ezra's several cousins who had interracial relationships, was married to a white man but bore Black children as well as white.[24] Although the whole family lived together and crossed the color line in private, they made a public show of segregation during Belle Marie's funeral.[25] Another meaning of queer was "counterfeit." Under that meaning, the state might consider Ezra's relationship to settler colonialism to be queer, as the family had dispossessed Indigenous people not by going through the formal homesteading process but by directly squatting on Indigenous land. "Queer" could have conveyed any or all of these meanings. But most deliberately, the writers used "queer" to name the disjuncture between Ezra's insight into his circumstances and their expectations of a man who shared such genetic and geographic intimacy with "feeblemindedness."

Ezra and the other subjects of *Peculiar Places* are frequently out of sorts, abrading the edges of fields like queer studies, transgender studies, disability studies, and working-class studies without fitting into them neatly. Examining the varied meanings of "out of sorts," Sara Ahmed contends that when "experiences (human or otherwise) are messy there is little point in making distinctions that are clear."[26] I use *white rural nonconformity* to analyze rural white colloquial ways of naming social difference without trying to parse and set the meanings of those colloquialisms in relation to twenty-first-century categories. The heterogeneous subjects observed through the lens of the anti-idyll do not belong to a single shared category of aberrance, let alone a coherent sense of self-identity. Although they may use vernacular language, they do not constitute a "vernacular culture" or "vernacular epistemology" like the queer Black vernacular theorizing that Matt Richardson analyzes.[27] I therefore cannot offer a straightforward historical context for the broad scope of social difference in rural white communities of the United States, nor of rural whiteness writ large, nor even of the subjects of this book—though I hope the close analyses of particular circumstances in each chapter offer depth and nuance. The subjects of the anti-idyll are eccentric to social expectations for rural whiteness but in ways that defy easy categorization.

What the subjects of the anti-idyll shared was their relationship to the normalizing power of the white rural idyll, rooted in the subjects' white, settler, citizen privileges; public expectations that they would embody white rustic virtue; and common understandings of their failures to meet those norms and expectations. After examining the powerful white myth of "rural America" and the material benefits it bestows, I elucidate heteronormativity and ablenormativity before circling back to elaborate how whiteness functions as a consolation prize even among white rural nonconformists.

The Powerful White Myth of "Rural America"

The idea of the "rural," burdened as it is with white, heteronormative set-tler colonial myths, exceeds simple definition by "empirical geographic specificities" such as population density.[28] The rural has typically been defined in opposition to the urban or the metropolitan, by both census-makers and queer theorists alike. During the formative decades of US queer theory, queerness was decisively placed in the cosmopolitan city of the Global North. In more recent years, queer studies has generated an im-pressive set of critiques of "metronormativity," not just from the vantage of the countryside but that of the suburbs and the diasporic formation of the "region."[29] At the heart of metronormativity is a teleology that envisions the countryside—and colonial "peripheries"—as sites of backwardness and repression, while envisioning the cosmopolitan city of the Global North as a lighthouse of freedom and tolerance to which rural and colonized queers are obliged to move. Yet, as Martin Manalansan et al. remind us, other tel-eologies conjure the city differently, particularly when it is racialized and understood as home to working-class migrants of color rather than cos-mopolitan white globe-trotters.[30] In those circumstances, the city, as spa-tial emblem of modern civilization and its concomitant social problems, is imagined to be what Roderick Ferguson terms the "racialized scene of heteronormative disruption," consequently subjected to intense state and social regulation.[31] Just as "the city" is imagined in contradictory ways, so is "the country." The rural white idyll is not only defined against the city or "metropolitan," but through opposition to the purportedly "unsettled" wilderness. In anti-idyllic renderings, the latter is imagined as a threat and temptation, a hazy space where the rules of "civilization"—including sex-ual norms—do not apply.

Whitewashed visions of the country functioned to shore up the apparent naturalness of white heteronormativity and ablenormativity. To disturb the rustic idyll and the disciplinary power that attends it requires not simply locating same-sex sexuality and gender transgression in rural areas, but understanding how and why rural white sexuality, gender expression, and disability have been granted the power to seemingly subvert the rural idyll. When it is imagined to be white, "the country," a name for rural life, func-tions seamlessly as a metonym for the "country," the name for the US na-tion. In the early twentieth century, as the United States was beginning to understand itself as an urban nation, President Theodore Roosevelt spoke before Congress to underscore the continued importance of rural Ameri-can life. In doing so, he appealed to the centuries-old national myth that the United States was "founded as a nation of farmers," and therefore, that the "strengthening of country life is the strengthening of the whole nation."[32]

The ideal "American type," Roosevelt and others contended, was white and US-born; raised in fresh air and good health, with a strong, able body; and steeped in virile white heteromasculinity.[33] White women were fundamental to this pastoral mythos as well, envisioned as naturally domestic guardians of the hearth, selfless mothers who promoted the health of the white race, and moral arbiters of their communities.[34] Yet, as Sarah Wald contends, these myths, derived from the Jeffersonian ideal of agrarian virtue, required three colossal but quite common historical erasures: the dispossession and genocide of Indigenous peoples; the enslavement of people of African descent, who were forced to do much of the nation's agricultural labor; and the socio-legal construction of the "abject alien farm laborer," who was also compelled to do agrarian labor considered "beneath white U.S. citizens" but in the "natural domain of undocumented laborers."[35]

Expectations, opportunities, and opprobrium for rural white folks in the twentieth-century United States were thus rooted in settler colonialism, anti-Blackness, and citizenship claims—three racialized and interconnected national histories that are deeply entwined with heteronormativity and ablenormativity. Together, these racialized historical ideologies promised that rural white people were uniquely able, destined to "succeed" in the country and fulfill the dream of the Jeffersonian yeoman farmer; that is, to settle and farm the land as healthy, rooted, "independent" farm families. This had both material and representational benefits. As legal scholar Cheryl I. Harris attests, whiteness is a legally protected form of property that has been "used and enjoyed" by white people across the socioeconomic spectrum.[36] Whiteness has meant freedom from being enslaved, entitlement to legally possess property (and not be dispossessed of it), and access to naturalized citizenship.[37] Whiteness has also been accompanied by what W. E. B. DuBois characterized as a "public and psychological wage" that compelled poor whites to ally themselves with wealthy whites who economically exploited them.[38] Whiteness—even for those with little to no material resources—conferred public respect and deference, lenient treatment from police, admission to public functions and better schools, freedom from lynch mobs, and even a positive reflection of oneself in the media.

Another material benefit of whiteness, according to Nayan Shah, is the "privileged autonomy of gender and sexual propriety."[39] The racialized myth of the nuclear family "renders any other form of kinship and household structures"—from South Asian male migrants to poor single Black mothers—"pathological, aberrant, and incompatible with cultural support and political privilege."[40] Further, as European settlers colonized the lands that would become the United States, they dispossessed Indigenous peoples not only of land, but of kinship systems and gender formations.[41] The

Dawes Act of 1887 divided reservation lands, which had been held communally, into individual allotments parceled out to a "head of family." As Beth Piatote contends, this transformed "Indian economies, lands, kinship systems, languages, cultural practices, and family relations—in short, all that constituted the Indian home."[42] In other words, while some white Americans depart from white gender and sexual norms, white Americans as a group have not systematically had their kinship systems dismantled or been structurally forced into ways of life that render their households and pleasures pathological.

Heteronormativity, Ablenormativity, and Their Discontents

Nonheteronormativity, according to Ferguson, names the "intersection between the racialized multiplication of gender and sexual perversions and the dispersion of capitalist property relations."[43] Capitalism's demands for a mobile labor force—and maneuvers by the state to manage attendant social disruptions—valorize the myth of the white nuclear family, while structurally disadvantaging communities of color for failing to meet white heteronormative demands. This is true for racialized subjects in the country just as it is in the city, as rural landscapes are also subjected to racialized capitalist forces and state strictures.[44] Likewise, rural places are among the sites where communities of color often manifest alternative familial arrangements, "thereby violat[ing] a racialized ideal of heteropatriarchal nuclearity."[45] Shah demonstrates that the conditions of migrant agricultural labor in the early twentieth century fostered interethnic "border intimacies" and "webs of dependency" between strangers and acquaintances.[46] Deemed pathological, these transient formations of kinship, eroticism, sociality, and interdependence were structurally excluded from the "privileged model of social organization and political participation" that took the form of the "settled heterosexual household."[47] Charlotte Karem Albrecht's examination of rural and urban Syrian migrant women peddlers shows how the household and kinship structures of the peddling economy—a peddler leaving her or his family for periods of time, the possibility of "sexual dishonor" when a woman was on the road, and the family interdependencies required to care for children and make lace or other products to sell—were considered to be a "dangerous disruption of the American heteronormative family unit."[48]

Just as whiteness promised—and demanded—the possibility of heteronormativity, it promised and demanded the possibility of ablenormativity. According to Lydia X. Y. Brown, "hegemonic ablenormativity" names a dominant, racialized cultural paradigm that simultaneously "assigns values of health, normality, worth, and functionality to normatively abled bodies" while "marginalizing and medicalizing deviant bodies."[49] Ablenormativity, and ableism more broadly, are racialized in multiple ways. People of color in the United States are more likely than whites to be disabled, and some—not all—of their disabilities result from the physical and mental harm of settler colonialism, enslavement, global imperial war, mass incarceration, "border enforcement," environmental injustice, and educational deprivation.[50] People of color are also more likely to be classified as "disabled" and subjected to ableism regardless of their bodyminds—a legacy of eugenics and other forms of scientific racism that deployed categories of disability and incapacity to justify considering Black and Indigenous people, in particular, to be "subhuman."[51]

Ablenormativity has not just selectively denied some groups the privileges of abledness; it has undermined the joys of anti-ableist approaches to bodymind difference, just as it undermined the pleasures of nonheteronormative ways of living. In other words, bodymind differences have always existed, and it is not necessary that bodymind differences should be used to justify pathologization or exclusion from full participation in society. The origins of compulsory ablebodiedness in white Western societies, as Robert McRuer contends, lie in the nineteenth-century rise of industrial capitalism.[52] Ableism flourishes in a capitalist system that devalues those who fail to meet manufactured expectations for productivity while enforcing a scarcity politics that actively withholds basic resources, like healthcare and shelter, from those who need them to survive.[53]

Whiteness as Consolation Prize for the Nonnormative

Rural white Americans have benefited in at least two ways from myths of white rustic virtue and health: first, they are granted greater material access to the privileged lives of heteronormativity and ablenormativity, should they desire such lives; second, white rural nonconformity typically receives less scrutiny than nonconformity in communities of color does. These are social and material benefits of whiteness. Yet white people need not actually live up to normative expectations to benefit in some way from whiteness. Whiteness itself functions as a "consolation prize."[54] Historically, whiteness was a guarantee that no matter how poor they were, a white person, by virtue of race alone, would be legally treated as superior to those racialized as nonwhite, even if they fell well below the social norms and economic standards expected of them. Despite the many material benefits of whiteness—freedom, citizenship, and not being dispossessed—white supremacy could not guarantee individuals' economic success or material goods beyond the value of white identity itself.[55] Throughout the twentieth century, the tragedy of white rural American poverty was depicted as the tragedy of opportunities left unmet—opportunities that had been afforded to white people based on the unearned, yet legally ratified, value of whiteness.

Indeed, on the rare occasions when white people named *whiteness* as such, it was to describe a white person who did not take proper advantage of their privileges. In 1939, for example, a poor white man photographed by Dorothea Lange told her, "We're not paupers, we hold ourselves to be white folks," naming his racial pride as the property he knew it to be.[56] Likewise, in the 1960s, a white West Virginian, the prototypical "hillbilly" migrant to cities like Detroit and Cincinnati, expressed that even though he was poor, he did not "see himself as lower class," because he was "free, white, and twenty-one." By the 1960s, that phrase, which had been common three decades earlier, was regarded as "raw ethnocentrism"—an explicit appeal to the legal property and privileges of whiteness in an era when white appeals to racial entitlement were typically more coded.[57] Even in the 1990s, a *New Yorker* writer covering a triple homicide in Nebraska remarked on the paradox of poor white folks "trapped by the tyranny of class" in, of all places, "white America, where class distinctions are not supposed to exist."[58] Yet this "tyranny of class" was not so much that there were supposed to be no class distinctions among white people, but that whiteness was supposed to guarantee a higher economic baseline and therefore easier access to both heteronormativity and ablenormativity.

The social formations indexed by the rural white anti-idyll seem to be in stark contrast not just to normative behaviors and bodyminds, but to the mythologies at the heart of the white American nation. These social formations have been known by different monikers, attributed to different regional histories, and ascribed variously to large classes or to archetypal individuals—"the unfit," for example, or "the culture of poverty," "poor whites," or "the Heartland psychopath," among countless others. These social types are rarely, if ever, distinct to rural whites. "The unfit" and "the culture of poverty" are more commonly associated with people of color and "psychopath scares" have more prominently been associated with the city. Even categories like "poor whites" or "Okies" were formed through and against association with Black Americans in the South or the California figure of the "Asiatic," respectively.[59] Further, as Tiffany Willoughby-Herard contends, writing about South Africa, the "abject status assigned to poor whites" often "incites a false equivalency," co-opting and displacing "contemporary and historical Black suffering and Black flourishing for the sake of sympathy, albeit with white supremacy"—a process that likewise occurs in the United States, particularly in political discourse.[60] Thus, the mere existence of rural white people who contradict the promises of rural whiteness—those who do not own land, have not "achieved" a normative nuclear family, and do not have "productive," unremarkable bodyminds—cannot unsettle white national mythologies and the social hierarchies that those mythologies erect.

"IT'S ALWAYS SOMETHING"; OR, A QUEERCRIP HISTORICAL METHODOLOGY

Colloquialisms like "peculiar," "odd," "out of sorts," or "none too stout" may function euphemistically at times, but they are not used only to smooth blunt edges: they are, like "queer" and "crip," alternative ways of naming and knowing. Yet those colloquialisms differ substantially from *queer* and *crip* as they are used by activists and scholars. "Queer" and "cripple," as Clare contended in 1999, are "words to help forge a politics."[61] The shorter "crip" comes from disability communities who have "taken the word into our own mouths, rolled it around, shortened it, spoken it with fondness, humor, irony, recognition."[62] Both the word "crip" and the political analysis it names emerged from disability communities, even as the academic field of queercrip theory has been popularized by scholars (such as Carrie Sandahl, Robert McRuer, and Alison Kafer).[63] The politicized, contrarian approach of queercrip analysis is a necessary methodology for reading against the grain of anti-idyllic texts—for finding the material and the mundane in what is represented to be monstrous. I begin with a genealogy of disability studies, then fashion a queercrip methodology for historical research.

Disability studies and disability history have historically congregated around the social model of disability, which locates the supposed "problem" of disability within social and spatial exclusion rather than individual differences of body and mind. This epistemological critique of medical and scientific knowledge has been valuable to disability historians, asking us to "reconsider the basic criteria by which sources are measured" and to question the authority of medicine, social work, education, and many of the archives where written histories of disability might be found.[64] As a method of historical inquiry, it is rooted in the work of historians such as Paul Longmore, Cathy Kudlick, David Serlin, Susan Burch, Katherine Ott, Dea H. Boster, Jaipreet Virdi, Sarah Rose, and Audra Jennings, among others.[65] Although crip history is not synonymous with disability history, they are not at odds, either; crip history would not be possible without disability history.

From the small seed of one radical idea—that disability need not be an individual flaw or failure—approaches to the study of disability have continued to proliferate, growing new shoots and blossoms, reseeding themselves, and mutating into new forms. Three overlapping intellectual and social movements—crip and crip of color critiques, critical disability studies, and disability justice—have emerged to challenge what disability justice advocate Patricia Berne characterizes as the "critical, but fairly limited framework" of early disability studies and disability rights activism.[66] Collectively, these movements impel us not to elide embodiment in our haste to contest medical authority; to recognize disability experiences and culture as sources of knowledge and ways of knowing; to fight not for rights and inclusion, but for collective liberation led by those who are most marginalized; and to address material, structural differences within the category of "the disabled."[67]

One manifestation of these new approaches to disability studies is that "disability" has grown more capacious, inclusive of many kinds of "stigmatized bodies and minds."[68] This broader scope better positions the field to de-center the medical with its requisite diagnoses—to instead consider how disability functions in communities of color, who might, for good reason, be reluctant to identify as disabled or even acknowledge a "compromised relationship to labor and the ability to generate capital."[69] Thinking about disability more expansively means more than adding disabilities to a list; it means fundamentally transforming what it takes to ascertain what "disability" is and who subjects of disability studies are. (It also requires changing the language scholars use in order to be inclusive of mental disabilities— "bodymind" rather than "body," for example, or "abled" rather than "able-bodied.") One consequence of this shift toward a broader framework of "stigmatized bodies and minds" is that it is more inclusive of the colloquialisms through which many people in poor rural communities speak as they refer to their "nerves" or grumble that it's "always something."[70]

As such vernacular language suggests, everyday understandings of what a historian might term "disability" often melt into gender, sexuality, class, and race. *Disability*, *gender nonconformity*, and *sexual difference* function as "useful touchstones for analyzing the past" but "need not be [understood as] discrete historical categories." As Susan Burch and Lindsay Patterson contend, historians and other scholars must focus how categories such as gender and disability have been "naturalized, normalized, and segregated from one another in scholarship."[71] It is not just a matter of "expanding" our understandings of disability; after all, as Kafer acknowledges, this new "inclusiveness" in disability studies "is often more hope than reality."[72] It is knowing that a subject that is in need of a disability historian's attention might at first seem to belong to "gender history" or "the history of sexuality" instead (or vice versa). Understanding disability as an analytic, rather than a physical-mental trait, allows us to consider questions of welfare and socioeconomics, social proximities and intimacies, extraordinary violence and ordinary struggle.

Sexuality and gender, like disability, must be understood as analytics rather than purportedly empirical classification systems. This allows queer historians to contemplate subjects who are not interpellated by the label "queer" and those whose erotic practices or gender expression defy simple, static, binary oppositions of hetero/homo and male/female.[73] In other words, it focuses on the "idiosyncratic, messy, and contradictory" ways that sexuality and gender undergird social norms and functions of power.[74] This emphasis on norms and power structures rather than individual classification has been led by Black lesbian feminist theory and queer of color critique. In 1997, building on the scholarship of Barbara Smith and other Black lesbian feminists, Cathy Cohen urged queer studies to center political demands around "all those who stand on the outside of the dominant constructed norm of state-sanctioned white middle- and upper-class heterosexuality," rather than simply opposing straightness.[75] Trans studies also urges scholars to consider normativity along different axes. As Susan Stryker contends, although queer studies is "putatively antiheteronormative," it fails, at times, to "acknowledge that same-sex object choice is not the only way to differ from heterosexist cultural norms, that transgender phenomena can be antiheteronormative, or that transgender phenomena constitute an axis of difference that cannot be subsumed to an object-choice model of antiheteronormativity."[76]

A queercrip historical methodology must read historical texts imaginatively, infusing them with crip knowledge and queer questions that become pry bars.[77] I use *queercrip* not to describe the individuals or communities who make up this book, but to describe a method of historical inquiry into the intersecting structural forces of disability, gender, sexuality, class, and race that constitute the circumstances of their lives. Queercrip ways of looking and knowing provide a potential alternative to the normative gaze and assumptions of the anti-idyll. "Cripping," according to Carrie Sandahl, "spins mainstream representations or practices to reveal able-bodied assumptions."[78] Historical research offers vital tools to supplement textual interpretation in this work. It may not seem particularly strenuous to identify the ableism in, say, a horror film that explicitly uses a disabled person to evoke fear and disgust. Yet to *spin* that kind of representation, to generate the force to work against deeply engrained ableism, requires imagination that is grounded in the material circumstances of the film's creation. Queercrip historical methodologies reconsider what kind of historical "evidence" qualifies as disability history. To put this into practice, rather than seeking to identify anomalous bodyminds, I observe disability in other ways: how people lean on one another for both support and intimacy; the flexi-straws, shirt cuffs, canes, and other assistive devices left within the frame of a photograph; or the withdrawn affect of a person returning from the welfare office.

The subjects who populate a queercrip history often live messy, contradictory lives, making them "bad subjects" of disability history and LGBT history. They might reject disability politics, desiring a cure or an end to pain.[79] Perhaps they refuse to identify as transgender, instead offering their girlfriends embarrassing, outdated, and inaccurate explanations about being a "'morphodite."[80] Perhaps they have an addiction, or a disability caused by an accident or act of violence for which they are culpable.[81] Maybe they have committed violence against someone who is also marginalized, frustrating our desire for black-and-white morality. They may be labeled lazy, inefficient, or malingering; perverse, antisocial, or embarrassing; lonely, isolated, or friendless; and some of those labels may not be inaccurate.[82] They may experience variable symptoms, have multiple disabilities, or form social and romantic relationships that we cannot easily categorize. In other words, they support Gordon's "theoretical statement," drawing from Patricia Williams, that *life is complicated,* and that "race, class and gender dynamics and consciousness"—with which we might consider sexuality and disability—are "more dense and delicate than those categorical terms often imply."[83]

If we do not require our subjects to meet certain standards of legitimacy, transparency, and belongingness, then we can focus less on categorical terms and more on how power flows, as well as the "creative negotiations" and "modes of existence" that characterize life on the margins.[84] Kim, drawing on the insights of disability justice activism and grounding her analysis in women of color feminism, proposes a crip of color critique that "honors vulnerability, disability, and inter/dependency," and reads for "relations of social, material, and prosthetic support."[85] Despite the myths of independence and self-sufficiency that infuse the idea of the yeoman farmer, poor rural white people live interdependent lives, seek mutual aid, and receive welfare. The public and private narratives around these life circumstances, however, are often carefully coded to avoid overt associations with communities of color. A queercrip history of bad subjects reminds us that these are mere myths, reaffirms the widespread value of social safety nets and interdependent values, and critiques the white politics of racial resentment that would deny this.

Throughout this book, I examine subjects that are ethically vexed if not deeply controversial. I cannot always know, for example, if language like "sex perversion," which appears frequently in eugenic texts (chapter one), refers to consensual same-sex sexual acts or opposite-sex sexual assault. To discuss Ed Gein (chapter three) in the context of mental disability and trans identity risks entrenching dangerous stereotypes about the relationships between violence, mental disability, and trans experience, despite my intent otherwise. Yet grappling with these difficulties is necessary. For example, in the case of Delbert Ward (chapter six), it could be true that police took advantage of him because of his intellectual disabilities *and* that he killed his brother Bill because of Bill's disabilities; yet disability studies has only been able to grapple with the former by ignoring the possibility of the latter.[86] These deeply problematic histories of shared stigma create tension that is impossible for a historian to neatly resolve.

"A PARTICULAR PLACE AND A PECULIAR PEOPLE": THE OPTIC OF THE ANTI-IDYLL

The rural white anti-idyll—like its longtime counterpart, the idyll—is not a moniker for real people or places but a name for an optic, a way of looking at white rural nonconformity with an estranged and sensationalizing perspective. The anti-idyll distorts by degrading or degenerating, while the idyll distorts by idealizing or romanticizing. Each is shifting, contradictory, and unreliable. Together, the anti-idyll and idyll shore up the myths that casually equate rural life with normative, healthy, and virtuous white communities—myths that isolate nonconformity to "a particular place and a peculiar people," apart from "typical" rural white people and communities.[87] But the anti-idyll is not merely an abstraction. Anti-idyllic optics are created through encounters, real or imagined, with someone visiting from afar: a social worker or politician, a filmmaker or journalist. These encounters have material consequences. Would the child of a woman visited by a eugenic field worker be involuntarily institutionalized? Would the entertainer accosted by a flirtatious traveling photographer be able to protect her intimate female companion from his advances? Would the man who froze up at the welfare office be able to sign up for relief? Would the elderly woman whose potato patch was destroyed by a film crew find enough food for her and her disabled granddaughter to subsist on? Given these stakes, we must examine anti-idyllic encounters with care, attentive to the thorny circumstances of their production.

In the short essay in which cultural geographer David Bell introduces the concept of the anti-idyll, he contends that in contrast to the bourgeois "armchair countryside," the anti-idyll is the *"behind the sofa countryside, a place far, far from idyllic"* and hidden from view.[88] Of course, there is an entire world of rural existence in between and beyond the white landowners sitting leisurely in vacation home armchairs and the poor, disabled deviants who are hidden off the main roads and behind metaphorical sofas, by social practice or local policy. Yet it remains true, as Raymond Williams asserted in 1973, that much of our knowledge about "the country" is not simple, transparent, and authentic as is often popularly assumed, but in fact reflects "the observer's position in and towards it."[89] Thus, the substantial difference between an idyllic "armchair countryside" and an anti-idyllic "behind the sofa countryside" lies in the subject's orientation to and feelings toward the metaphorical furniture and the material landscape.

In this book, I examine the kinds of stories told about rural white communities in the continental United States, stories that were told, for the most part, by white professionals who were "passing through." Of course, this is not the only vantage from which one might observe poor white rural communities. For their own survival, Native and Black communities have learned, over centuries, how to observe and appraise white people, including those on the economic margins. The anti-idyllic ways of looking deployed by middle- and upper-class whites may have originated, in part, in the critical forms of knowledge necessary for the survival of Native people who were threatened by white settlers and Southern Black folks who were threatened by violence enacted by those whom they knew as "poor whites" or "white trash." In the nineteenth-century United States, the "logic of elimination" that characterizes settler colonialism, according to Patrick Wolfe, was enacted in part through the lawless, "murderous activities of the frontier rabble"—poor white people, typically immigrants from among Europe's landless.[90] Likewise, poor white Southerners were put into service by planters as overseers, slave drivers, and the patrol system that actively subjugated enslaved Black people. As DuBois contends, "poor whites" held tightly to the social status afforded them merely based on race, eschewing potential economic alliances with Black people and enacting vicious violence—driven in part by frustration with the planters' economic system that they chose to ally themselves with—onto Black communities.[91] By the 1970s, when Black film viewers enthusiastically embraced anti-idyllic horror films featuring poor rural white antagonists (chapter five), they brought a different history to and way of looking at the films than white viewers did: for Black viewers, the banjo-picking "mountain men" of *Deliverance* were menacing not because they evoked a failure to meet norms of white rustic virtue, but because they evoked the violent legacies of overseers and lynch mobs.[92]

I address the optic of the rural white anti-idyll as it is framed by those who are white and in positions of authority or socioeconomic privilege. Though anti-idyllic stories are not limited to a particular region, they are often narrated as regional tales. The idea of the "region" itself has functioned as a way of looking, a way of demarcating those who are different. As Ardis Cameron contends, regions as seemingly disparate as New England and Appalachia have been rendered "topographies of strangeness" through the "voyeuristic practices of cosmopolitan storytellers," ranging from writers of regional fiction to documentary photographers and filmmakers.[93] The most enduring anti-idyllic narratives about the white United States, of course, are associated with the plantation South and the southern

Appalachian mountains—regions that are proximate to one another but have different racial and economic histories.[94] Yet those narratives began as local particularities, coming to refer to broad swaths of the United States only after decades and centuries had passed. When Virginian William Byrd described a "peculiar status of marginal whites" in 1728, he did not ascribe it to the entire South: just the North Carolina side of his state's border.[95] Likewise, when Nathaniel Shaler denigrated the poor whites of Tennessee in 1885, he insisted that his own Kentucky had largely been spared such shiftless types.[96] All across the United States, from New Jersey to Wisconsin to California, people have told stories about "those people over there," the poor folks with irregular bodies and unusual intimacies who live in the next town, or state, or branch of the family. It is only when those stories begin to circulate more widely that they take on a larger representational burden, becoming affixed to an entire region or nation, rather than a solitary valley spied by a nurse or writer on her travels.

The germ of anti-idyllic tales was typically local gossip, elicited by social and cultural workers during their travels, and then conveyed to others second- or thirdhand. Gossip can function, as Eve Kosofsky Sedgwick contends, as a "nonce taxonomy," informal ways of knowing and navigating power structures that allow marginalized people to get by on a daily basis; gossip can also work, as Kwame Holmes asserts, as an "archive of experience" that "resists recognition and institutionalization."[97] The gossip that circulated in predominantly poor, rural, white communities functioned in those ways some of the time. Yet in the encounters that produced the anti-idyll, gossip was deployed differently: it was dislodged from the front porches and welfare offices where it was first relayed, and it was put to work for a scientific study or documentary film, circulating through different channels than casual gossip typically did.

Often, the scandalous anti-idyllic tales that are taken to be "authentic" local depictions are in fact several degrees removed, conveyed by someone who purports to speak for people who in fact live in much different circumstances from him or her. For example, photographer Shelby Lee Adams was "introduced to this world [of poverty] . . . by his uncle, a doctor, who had some of these people as patients," or *Hillbilly Elegy* author J. D. Vance, who has become the apparent voice of white Appalachian cultural "pathology" despite being a hedge-fund manager two generations removed from Appalachia.[98] As Karl Jacoby contends, the "American rural periphery" eludes the methods of the predominantly urban field of social history, even though the official documents in which rural folks appeared often functioned as "little more than official attempts to eavesdrop on the 'hidden transcripts' of the local populace."[99] Whether or not they are routed through local elites and distant grandsons, anti-idyllic tales are not reliable claims to truth. The power of the anti-idyll's gaze lies less in whether the story it composes *is* true than whether it *could be* true: in the words of *The Texas Chain Saw Massacre* actor Gunnar Hansen, "You watch this movie and you think, there are people like this in the world."[100] The anti-idyll combines fictive elements—whether intentionally so or made so by repeated tellings and misunderstandings—with truth claims grounded in science, journalism, and documentary.

Since I cannot take anti-idyllic sources at their word, I must follow the methodological lead of postcolonial scholars in reading "against the grain," disidentifying with the ways of thinking that led to their creation. By bringing feminist queercrip analysis to bear on documents created under vexed and exploitative conditions, I reframe the story to focus the mundane and the material rather than the sensational. Reading against the grain of the anti-idyll is tricky, of course. The conditions of the anti-idyll's creation are rooted in exploitation, and the people whose lives make up the fabric of anti-idyllic stories are typically quite vulnerable; they are rendered (partially) legible to me as a researcher through the same forces that rendered them (partially) legible to the state. To note that these subjects are vulnerable is not to suggest that they are sympathetic. Interpersonal violence appears and reappears in anti-idyllic texts. Poor white Americans' complicity in the violence of colonial conquest and enforcement of enslavement haunts their interactions. But to accept the anti-idyllic view of a community is to deny its internal power dynamics. It allows, for example, a sexually violent father and the daughter he abuses to be rendered interchangeable symbols of a "certain type of family" (as in chapter four), or for a Black homicide victim in a predominantly white community to be written off as being in the "wrong place"—as though his killers were not both familiar to and estranged from him (chapter six). Focusing on the mundane moments in anti-idyllic sensationalism allows us to more carefully attend to relations of power, including the quotidian ways in which white supremacy, sexism, trans-antagonism, and ableism function.

CHAPTER OVERVIEW

Chapter one, "Harlots from the Hollow: Eugenic Detectives on the Lookout for the Rural White Hovel Family," begins in the 1910s and 1920s, when the rural white anti-idyll emerged as a national optic. As the US population officially became more "urban" than "rural"—and as racialized concerns about vice and immigration heightened concerns about city life—long-mythologized notions of rustic virtue and health came under increasing scrutiny. Chapter one analyzes what Nicole Hahn Rafter terms "eugenic family studies" as a form of popular science that oriented the US public to an anti-idyllic gaze. Eugenics, the racial science of determining the "fit" and the "unfit," was used to justify restrictive immigration legislation, renew bans on interracial marriage, and involuntarily sterilize women of color and women with disabilities. The project of shoring up white supremacy also required that eugenicists manage the "unfit" among white, US-born populations. During the 1910s, the notorious Eugenics Record Office trained hundreds of women and dozens of men to become eugenic fieldworkers, who combined scientific investments in the notion of "better breeding" with social impressions of white rural depravity. Fieldworkers traveled across the northern rural United States, tracing genealogies of people institutionalized for "feeblemindedness" and "insanity" and dutifully recording tales of "queer" grandmothers and "peculiar" uncles. These studies were often published as monographs or magazine articles; some, like *The Kallikak Family*, became widely read exemplars of popular science and inspired hundreds of amateur sleuths to conduct their own investigations. Chapter one contends that by proliferating the image of the rural white "hovel family," eugenic family studies popularized the anti-idyll as a way of looking for nonconformity in the rural white United States.

Chapter two, "Curious Scenes: The Fringes of Rural Rehabilitation in 1930s Documentary Photography," examines how the documentary photography project of the Farm Security Administration (FSA)—the defining federal photography venture of the Depression—sought to rehabilitate the image of the idyll that had been damaged by eugenic narratives of rural white social and sexual depravity. Between 1935 and 1943, through hundreds of thousands of FSA photographs from across the United States, the agency represented the white rural idyll as alive and achievable. Simultaneously, however, the FSA documented anti-idyllic scenes in photographs that never circulated widely or ascended to iconic status. Popular and organizational demands caused the FSA to prioritize photos of sympathetic, abled white women and children, but its photographers also told photo-stories of disabled bachelor lumberjacks in the far reaches of the upper Midwest, and of sex workers and their companions in small towns of the Western Great Plains. Analyzing these rarely discussed photo series, chapter two argues that Depression-era attempts to rehabilitate the image of rural whiteness were undermined by continued prurient interest in the lifestyles forged by unmarried, disabled, and poor women and men across the United States.

In 1957, when a blockbuster *Chicago Tribune* article reported that farmer and alleged murderer Ed Gein had confessed to having a "feminine complex," the anti-idyll's associations with gender transgression and violence deepened, fusing together with popular understandings of mental illness.[101] Chapter three, "Madness in the Dead Heart: Ed Gein and the Fabrication of the Transgender Heartland 'Psycho' Killer Myth," examines media coverage, court documents, and the confession of Ed Gein, the Wisconsin farmer, grave robber, and human taxidermist whose reputation inspired "psycho trans" characters from Norman Bates to Buffalo Bill. As national media became preoccupied with the lay theories of psychopathy, schizophrenia, and transsexualism, it was the weekly papers of neighboring towns that cast an anti-idyllic gaze on local landscapes occupied by poor people and poor soil purportedly known as the "Dead Heart" of Wisconsin. A few years later, the Wisconsin farmer was transformed into California hotelier Norman Bates in Alfred Hitchcock's *Psycho*. Stripped of particular relational, regional, racial, and economic contexts, the fictionalized story staged a relationship between gender transgression and violence. The film popularized the deeply damaging cultural trope of the "psycho trans" killer—a formulation that falsely equates being a murderer with both mental illness and being transgender—and the fear that such killers might stalk any rural US landscape.

By the early 1960s, racialized political concerns sent "poverty tourists" flocking to West Virginia, eastern Kentucky, and other parts of the central and southern Appalachian Mountains. In chapter four, "'Maimed in Body and Spirit': The Spectacle of White Appalachian Poverty Tours during the 1960s," I analyze the poverty tours or inspections embarked upon by politicians, social workers, journalists, volunteers, and college students to predominantly white communities. Instead of urging Americans to scrutinize rural landscapes for signs of gender nonconforming psychopathy, 1960s poverty warriors attributed the social problems of white rural America to a more muted form of mental and economic depression. Michael Harrington claimed, in expanding the scope of the culture of poverty to include poor whites in Appalachia, "Everything about the poor, from the condition of their teeth to the way in which they love, is suffused and permeated by the fact of their poverty."[102] In chapter four, I offer a queercrip analysis of Appalachian culture-of-poverty theory, analyze two poverty tour visits—one by a president, one by a social worker—and examine how the poverty tours were whitewashed.

As it became clear that the War on Poverty had not succeeded in rehabilitating rural white communities, the anti-idyll surged in popularity again, projecting cultural fears to the big screen. Chapter five, "Banjos, Chainsaws, and Sodomy: Making 1970s Rural Horror Films and the Apex of the Anti-Idyll," analyzes anti-idyllic rural slasher films known as "urbanoia" films.[103] Urbanoia films emerged in the early 1970s just as television networks like CBS initiated a "rural purge" and shifted toward "relevance programming" (e.g., *The Mary Tyler Moore Show* and *All in the Family*) that was aimed at more youthful, urban audiences. Urbanoia films appealed to these same audiences, using rural landscapes and their white inhabitants to enact epic battles pitting the privileged (rich white people from the cities and suburbs) against the disenfranchised (poor white people living in desolate rural settings). This chapter examines the films *Deliverance* and *The Texas Chain Saw Massacre,* addressing their material impact by analyzing them alongside reviews, circulation data, and public commentary about racial and demographic concerns that are implicit in the films. Although horror films have typically been read as a form of psychoanalytic catharsis, I argue that urbanoia films directly engaged with certain contemporary social issues—such as postindustrial economic change—while studiously avoiding others—such as emerging gay and trans social movements. Chapter five claims that, through the fearful spaces of the theater and the drive-in, urbanoia films seared the anti-idyll into the American cultural consciousness for decades to come, while simultaneously ensuring that rural sexual and gender difference remained in the cultural realm of the anti-idyll, rather than in the social realm of gay rights.

By the 1990s, the anti-idyll was a residual formation, challenged by and uneasily coexisting alongside the rise of identity movements from transgender and disability rights to the reclamation of "white trash." Chapter six, "Estranged but Not Strangers: Nonconformity Encounters Identity in 1990s Hate-Crime Documentaries," examines the period when rural LGBT life was starting to become imaginable and thereby had the potential to disarticulate anti-idyllic views of rural nonconformity. *Brother's Keeper* and *The Brandon Teena Story,* two documentary films from the 1990s, typified the divergent understandings. *Brother's Keeper* portrayed "a bunch of queer old farmers" in the older manner of the anti-idyll, broadly locating their social difference in their poverty and intellectual disabilities as much as their fraternal intimacy. In sharp contrast, *The Brandon Teena Story* constructed a narrowly focused story of transgender identity out of the triple homicide of three acquaintances—a white-passing transgender man (Brandon Teena), a physically disabled Black man (Phillip DeVine), and a white single mother (Lisa Lambert)—in Humboldt, Nebraska. Outside of LGBT media, however—in everything from pulp paperbacks and *Playboy* articles to the *New Yorker*—the "Humboldt murders" were viewed through the prism of the anti-idyll. National media saw it as self-evident that violence would erupt among a ragged circle of young social misfits raised by single mothers on welfare. In the 1990s and into the 2000s, chapter six concludes, the broad scope of the anti-idyllic lens began to fracture and split into discrete and particular identities.

I: HARLOTS FROM THE HOLLOW

Eugenic Detectives on the Lookout for the Rural White Hovel Family

In the 1910s, researchers across the northern United States traipsed through rural communities, knocking on doors and making small talk to induce town elites and ordinary folks alike to share gossip about their ancestors' peculiar traits and their neighbors' queer proclivities. In rural New Jersey, a woman named Ada was said to be "extremely masculine in appearance," a characteristic that was especially suspicious given that her brother was a "sexual pervert" institutionalized at a West Virginia hospital for the insane.[1] In Wisconsin, researchers described a number of "peculiar" rural women and bachelor farmers who never married.[2] In Maine, a convicted sodomite with a "somewhat feminine type pelvis & hips" was reported to be the "leader of a gang of loafers and degenerates" who tilted the balance of politics in his rural community.[3] In Arkansas, a woman was written up for having illicit intercourse with several men "up yonder," at a county poor farm.[4] In Utah, a college student recorded the sordid history of three generations of sexually deviant rural white women: a sexually precocious girl who enjoyed buggy-riding with boys; her mother, who was known to consort with Black men and had borne a mixed-race child; and her grandmother, who had been "considered queer" because she was indifferent to marriage.[5] Eugenic researchers of the 1910s collected gossip as a form of local intelligence, indexing interrelated forms of white rural nonconformity and writing them up as "eugenic family studies." In doing so, they linked together notorious "local" families across the country—starting with the Northeast and Midwest and expanding fitfully from there—into a single national problem. In other words, they popularized an anti-idyllic way of comprehending white rural nonconformity and made it into a nationwide concern. Through the late twentieth century, long after eugenic family studies themselves were more or less forgotten, simply the word "Kallikak"—from the title of the popular monograph *The Kallikak Family: A Study in the Heredity of Feeble-Mindedness* (1912)—evoked the gaze of an entire imagined world of rural white deviance, much like the sound of a banjo would after the release of *Deliverance* in 1972.[6]

Eugenic family studies focused primarily on white families and the boundaries of whiteness, but as Dorothy Roberts contends, eugenicist interest in whiteness still emerged from a "racist ideology" that functioned to justify the subjugation of Black people, Indigenous people, and other racialized subjects.[7] Adherents of eugenics, a racial science concerned with managing the "biological stock" of the nation, sought to prevent the "unfit" from populating the United States. Eugenics—and the very idea that "race" is an innate or biological characteristic—emerged from scientific racism, an ideology with roots in the seventeenth century that used claims of innate white racial superiority to defend "domination by one group over the other as the natural order of things."[8] The eugenics movement of the early twentieth century sought to enact policies such as immigration restriction, compulsory sterilization laws, interracial marriage bans, and the use of state institutions to segregate the "unfit" from the rest of society.[9] Eugenic family studies shored up these claims to white superiority by regulating and preventing reproduction among white communities whose economic standing, morality, and heterogeneous bodyminds might reveal the sham of white supremacy.

Eugenic family studies flourished in the 1910s and early 1920s, as professional and amateur researchers flocked to peculiar places populated by marginal people, the "breeding places of those whose minds are feeble and without inhibitors to their impulses."[10] These places were impoverished sections of rural areas, home to white or mixed-race communities who dwelled in rudely constructed homes described as huts or hovels—those who were designated "feebleminded," "defective," "dependent," and "delinquent." Such locales were reported to be "out of the way" and beyond social surveillance, yet somehow found themselves surveyed by countless social researchers. Family studies situated harlots from the hollow and their queer kin within the archetype of a poor, disabled, shack-dwelling social unit: the hovel family. The hovel family functioned as the "confirmational image" of eugenic family studies and far exceeded the reach of the studies themselves.[11] Professional researchers and the institutions that funded them often published studies, sometimes as monographs and sometimes as journal or magazine articles. Amateur volunteers, often students, read these published studies and conducted their own, sending copies to the Eugenics Record Office (ERO) that employed most of the professional researchers. These published studies about sprawling families of rural white "degenerates" compelled readers to check out and write up the deficient families near their own hometowns.[12] Eugenic family studies instructed the middle- and upper-class public how to look at nonconformity and bodymind variation in rural white communities.

As a genre, eugenic family studies popularized and nationalized the rural anti-idyll by consolidating the more ragged, haphazard anti-idyllic gossip and stories that were situated in specific regions and localities. Members of the archetypal hovel family conducted themselves on the fringes of sexual decency, subsisted on the margins of the wage economy, and demonstrated only borderline intelligence. Yet as white, native-born residents of the rural North, the subjects of family studies were supposed to constitute the racial and geographic heart of the US nation and its claims to white racial and civilizational superiority. Volunteer eugenic investigator Bernice Reed succinctly described the problem when she explained, "The country is not usually thought of as being a harbor for vice and crime, and yet every rural community offers its problem of a defective family."[13]

Progressive reformers frequently invoked the rural white idyll as a rhetorical and literal counter to the nation's gendered and racialized problems. Sociologists posited that most white Americans, with their deep roots in farming and their vigorous experiences on the frontier, had not yet been exposed to the "deteriorating influence of the city and factory."[14] At the heart of the early twentieth-century US pastoral was a nostalgic, heteronormative, and ablenormative vision of the rural white American family as the natural embodiment of national social ideals: a hardworking male breadwinner married to an efficient female housekeeper who oversaw a plentiful and orderly brood of healthy white children.[15] Norms of heterosexuality, white feminine sexual restraint, white masculine industry, health and physical fitness, and mental acuity supposedly distinguished rural white families from Black Americans, immigrants from Asia and Eastern and Southern Europe, and urban white laborers.

Rural American whiteness was also idealized through its relationship to an emerging ideal of white masculinity forged through the act of violent colonization, or what Theodore Roosevelt famously called the "strenuous life."[16] As rural minister and country life reformer George Walter Fiske alleged, "our pioneer days certainly developed a sturdy race of men," a "remarkable race of continent conquerors."[17] As Roosevelt yearned to restore white masculinity to a "primal vigor by subduing primitive men" in imperial territories such as the Philippines, Fiske glorified the rural white masculinity of past generations for the same basic undertaking—subduing "continents," and, left unspoken, their Indigenous inhabitants—in North America.[18] When Fiske pronounced that "Effeminacy is not a rural trait," he was not making a simple statement of fact, but announcing an intention, while romanticizing and venerating the violence of the fathers and grandfathers of the rural white men he knew.[19]

Eugenic family studies drew national attention to the white hovel families who failed to live up to the lofty racial expectations they bore. Roosevelt's fear of "race suicide" did not merely register alarm over the possibility that the white race might be "overtaken" by nonwhite races, or that whites were becoming "overcivilized," but that the most fecund white families—those in rural areas—were those that held the least potential.[20] As eugenicists regulated the external boundaries of whiteness through immigration restriction, they regulated the internal boundaries of whiteness through eugenic family studies.[21] Twentieth-century investigators who focused on rural white hovel families did so in an attempt to "improve" the white race, investing white communities with optimism that came at the direct expense of communities of color—and Indigenous peoples.

To regulate the internal boundaries of whiteness required identifying the "unfit" among white, rural, US-born Americans. Under scrutiny because of the mundane realities of their poverty, condemned for their sexuality, and institutionalized on the basis of disability, the subjects of eugenic family studies were never identified by only their sexuality, disability, or class, but by the intersections of all three. As Susan Burch and Lindsay Patterson assert, at the heart of eugenic determinations of unfitness were "expectations of what bodies and minds should do—at work, in family and daily life, in social settings, and the like."[22] Eugenicists deployed malleable categories like feeblemindedness to judge people deficient according to normative notions of productivity and morality. Feeblemindedness was used to identify the "concept of substandard labor capacities" that still legally defines disability in the United States, but labor capacity was deeply gendered.[23] For white women in the 1910s, labor capacity was judged not to work outside the home, but to marriageability, morality, and household management skills. Feeblemindedness did not just designate someone immoral—although it also did that—but denoted that she was "unable to live and act in sexually deliberate ways."[24]

As a sign of morality, feeblemindedness functioned as much more than a heteroreproductive vector of transmitting hereditary "flaws." Even among the "unfit," nonreproductive sexuality—from same-sex intercourse to masturbation to abstention from sex—was of concern to eugenicists. So while it is true, as Siobhan Somerville contends, that "most eugenicists did not emphasize questions of homosexuality," it is also true that they did not emphasize questions of "heterosexuality" as such.[25] More interested in broad ideas of morality or vice, eugenicists did not focus on specific taxonomies of sexual deviance in the way that their sexologist colleagues did.[26]

Nonconformity, however, was well within the purview of eugenicists, and sexual and gender nonconformity of all kinds, including same-sex sexuality and cross-gender identification, intersected with their understandings of disability and racial degeneration. The dense, tangled categories of deviance that researchers catalogued as "feeblemindedness," "sex immorality," and "perversity," among others, were produced through the anti-idyllic acts of searching, listening, and taxonomizing in eugenic style.

As I analyze the emergence of the national white anti-idyll, I use queer-crip analysis to read against the grain of eugenic family studies, focusing on mundane social interactions and material circumstances of the families that fieldworkers purported to describe.[27] Eugenics, as Tobin Siebers contends, wed "medical science to a disgust with mental and physical variation."[28] Yet much of what eugenicists derided is valued much differently by crip, queercrip, and crip of color analysis. Crip of color analysis, according to Jina B. Kim, honors "relations of social, material, and prosthetic support—that is, the various means through which lives are enriched, enabled, and made possible."[29] Mutual support, nonnormative kinship arrangements, and part-time work in the informal economy constituted the "ingenuity of living" that being poor and disabled required—and this system horrified eugenicists.[30]

Queercrip analysis also allows us—requires us—to hold space for moral complexity. To remove the disgust that eugenics wedded to variant bodyminds, or even to recognize crip values like interdependence, does not require holding up people who evince those values as heroes. Eugenic family studies are thorny materials to work with. For example, the ambiguity of historical terms like "sex perversion" makes it impossible to distinguish between a person who had consensual same-sex affairs and a person who committed opposite-sex sexual assault. And unlike the women of color who constitute the focus of crip of color analysis, the white US Americans targeted by eugenic family studies benefited from the material value of whiteness, regardless of their poverty.[31] Poor white people were complicit in settler colonialism, as well; indeed, squatting on Indigenous land rather than going through the formal homesteading process was one of many concerns registered in eugenic family studies.

Eugenic family studies provided an anti-idyllic way of looking at poor white and mixed-race families, as well as the scientific validation necessary to imbue local gossip about rural white disabilities and sexual practices with national significance. I begin the chapter by tracing the establishment of the rural white hovel family as a national concern between the publication of *The Jukes* in 1877 and the rise of eugenic family studies as a genre in the 1910s. I then consider how the ERO trained professional fieldworkers to use gossip and geography to identify the hovel family and how popular sources trained nonprofessionals to do the same. Finally, I analyze how tests of sexual and social conduct were used to diagnose feeblemindedness in medical, legal, and popular spheres.

FROM THE JUKES TO THE KALLIKAKS: THE PROBLEM OF RURAL WHITE DEGENERACY

Progressive Era interest in the moral, intellectual, and physical problems of "hovel communities" emerged at the juncture of scientific concerns about peculiar morality and social concerns about the decaying quality of "pioneer stock" in rural white New England communities. Between 1877 and 1912, the hovel family crystallized as the primary site of rural white racial perversion in the US North—as fallen pioneers who brought down the moral values of everyone around them. The gendered economic failures of rural white hovel families first attracted popular attention through the social optic employed by Richard Dugdale's 1877 publication of *The Jukes: A Study in Crime, Pauperism, Disease, and Heredity*, and they became categorically tethered to white rural landscapes through prominent 1890s debates about the degeneration of New England pioneer stock. By the 1910s, the anti-idyllic hovel family was becoming a popular national imagination of rural white poverty, inaugurated by publication of *The Kallikak Family* and the founding of the ERO.

The Jukes, based on the legend of the notorious eighteenth-century woman known as "Margaret, Mother of Criminals," did not mark a new interest in gendered rural white poverty so much as it indexed a transition from the figure of the individual fallen woman to the social type of a sprawling hovel family.[32] Both were notable for wayward reproduction and disrespect for marriage, but the hovel family augmented the sexual and social problems of the fallen women with disability, criminality, and much more: Maggie, the poor waif "left adrift" in a Hudson River Valley town in the late 1700s, was transformed into Ada Juke, one of five sisters who together spawned 900 descendants, of whom two hundred were criminals and many more were "idiots, imbeciles, drunkards, prostitutes, and paupers."[33] The aspiring social scientists who "discovered" the Jukes in the 1870s suggested that unlike Margaret, who had functioned as an infamous but ultimately local cautionary figure, the Jukes were metonymic for a much more widespread threat to the social order. As William Round declared in his 1884 introduction to the seventh edition of *The Jukes*, "There is not one 'Jukes' family alone in the state—but the 'Jukes' family is the type of a great class."[34]

The existence of a "great class" of rural white hovel families posed a social threat to the work ethic and related moral values that white elites believed were already under siege in the 1870s and 1880s, since excessive sexual instincts were interpreted as a major threat to the work ethic.[35] The Jukes were described as backwoods squatters, thieves, and harlots—men and women who lived beyond the controlling reach of work and were indifferent to the state regulation of property and marriage.[36] Their idleness and refusal to work, Dugdale asserted, was closely associated with the hypersexuality and licentiousness that he defined as their principal failure. Contending that the chief problem in training "idiots," a subcategory of the feebleminded, was the "sexual orgasms to which they are addicted," Dugdale insisted that physical labor would "produce fatigue, so that when laid down they fall to sleep at once without chance of sexual abandonment." Yet, since idiots were characterized by the misdirection of their "vital forces" toward sex rather than industry, simply giving them laborious tasks would not produce a change in their character. Dugdale's proposed solution was to forcibly "compel the flexion of the members," either by a nurse or "sometimes by mechanical contrivances." This would not only fatigue incorrigible subjects but would also train their apparently feeble minds and senses to be "arbitrarily excited" by labor rather than sex.[37]

Thus, for Dugdale, only forced industrial training and hard labor could restrain the feebleminded Jukes family's wild "sexual indulgence" to a more "healthy periodicity."[38] Idle, dull minded, and sexually indulgent, the Jukes embodied moral values that had no place in an industrial capitalist society—particularly not one that was already being challenged by an economic depression, massive urban labor unrest, and the end of Reconstruction. While the Black Codes, vagrancy laws, and scientific charity efforts forcibly imposed labor discipline and domestic norms on men and women of color and poor urban immigrants, Northern rural white communities were typically invested with greater moral optimism.[39] Much to the chagrin—and titillation—of reformers, however, the Jukes' unexpected "lack of moral stamina" presented a "remarkable and revolting spectacle" of a rural white community.[40] *The Jukes* and later eugenic family studies spatialized scientific concerns with immorality, locating "moral disability"— known as "moral imbecility" or "moral insanity" in the nineteenth century and popularized as "moronism" in the 1910s—in rural places.[41]

The Jukes served as a blueprint for future studies of the rural white hovel family, but it was not until the crisis of the New England village in the 1890s that the hovel family became irrevocably framed as rural. The Jukes' rural "breeding-spot" was a backdrop for their sordid lives, important primarily because rural hovel communities were imagined as "crime cradles" that incubated future urban migrants sure to introduce their disorder to a nearby city. During the late nineteenth century, social reformers and social scientists used Dugdale's monograph as a guide for studying white poverty in urban and rural areas alike, from Oscar McCulloch's Ishmaels of Indianapolis to Frank Blackmar's neighbors in rural Kansas.[42]

As the twentieth century approached, a series of popular magazine articles penned by New England ministers brought public concern back to the rural communities that had initially characterized the iconic Jukes. Remarking on the moral, intellectual, and economic stagnation that afflicted even "good stock," or rural Americans "of pure English descent," rural pastors like Rollin Lynde Hartt and urban reformers like Alvan Sanborn lamented that rural white New Englanders had been left behind by more adventurous spirits seeking to make their profits in nearby cities or faraway frontier towns, appealing to colonial notions of adventure and conquest as white racial progress.[43] The white rural New Englanders who remained, they claimed, lacked ambition, were too individualistic to submit to religious institutions, too provincial to understand the sanctity of marriage, and too seduced by cheap knockoffs of urban luxury goods to properly manage their debt.[44] Further, the degraded moral and social conditions of these "decadent hill towns" were causing "good stock" Americans to decay intellectually and physically.[45] Ministers wrote disability metaphors onto social and moral landscapes, describing rural New England as "cursed with an abnormal heredity, dwarfed and crippled and malformed" and home to many "high-grade idiots."[46] As they chronicled the plight of the decadent New England hill town, these ministers created a potent image of rural white degradation—physical, mental, and moral—that would soon be applied beyond New England.

By the 1910s, the moral threat posed to the white rural idyll by the Juke family and the New England hill town had been generalized into a social problem that could be found anywhere in the northern United States, if one knew how to look.[47] With the ERO's founding in 1910, hundreds of women and dozens of men were professionally trained to identify and report on "harlots from the hollow" and other aberrant types associated with rural white communities.[48] The ERO's fieldworkers began by investigating the familiar terrain of New England but soon expanded westward, regularly writing up families as far away as Minnesota or Arkansas and occasionally traveling as far as California. Inspired by tremendously popular eugenic monographs like *The Kallikak Family*, amateur investigators learned to identify the anti-idyll in communities across the nation and further expanded the geographic scope of the family studies. Although eugenics was a serious biological science with profound political and scholarly influence, the family studies constituted a genre of popular scientific writing that appealed to a broad audience by setting sensational morality plays in the pastures and woods just beyond the heart of US civilization. By the time eugenic family studies began to proliferate in the 1910s, the hovel family was an established social type, marked by sensational sexual difference that was inextricable from poverty and intellectual disabilities, and associated with particular rural white communities.

SOCIAL MISFITS IN SECLUDED VALLEYS: THE GEOGRAPHY AND GENEALOGY OF THE HOVEL FAMILY

Behind the science and the political significance of eugenics—a social movement with severe and even deadly consequences, particularly for poor women, women of color, and immigrants—was simple small-town gossip being transformed into scientific pathology. Eugenic fieldworkers, both professional and amateur, began their surveys of hovel families by spotting an economically depressed rural area and chatting up its residents, inquiring about the sickly, troubled, and odd. They were taught two main skills: to recognize the peculiar places that bred rural white deviance—to discern landscapes in an anti-idyllic way—and to draw out rumors from the people who resided in those places. Some researchers studied these skills formally, through the ERO's six-week summer training program, while others learned them through the public instruction of popular culture.

The search for hovel families began at "institutions concerned with social misfits."[49] In practice, these "social misfit" institutions included institutions for the "feebleminded, epileptic and insane," the "deaf, dumb, and blind," "inebriates," and "juvenile delinquents." A professional fieldworker would first be trained at the ERO, which biologist Charles Davenport had established partly as a repository for information serving "eugenical interests," and partly as a training school for college-educated women and men interested in eugenic field research.[50] The fieldworker was then paired with a state institution, hired jointly by that institution and the ERO, and eventually, they intended, paid directly by the state legislature. The fieldworker was sent into a rural area to "study, at their *homes*," the "personal and family history of those who are wards of the State." If she found a more "interesting" family along the way, however, she—only occasionally he—was encouraged to write up that family instead.[51] Although institutionalized patients came from urban and suburban areas as well as rural areas, fieldworkers only studied patients from rural communities. From the outset, their target was the broad field of rural nonconformity.

On the lookout for misfits and nonconformists, fieldworkers were trained and chosen for their ability to tactfully incite conversation about such local eccentrics. Davenport instructed students in the ERO's summer fieldwork training program to "engage in conversations at random houses in a given rural community" to learn if they might have information of interest to the study.[52] And, with a few minor exceptions, that is precisely what eugenic fieldworkers did: they set out for the countryside, spoke with "leading citizens" like doctors and judges, attempted to befriend the families under investigation in order to obtain more truthful genealogical information from them, and dutifully sent their notes back to the ERO, even when they were not officially employed by the office. The ERO trained fieldworkers in the way of gossip, or, as they described it, the art of "quietly and tactfully draw[ing] out all the information that it is possible to get" from the socially inadequate families under study.[53] Amateurs, trained by the example of published ERO studies or by magazines like *Popular Science* and *Atlantic Monthly,* also ventured into the countryside, notebooks in hand, hoping to find their very own hovel families.

Fieldworkers understood this process to be applying the rigor and taxonomies of scientific research onto important genealogical knowledge disguised as small-town chitchat. Elizabeth White described the difficulty of the work carried out by Elizabeth Kite, one of the first professional eugenic fieldworkers:

> Miss Kite's mission was to gather up the tiny bits of knowledge possessed by the pineys. Such trivial and apparently unimportant bits possibly as that "Joe Boy's aunt Jane was awful queer," and fit them together with bits obtained from other sources until she had all these genealogies and character sketches worked out, not perfectly to be sure, for she could not find all the pieces, but sufficiently so.[54]

"Tiny bits of knowledge" about the queer and peculiar were at the heart of eugenic fieldwork and the tale of the hovel family's social problems, however incomplete. Kite, a high school teacher hired by psychologist Henry Goddard to conduct the research that became *The Kallikak Family* and several articles in social welfare journals, developed the prototype for future fieldwork. As professional and aspiring fieldworkers followed her lead, they likewise gathered up bits of gossip about local misfits and placed them into a national narrative of rural white moral degeneracy.

While women fieldworkers like Kite and White stressed the scientific synthesis of their work, the men who directed them emphasized their "feminine tactfulness" and ability to elicit confessions of peculiarity.[55] Between 1910 and 1924, Davenport and Harry H. Laughlin trained 258 field workers, most of them women, in their six-week eugenic fieldwork summer courses. In some ways, the ERO's fieldworker trainees resembled other highly educated white women of their time who were employed in professions like social work.[56] Yet, unlike social workers, fieldworkers were not expected to help the families they worked with or alleviate their suffering.

For example, when a mother asked a fieldworker from the Minnesota State School for the Feeble-Minded to convey to the superintendent that she would like for her daughters to be allowed to visit home more, the fieldworker conveyed the message—but only as an amusing anecdote.[57] Female fieldworkers also complicated the maternalist model of women's professionalization by exerting authority over less privileged men and participating in professional conversations about labor and medicine that were typically considered the "male dominion."[58]

Published eugenic family studies were part biological manifesto, part sociological study, part travel diary, part reformist call-to-arms, and part publication of local gossip. But the appeal of investigating the hovel family was not limited to professionals or even to those with knowledge of the ERO. Potential "sociological detectives" encountered the hovel family in fiction and popular magazines, in high school classrooms and state fair expositions, and by reading published family studies like *The Kallikak Family* and *The Hill Folk*, pseudonymous titles that functioned metonymically for the social type they purported to represent.[59] Notorious hovel families like the Jukes and Kallikaks were explicitly named in public health directives to teach students about the "sociological aspects of sex," public exhibits lobbying for more institutions for the feebleminded, and popular novels like *Bram of the Five Corners*.[60] *The Kallikak Family* became such a cultural touchstone that it nearly inspired a Broadway play, was discussed as deserving matter for a film, and became the name of a short-lived 1977 television show.[61] Reviewers described monographs like *Dwellers in the Vale of Siddem* as "intended for popular consumption."[62] Sometimes the people interviewed by professional fieldworkers had already encountered family studies and were familiar with the "very field we are investigating."[63]

As Davenport trained fieldworkers, he impressed upon them that the hovel families they were looking for might not always be linked to state institutions. As they traveled through the countryside, he urged them to "Be on the lookout, all the time, for interesting families."[64] In published studies, authors like Goddard and Arthur Estabrook similarly implored their lay audiences to look for "interesting" families. "There are Kallikak families all about us," Goddard proclaimed, inspiring spin-off studies like the "Canton Kallikaks" and "The Kallikaks of Kansas."[65] "These country slums are not restricted to such groups as the Jukes and the Nams and Kallikaks," Estabrook contended, informing the readers of popular science magazine *Eugenics* that although their leisurely travels up and down the Hudson River might only reveal good people living in fertile valleys, a few days in the foothills and the "back country sections" would show a much different side of rural life.[66]

In practice, key to distinguishing between the idyllic and anti-idyllic was watching for "interesting"—perhaps queer, peculiar, misfit—families, identifying the kinds of locations where such people lived, and searching for those particular topographies. This was particularly true for amateur researchers, who did not have an institutionalized subject with whom to begin a study. Just as professional researchers had to parse gossip into biological taxonomies, amateurs had to practice ways of seeing that could distinguish scenic landscapes of rural leisure and efficient farming landscapes from impoverished landscapes that would later, in the 1930s, be termed "submarginal." Estabrook, the most prominent fieldworker trained by the ERO, explained retrospectively in 1929 that

> It was soon apparent from the reports of these field workers that there were many people living in out-of-the-way places in the country, on the hillsides, in the secluded woods, along the river banks, who did not measure up to the economic, social or intellectual level of the farmers on the more productive farms or the people in the small villages of the country.[67]

Distinct from "hillbilly" and "white trash" families, the hovel families of interest to fieldworkers were rarely in the hills or mountains of Appalachia or the Ozarks, although they were very often in hilly areas. Amateur Sadie Myers in 1912 sent her research on a "very interesting" family in Cache County, Utah, to the ERO, explaining that "in glancing over the topography of the state one would naturally pick out this valley" as one that fostered feeblemindedness.[68] Primarily, the hovel family was found in geographies defined by isolation and seclusion.

Yet, as advocates of eugenics tried to persuade ordinary citizens to look for particular sorts of landscapes that were more likely to foster dysgenic traits, they emphasized that degeneracy could strike any rural community, even in a "flourishing" and "scenic" agricultural area of the Midwest.[69] In a 1913 magazine article entitled "Village of a Thousand Souls," Wisconsin psychologist Arnold L. Gesell made visible and spatialized the hidden degeneracy of the scenic small town by rendering a eugenic pedigree chart in the form of a village map (fig. 1.1). Gesell's village map is a striking contrast to Progressive Era maps of the ideal, "beautiful" imagined city. In Ebenezer Howard's "Garden City," as Susan Schweik contends, people with disabilities were displaced from and "perfectly segregated outside the urban garden," in asylums for the blind and deaf, a farm for epileptics, and convalescent homes, while the heart of the city offered the "promise of disability-free boulevards to everyone else."[70] Gesell's map, in contrast, represented degeneracy running amok—and not in an isolated country area, but in a small town, with blocks and churches. Gesell rendered icons of churches, saloons, and homes with symbols for supposedly inheritable conditions

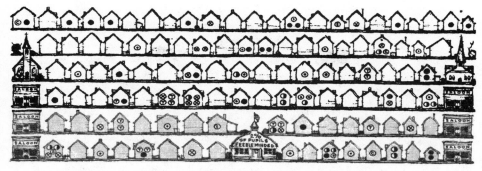

1.1 A drawing depicts an abstract "typical" small town with six rows of generic houses—many containing symbols that represent "defective" traits—as well as saloons, churches, and a school labeled "2% of pupils feebleminded." The caption reads "Eugenic map of The Village of a Thousand Souls—220 families (1880–1913)." *American Magazine.*

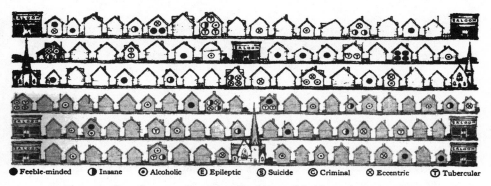

1.2 The town from figure 1.1 is continued with an added legend naming the types of "defects" that symbolically occupy the town's houses: "feeble-minded," "insane," "alcoholic," "epileptic," "suicide," "criminal," "eccentric," and "tubercular." *American Magazine.*

like feeblemindedness, insanity, suicide, alcoholism, epilepsy, criminality, eccentricity, and tuberculosis (fig. 1.2).[71] By circumscribing the symbols for "defective" unit traits in homes rather than individual pedigree charts, and by emphasizing the typical nature of the community profiled, "Village of a Thousand Souls" urged readers to profile nearby rural communities in similar ways—to document the social, economic, and intellectual failures of rural villages, and to use eugenics to address the problems thus recognized.

As Gesell emphasized the ubiquity of degenerate rural towns and the ways that degeneracy hid within even the most serene pastoral landscapes,

1.3 "A Sociological Contrast" juxtaposes photographs of two homes. In "Evidence of a Feeble Mind," a man sits outside a small, roughly constructed home atop crude stairs. In "Evidence of a Vigorous Mind," several well-dressed figures lounge in the yard of a stately white home. *American Magazine.*

he made it very clear that there was a particular *type* of person or family who threatened rural and implicitly white communities from the inside. In a photographic juxtaposition entitled "A sociological contrast," *American Magazine* presented, as "Evidence of a Feeble Mind," an image of a dilapidated one-story log shack with a lone white man posed in front of the home's single window (fig. 1.3). Beside it, a photograph captioned "Evidence of a Vigorous Mind" featured a stately, two-story Victorian home, decorated with three white women and one white man, dressed, respectively, in immaculate ankle-length gowns and a fine suit, and engaged in leisurely activities like watering a flower and reclining in a hammock. The text of the article confirmed that class and sexuality were the primary differences between the typical feebleminded family and a family of the better sort. Gesell's man "of doubtful mental caliber" was deemed feebleminded partly because he "dwelt in a tumbledown house" and "drove a disreputable horse," and partly because his "unattractive" yet sexually assertive daughter was proof that his condition had been inherited.[72] Gesell's "Village of a Thousand Souls" depicted an exemplary " 'slumlike' village hovel in a land of plenty," popularizing the work of published family studies and showing a lay audience that mental deficiency could be recognized through sexual and economic difference in rural white communities.[73]

American Magazine readers should not be blamed if, in reading Gesell's story, they felt that they too could conduct a study like the one conducted by a professional psychologist. Unlike ERO studies, which were at least based on gossip from multiple sources, Gesell's primary source was simply the gossip of his own mother. The photograph Gesell chose to represent the vigorous-minded family resembled the Gesell family's own house enough as to "infuriate local residents."[74] The photograph of the "tumbledown house" was not as Gesell represented it, either. The photograph of the home of Abraham Schmocker, a Swiss immigrant, was from 1885—twenty-five years before the photo it sat alongside for comparison— even though Gesell had another photo of Schmocker. In the second photograph, his house appeared coarsely made, his windows stuffed with rags to keep out the Wisconsin cold (fig. 1.4). Yet the photo was framed tightly, so instead of gazing at his ramshackle stairs, viewers encountered Schmocker himself, posed next to his front door. He sat unassumingly beside a washboard and bucket, hands grasped loosely around the small cat in his lap.

1.4 In front of his humbly made log home, Abraham Schmocker sits on a bench next to a washtub, holding a small cat on his lap. Wisconsin Historical Society. WHS-25660.

The scene was striking in its ordinary domesticity rather than in the shock value of rudely constructed stairs. On paper, Schmocker lived out the kind of white masculinity that Roosevelt and others idealized: he was a European immigrant who had moved to the "frontier" of Wisconsin in the nineteenth century, a settler of the first generation to directly colonize and lay false claim to the land his humble home was built on, implicated in the direct dispossession of Native people. But the "strenuous life" that Roosevelt was so enamored of was not all fighting and toiling. Even those with the "manly and adventurous qualities" necessary to move halfway across the world and colonize another's land for himself, like Schmocker, might enjoy sitting quietly outside his home, petting his cat.[75]

"Interesting" families of eccentrics living counter to social norms in secluded valleys and hillsides, on the edges and outskirts of more "attractive" communities—this was the stuff of eugenic family studies, the evidence of moral and intellectual disabilities, of the need to sterilize, institutionalize, and restrict. But minus the voyeur's interest in topography and minus the neatly drawn diagrams charting each and every form of difference, this was the stuff of ordinary life in rural white communities—ordinary life that was enmeshed in the power relations of settler colonialism and underwritten by the often-invisible property of whiteness itself. The mundane domesticity of most "interesting" gossip ran counter to the anti-idyllic optic, yet eugenic researchers elicited that gossip, turned it into science, penned popular articles and monographs, and inspired amateurs around the nation to join the hunt for rural "defectives." While rural denizens apparently shared their knowledge of friends' and family members' peculiarities with researchers, it was eugenics advocates who transformed those peculiarities into pathologies and remade those local pathologies into a national crisis.

FROM GOSSIP TO DIAGNOSIS: SEXUALITY, RACE, AND THE CONDUCT TEST

Judging a person's intelligence based on their social conduct was not just a facet of eugenic fieldwork, it was part of the state machinery for determining who should be institutionalized, sterilized, and prohibited from marrying. Medical practitioners, heads of institutions for the disabled, and legal representatives such as county clerks used an anti-idyllic "conduct test" to assess and identify feebleminded people by examining not only their visual appearance, but their lifelong history of social and sexual behavior as well. The conduct test allowed people with medical and legal authority, not just fieldworkers, to use stories about refusals to marry, poorly kept homes, or flings with homeless men to support their diagnoses of feeblemindedness. Eugenicists understood same-sex sexuality, interracial sex, and gender transgression, among other forms of deviance, to be evidence of low intelligence and irresponsibility that afflicted individual white people but not the entire white race. Concerned most with the problem of the "unrecognized moron," the irresponsible white woman who could pass for normal, eugenicists compelled community action both to identify peculiar local folks and to support legislation that would restrict their ability to live freely, reproduce, or marry. Conduct tests searched for the kind of domesticity, intimacy, and sociality that we might also deem queercrip domesticity.

Eugenicists were concerned with queer behaviors because they evidenced a mental disability like feeblemindedness, not because "homosexuality" itself was considered a disorder. It was not only queer behaviors that raised the specter of feeblemindedness, of course. Public concerns about the feebleminded reached a "near hysterical pitch" during the 1910s, largely because the feebleminded came to encompass a new and much larger category of moral defectives than had previously existed: those who purportedly had the intelligence to know right from wrong but lacked the mental power necessary to resist wrongdoing.[76] Eugenicists were worried that feebleminded women might transmit their hereditary "mental deficiency" to their children biologically, but they were also motivated by the "universally recognized fact" that a defective adult would tend to "lower standards of living among the normal people who come in contact with him,"[77] and that a feebleminded child would "poison morally the children of an entire neighborhood."[78] Of the "idiots," "imbeciles," and "morons" who constituted the feebleminded—in order of ascending intelligence—it was "morons" who attracted the most attention, as they were nearly impossible to detect.

A conduct test was deemed necessary by psychiatric and social welfare professionals because intelligence tests failed to classify many nonconforming people as feebleminded. As psychologists developed intelligence tests that wildly overestimated the preponderance of intellectual impairments among the US population, "morons" were among the minority who were actually able to pass written and oral intelligence tests—yet, on the basis of their moral conduct, they were diagnosed as feebleminded.[79] "Intelligence" is not a neutral concept, and quantitative intelligence tests were culturally biased attempts to prove the superiority of white, middle-class, non-immigrant men.[80] It is especially striking, then, that even by their own measures, on tests of their own making, scientists struggled to definitively prove that their most worrisome subjects were indeed feebleminded. "Morons" who passed intelligence tests may or may not have been "more intelligent" than those classed as "idiots" or "imbeciles," but they certainly proved more frustrating for scientists.

The "conduct test" was a scientific name given to the observation of rumors of sexual misbehavior or failures of domesticity. Unlike intelligence tests, conduct tests were not standardized. Those identified as feeble-minded by conduct tests were women who made homes that were untidy or unchaste, men who did not work regularly or did not marry, women who slept with homeless men, and people who were identified as "sexual perverts."[81] The conduct test had wide-reaching power, as it was often used to censure and sometimes institutionalize poor and working-class white women for becoming pregnant outside of marriage or for simply having reputations as "loose" women. The feebleminded were considered unable to "manage [their] affairs with ordinary prudence," and the conduct test specifically focused on those who lacked "power of resistance to evil and of self-support"—in other words, the perverse and the poor.[82]

Conduct tests judged any "immoral" deviation from heteronormativity, not just improper reproductive sexuality. In Minnesota, institutional officials endorsed the use of a conduct test, including an examination of the patient's sexual history, to determine whether a person should be institutionalized for insanity or feeblemindedness; at their suggestion, the conduct test was written into a statewide compulsory institutionalization law. R. M. Phelps, the superintendent of the St. Peter Hospital for the Insane, justified the need for a conduct test by arguing that there were a number of people who could pass the intelligence test despite intrinsic defectiveness: such people were "often moral perverts—or moral imbeciles—sexual perverts—perhaps kleptomaniacs. A larger number are known as 'always queer'—'always seclusive'—'always cranky'—'always eccentric.'"[83] Phelps employed a series of dashes, spaces, and unconventional punctuation to articulate the unsettled relationships between queer, eccentric, and moody behaviors that he could not communicate adequately through words. By repeating the word "always," however, Phelps made it clear that while the states of mind that led men and women to act queerly might lack precise names, he was certain that such disabled states were lifelong rather than temporary.

Thus, in order to judge whether someone was truly feebleminded, the conduct test had to be applied to their entire life history, not just the circumstances that brought them to the state's attention. In arguing for the adoption of a conduct test, Phelps contended that a life history was necessary to recognize the "always queer" feebleminded people who were "often without superficial defect," and he provided several examples to this effect. One in particular was a "rather youngish man" who had "courted a number of respectable girls, through all plans up to marriage, including ways of furnishing the house;—and then disappeared." In contrast to most references to feeblemindedness during this period, Phelps's man was from a respectable, educated, and middle-class background—he was marginalized not by class, but by his refusal to join a woman in forming a heterosexual household economy. Yet despite his privileges, and despite manifesting none of what Phelps called the "ordinary stigma of insanity," the man repeatedly got cold feet after making an initial commitment to a lifetime of intimacy with a woman. Whatever the man's reasons for bolting at the thought of lifelong heterosexual intimacy, Phelps found his refusal to participate in romantic heterodomesticity to be perverse. Although the man was of "good apparent intelligence," his history showed that "even in childhood, he showed sex peculiarities," and, with "apparent glibness," had refused to learn to abide by sexual norms.[84] Based on this history of a lifelong inability to conduct himself normally with regard to sex and romance, Phelps concluded that the man was not insane, as others might suggest, but instead suffered from a "life long 'defect'" that belonged to a "branch of feeble-mindedness." The conduct test looked not just for pregnancies or heterosexual intercourse out of wedlock, but for all kinds of "sex peculiarities," including those that might lead a man away from heterosexual marriage.

Both the popular press and amateur eugenic fieldworkers concurred that sex perversity was a symptom of feeblemindedness or high-grade mental defect. Although scholars have contended that the category of the feebleminded, and particularly that of the moron, were "almost synonymous with the illicit sexual behavior of the women adrift," early twentieth-century commentators stated that both categories had become nearly synonymous with sexual perversion, which itself often referred to homosexuality.[85] A legal analyst lamented in 1921 that Chicago newspapers had been using "moron," "which properly means a person limited in intelligence," to instead describe "a psychopathic person with psychoses of sexual perversion."[86] In the book *Race Decadence*, physician William Samuel Sadler asserted that "No discussion of feeble-mindedness, moronism, etc., would be complete with some consideration being given to the question of sexual perversions," suggesting that the relationship between moronism and "perversions that are more or less homosexual in their nature" was not out of the ordinary.[87] Even amateur eugenic investigator Bernice Reed described one of the men of "The Trix Family"—a nearby "hovel family" that she described in a study that she sent to the ERO—as "simple-minded" not because of an intelligence test, which she did not use, but because he was "very feminine" and enjoyed staying at home and doing housework—a negative judgment both of gender nonconformity and of "feminine" labor.[88] The conduct test created a way of viewing the division of labor that expanded definitions of feeblemindedness to include sexual deviants and gender transgressors of all intellectual abilities, despite occasional objections that such deviations belonged more properly to diagnoses of insanity or the classification schemas of sexology.

The most popular image of the "moron girl" was a poor, white rural woman who reproduced prolifically, but in the field, researchers attempted to name and record every kind of gender variance or sexual deviance they encountered. Although the people classified as feebleminded for being "sissies" and "sex perverts" were typically men, rural white women who rejected relationships with men or norms of femininity were also described as feebleminded. Fieldworker Z. E. Udell reported the case of a young person who frequently quarreled with her parents because she "did not care to hurry about marrying." Her mother, according to Udell, indicated that she had "acted queer from time to time for about five years," and her sister Lucy confirmed that her difficulties dated to the onset of puberty, telling Udell that "when she matured she was disgusted and would stop her courses by using cold water."[89] Perhaps the young person was claiming ownership over a body that had been subjected to childhood sexual abuse; experiencing what might later be understood as gender dysphoria, wishing for sexed markers like menstruation to go away; or feeling a compulsive need to be clean. Perhaps it was none of those, or a combination. Whatever caused the young person's fraught relationship to her body and desire to delay marriage, she was considered feebleminded and insane not because she threatened to spread her "defective germ plasm," but because she threatened not to want to.

A history of "sex perversion" often led a eugenicist to declare a person feebleminded or perhaps insane, but eugenicists also used sex perversion to ascribe other diagnoses. Describing a man who had embodied "the nature of a sex perversion," Davenport mentioned that his father had been the same way, but that, "much more to the point, his mother was given to epileptic fits."[90] Sexual deviance was represented as a sign of hereditary abnormality, to be sure, but researchers suggested it could have various causes. In this case, the man's "perverted acts," Davenport postulated, took place "in an abnormal mental state" resembling epilepsy, so the man could not help his fits "anymore than the mother could help hers."[91] Despite the fact that the man's father evidenced exactly the same condition, Davenport found a way to blame the man's mother for his hereditary faults, while insisting that the man was not responsible for his own sexual activities. He also understood sexual peculiarity as a symptom of mental disability, like fits or a low IQ test score, not as vice or illness itself.

Advocates of the conduct test asked states to write it into law in order to protect the "normal" man who might be deceived by a pretty but nonetheless "abnormal" young woman. As Goddard insisted to Davenport, the public needed to be informed that the "most dangerous children in a community are those that look entirely normal," and yet are "really feebleminded and incapable of taking care of themselves."[92] This "problem of the *unrecognized* moron" and its significance for normal men was particularly emphasized in fictional representations of feeblemindedness.[93] A short story published in *Atlantic Monthly* in 1917 conjured a courtroom "packed with grimy, lowering fathers, grimy, worried mothers, grimy, sullen, abnormal children," wherein a judge was committing a feebleminded woman's children to state homes. Emphasizing that the woman's husband was a good man, the story advocated for laws prohibiting the marriage of the feebleminded, suggesting that they were necessary to protect normal men from the threat of feebleminded women. "Shouldn't the law have protected him and his descendants from this blight?" several courtroom visitors asked. "How could he know that she was feeble-minded? And he had a right to know."[94] Arnold Mulder's 1915 novel *Bram of the Five Corners* related the story of a second-generation Dutch immigrant from a provincial village in rural Michigan who made the mistake of falling for a feebleminded girl named Hattie. "The girl was undeniably pretty," the narrator insisted, and her prettiness, combined with her penchant for giggling, allowed the male protagonist to recognize her fate and break off their engagement.[95]

Civic action was required not just to protect individual men from simple pretty girls but to defend and restore the intellectual and moral prowess of the white race. Among white people, diagnoses like feeblemindedness were used to explain immorality and maintain claims to racial superiority. Intrinsic to the diagnosis was the contention that mental deficiencies were the only reason a white woman might stray from racialized sexual and gender norms. As columnist Robert Quillen wrote in the *Washington Post*,

> The normal woman, made moral by Nature for her own good and the good of the race, is protected in chastity by a sense of modesty and purity; but this normal barrier is found only in normal women. The feebleminded lack the protection in proportion to their lack of intelligence and thus it is that the women of the half world are recruited from the ranks of the half wits.[96]

Ernest Bicknell, the secretary of the Indiana Board of State Charities, confirmed that the implicitly white feebleminded woman fell into vice only because she was "lacking the protection which should be her birthright."[97] One fieldworker excused the immoral and wretched home conditions of an entire Polish family by describing them as "feeble-minded and therefore not responsible."[98] When a white family—even an "ethnic" white family—was designated feebleminded, it meant that a woman's entire race was not held responsible for her moral failings. This allowed eugenicists to continue proclaiming the superiority of the white race, particularly white womanhood, even as they documented its many "deficient" individuals.

The traits that characterized individual mental disabilities among whites were taken as evidence of blanket racial inferiority in Black Americans and American Indians. This is most exemplified in *Mongrel Virginians*, the only prominent family study to center a community of color. Many family studies had described their subjects through racialized and orientalist flourishes—metaphors of "gypsies," tales of "dusky"-hued forebears, or rumors of a distant "Indian" ancestor—but they were explicitly concerned with white families and the protection of whiteness. Interracial sociality and intimacy were routinely chronicled in family studies, but merely as evidence that a white woman was feebleminded. *Mongrel Virginians* intruded on a community of Monacan Indians who had intermarried with Black and white people, seeking to reclassify them as "colored" per the recently passed Racial Integrity Act. This erased their Indigenous status, an act that Monacans and other Virginia Indians contested, and later described as "paper genocide."[99] Estabrook and sociologist Ivan McDougle claimed that two types of racial "stock" might lower a mixed white/Indian community's intelligence: "white stocks which are known to be below the average mental level" and "negro stocks, which are necessarily below the level of the whites."[100] Making explicit their assumption of white intellectual superiority, Estabrook and McDougle also stated clearly that the "average mental level" was by definition white. Any individuals who were measured inferior to the "average mental level"—the feebleminded—were implicitly white as well.

Eugenicists described Black people in many of the same ways they did the white "feebleminded," but the distinction of a medical diagnosis was considered unnecessary, perhaps even redundant. Even after controversial army intelligence tests reported the average "mental age" of Black recruits to be within range for a diagnosis of feeblemindedness, white eugenicists in the 1910s still rarely used the term "feebleminded" to describe Black Americans with or without perceived intellectual disabilities.[101] Before the 1930s, only Black social scientists like W. E. B. DuBois and E. Franklin Frazier expressed concerns about "feeblemindedness" within Black communities.[102] Even when people of color were given medical diagnoses and deemed in need of institutionalization, they were typically sent to almshouses or reformatories rather than institutions for the disabled.[103] The "conduct" constituting feeblemindedness was so broad that it was applied to all kinds of white women; yet, for Black women and girls, that definitional imprecision cast doubt on the legitimacy of their diagnoses. In Kentucky, "a colored girl" diagnosed as feebleminded on the basis that she "could not learn in school" was instead accused of being un*willing* to learn. "The girl was ablebodied," the journal reported, "yet her pension was making it easy for her and her mother to be 'parasites.'"[104] "Able-bodied but irresponsible" was the very definition of feeblemindedness among white women, but in a Black teenager, it became evidence of malingering.

The conduct test was devised as a method of looking for mental and intellectual disabilities among white people who, despite seeming otherwise mentally "normal," might undermine purportedly scientific claims to white racial superiority through their queer proclivities, odd kinship formations, unkempt households, and estrangement from the modern economy. If such women and men were understood to be feebleminded—that is, incapable of economic, social, and moral competence, rather than unwilling to submit to economic, social, and moral norms—then they could be institutionalized, sterilized, and removed from the white gene pool, thereby allowing white racial superiority to assert itself unimpeded.[105]

Eugenicists targeted poor backwoods families not in spite of the rural idyll, but because of its lofty impossibility. The popular nonfiction of eugenic family studies nationalized the trope of the anti-idyll by sensationally "revealing" that all over the countryside, sexual perverts were having "fits" and organizing gangs of local degenerates to vote; living interdependently and peaceably with kith and kin who had "temperamental peculiarities" or were "fond of talk and loafing about; or spurning marriage, work in the formal economy, and the competition" of modern industrial society.[106] Eugenicists lamented that "an increasing recognition of the value of mutual help" was making it more possible for the "inert, untrained, or ignorant"— the "constitutionally unsuccessful"—to survive and thrive.[107] In decrying mutual support, eugenic family studies chronicled the ways that interdependence characterized life in poor rural white communities, in contrast to idealized notions of Jeffersonian independence and "pioneer" masculinity. But for the person who was, say, socially proscribed from owning a more reputable horse—or did not care to marry, or enjoyed gathering blueberries because it allowed his mind to wander, or did not want her neighbors to discuss whether she was being sexually assaulted—encountering a fieldworker and finding herself in such a chronicle was sure to end badly. The poor families who most sensationally contradicted the notion of white rustic virtue were those who faced its most serious consequences: institutionalization, sterilization, or being prohibited from marrying for failing to meet the norms of the rural idyll.

By instructing Americans to be on the lookout for "interesting," "defective" families in the country, eugenic family studies created a purportedly scientific optic for diagnosing undesirable traits as evidence of a social disease that could only afflict white people. Family studies nationalized the anti-idyll at a historical moment when rural life seemed to be an afterthought among US elites, at the point in US history when the population became more "urban" than "rural." A few years later, however, the Great Depression—which, for many rural denizens, was not a new experience of poverty but a continuation of it—brought nostalgic yearnings for a more idyllic "rural America" back to the cultural forefront. Farm Security Administration (FSA) photography documented these hard times, acknowledging that social factors were at play. In doing so, the FSA piqued hope that poverty was temporary and that the people afflicted could be rehabilitated, even as photographs left traces of the anti-idyll that the project tried to disavow.

2: CURIOUS SCENES

The Fringes of Rural Rehabilitation in 1930s Documentary Photography

Mrs. Hale was standing with one of her sons outside their log cabin near Black River Falls, Wisconsin, when two men from Washington, DC, came visiting in June of 1937. Though she did not initially wish to speak with them, they induced her to. One of them, Russell Lee, had traveled to Wisconsin to photograph small farmers and loggers in the cutover region for the US Farm Security Administration (FSA). The other, Roy Stryker, was the director of the FSA's Historical Section and had joined Lee out in the field for a few days. Unlike the eugenic fieldworkers discussed in chapter one, who traveled through the countryside to tell anti-idyllic stories focused on individualized pathology, Lee was in Wisconsin to chronicle structural poverty: the struggles of poor families farming the stump-strewn "cut-over" land left behind by logging companies.[1] Yet Lee was well aware of the reputation that poor rural white communities had, and he knew that Hale would be aware of it as well. As Stryker recounted later, Lee, "with that first quick step of his," approached the "little old lady" and her son, who "wasn't too bright." Lee wanted to photograph them, but Hale rebuffed him belligerently. Lee had a second angle, though: "a lot of people in the city," he reminded her, thought that poor folks were "just a bunch of lazy loafers out here." Whether Lee's remark was taken as a threat or an assurance, Hale assented. She purportedly allowed Lee to take the photograph (fig. 2.1), invited him back for more photos of her entire family, and even permitted him to take photos inside her cabin. "I can find you lots of pictures," Hale promised Lee, "but we are not lazy."[2] In Lee's first photo of Hale, she stands in front of her cabin with a hand on one hip and a basin resting on the other; beside her, sitting in a stack of tires, her son is smoking a cigarette. It is not

2.1 Mrs. Hale and her oldest son outside their log cabin. The son smokes a cigarette and sits in a pile of tires. Library of Congress, FSA/OWI Collection, LC-USF34-030039-E.

clear whether Lee sought to visually document the son's perceived disability or why that detail lodged itself in Stryker's memory. The official caption strives to set Hale's family apart from the anti-idyllic representations of eugenic family studies. The caption emphasizes her married status, her family's physical capacity to build their own home, and the thrift with which they did so. Whether or not Lee believed the gossip that rural white folks were "lazy loafers" or "n[o]t too bright," he had promised to rehabilitate their image, and his caption did not betray that promise.

The Great Depression offered an opportunity for a new narrative about rural white poverty, one that might attribute social nonconformity to larger economic problems rather than moral defects and hereditary deficiencies. FSA photos, created between 1935 and 1943, were not anti-idyllic during their time, but they were not quite idyllic, either.[3] The FSA images that became enduring representations of the Great Depression evoked the potential and desire for the idealized white rural family but did not imagine such a family to be a transparent fact of rural life. Across fiction, film, and visual art, 1930s cultural production became increasingly invested in harkening "back" to imagined small-town values that were associated with an earlier era; this interest in "rural values" and "folksiness" shaped the popular arena through which FSA photographs circulated in the 1930s.[4] The FSA was a federal agency that provided welfare relief programs to poor farmers, in addition to administering the now-famous documentary photography program that was headed by Stryker and made famous by photographers such as Dorothea Lange and Walker Evans. In order to justify the agency's work, the photography program had to combat a misconception held by the "general public, and more specifically, the urban public": the "dream of the happy farmer."[5] The FSA photography program sought to make the public aware of the "appalling waste of lives and land" in places like the cutover lands of the Great Lakes states and the mountains of Appalachia and the Ozarks, which were threatening to "create a class of [white] American peasants." At the same time, they had to show that with successful government intervention, sympathetic white farmers and their families could be made happy and efficient once more.[6]

Within the vast FSA archive, however, are images that index alternative domestic and family arrangements, disrupting the "myth of the nuclear family," and telling different stories about 1930s poverty than their more iconic counterparts. The myth of the nuclear family, according to Nayan Shah, "renders any other form of kinship and household structures pathological, aberrant, and incompatible with cultural support and political privilege."[7] Most of the FSA archive reinscribed this myth, minimizing all sorts of family formations and "stranger intimacies" that characterized the lives of poor people during the 1930s. Poor rural families often formed interdependent households to share the burden of farm and domestic labor, for example, but as Wendy Kozol demonstrates, FSA photos rarely depicted households composed of multiple families, several generations living together, or even an adult child.[8] Yet there are exceptions to these general rules. In some FSA photo series, the material conditions engendered by particular vocations—seasonal labor like logging, for example, or the gendered labor of sex work and public entertainment—inadvertently reveal queer circumstances: nonnormative family structures and irregular bodyminds that resist visual normalization.

A queercrip approach to FSA photography traces how the cultural logic of visual rehabilitation worked in the 1930s and how, in spite of that, unrehabilitated queercrip domesticity, intimacy, and social life made their way into the FSA archive. This chapter begins by analyzing the deeply gendered pictorial rehabilitation undertaken by the FSA. I continue by analyzing the traces of white queer and disabled figures who appear in photographs by Lange, Marion Post Wolcott, and Arthur Rothstein, in spite of FSA rehabilitation narratives. In the last two sections, I focus on two sets of photographs that contradicted the gendered and sexualized rehabilitation narrative: a 1939 photo series from the Northern Minnesota Pioneers' Home, a retirement home for unmarried lumberjacks, and the 1938 Alamo Bar series, which featured a middle-aged saloon entertainer named Mildred Irwin and her female admirer.

FROM MADONNA TO MRS. AMERICA AND BEYOND: THE INCOMPLETE PROJECT OF REHABILITATING RURAL AMERICA

The discourse of rehabilitation required photo-stories that emphasized healthy, heteronormative families who did or could own farms, an emphasis that reflected FSA lending priorities.[9] Yet the rural denizens who were most economically disadvantaged were none of these things. Being landless, being disabled or ill, and living without a traditional family made a person much more vulnerable to poverty, and the idealized family farm system had never predominated in communities of color or in regions like the US South and California. Despite these lending and photographic priorities, FSA photographs that tell different kinds of stories do exist among the hundreds of thousands of images in the FSA archive. The "Madonna" and "Mrs. America" figures became iconic through social and cultural desires for a rehabilitated image of rural America, not simply through individual choices of photographers or program administrators.

If the happy farmer was the nostalgic symbol of the nation, then the mother/wife was the idealized symbol of the farm family. Rural white women came to bear a great representational burden, functioning as a barometer for the health of the nation and the success of the New Deal. Over the course of the 1930s, the ideal image of rural life conjured the trajectory of rehabilitation. The ideal shifted away from the destitute but worthy figure of the Madonna, and toward the capable figure of Mrs. America, an efficient poor woman who managed her meager resources admirably. Madonna and Mrs. America personified the "before" and "after," representing the sympathetic family who could be rehabilitated and the successfully rehabilitated family living modestly but getting by.

Rural rehabilitation was just one facet of New Deal agricultural programs, but the notion that struggling white farm families needed to be restored to their culturally privileged status appeared throughout representations of rural life in the 1930s.[10] In the 1910s and 1920s, as eugenic family studies popularized the view of racially and morally degraded rural white communities, the return of white disabled soldiers from World War I led to the development of physical rehabilitation—a science aimed at reversing "degradation" of a different sort, among those imagined to be racially capable of it.[11] While the white men returning from war were rehabilitated by "repairing" both their bodies and their reputations as workers, the women who represented rural white families were to be rehabilitated primarily, though not entirely, in reputation. Sometimes rural rehabilitation involved both cultural and physical components, particularly in the South, where a trio of endemic illnesses—hookworm, pellagra, and malaria—became known as the "lazy" diseases.[12] Since improved sanitation and diet could reduce the disabling effects of hookworm and pellagra, respectively, FSA public health and nutrition programs aimed to rehabilitate both ill bodies and the social stigma associated with them. Even on occasions when the cultural rehabilitation of white rural life did not involve the physical travails of rehabilitation medicine, it had many of the same goals: representing its subjects, in contrast to racialized groups excluded from it, as industrious, healthy, and capable of living in line with American economic standards.[13] Although the hundreds of thousands of images in the FSA archive represent nearly every kind of person imaginable, the photographs that became most iconic resonated with the rehabilitative narrative that rural white American poverty was aberrational and that the ideal of the hardworking middle-class white family farm could be restored.

If the aim of rehabilitation was the erasure of alterity within whiteness— making white people with disabilities "dissolve" into the "greater and single social whole"—then the late years of the FSA project evidenced the logic of rehabilitation in their move away from regional stories of feminized family poverty toward a generalized story about life in small towns.[14] Initially, the FSA desired photographs that would show that the white rural poor had the potential to be rehabilitated, and the downtrodden yet sympathetic Madonna figure did just that. The FSA's "Madonnas of the fields," most famously represented by Lange's "Migrant Mother," became the most iconic and enduring archetype of 1930s documentary photography. As Robert Hariman and John Louis Lucaites contend, the FSA's Madonna figures interpellated the public to step in and fulfill the "patriarchal duty" of a seemingly absent father.[15] The Madonna and child figures drew on Catholic iconography to represent poor white mothers as worthy, justifying the restorative uses to which state aid would be put. After a few years, however, the FSA needed images that would show the successes of the program, and the ideal archetype for rural white women shifted from the secular Madonna and child to a woman that Stryker called "Mrs. America."

Mrs. America was an accomplished and successful domestic figure who thrived while making do with less. This rehabilitated figure, also conjured by the "Mrs. America" pageant that began in 1938, was a highly recognizable symbol in the 1930s.[16] Mrs. America's home was modern and clean, and although efficient domestic labor was her defining characteristic, she never appeared burdened by the labor. While FSA Madonna figures were pictured caring for children, their toil in the fields and home was evident only in their lined, wearied faces. In contrast, Stryker wanted his photographers to capture Mrs. America at work. "To be specific," he wrote, "let us have more pictures of woman [sic] in the home, women in the kitchen, women gardening, women working."[17] Mrs. America was always working but never toiling. Further, as signified by her moniker, Mrs. America was not in need of further patriarchal support in the same way that the Madonna was. The Madonna figure had never been easy for FSA photographers to find, and the actual women behind the iconic images often led more complicated family and sexual lives than the photographs let on. But if Madonna images had to be carefully constructed to avoid visually referencing a husband or a lover, or more children than would be seen as "sympathetic," Mrs. America was even more elusive.

Behind the ideal of the family farmer who could be rehabilitated was a powerful, implicit, and incorrect understanding that the victims of Depression-era poverty were healthy, hardworking heterosexual families who had been struck by hard times but were not burdened by long historical legacies of slavery, colonialism, or capitalist exploitation, nor by the social consequences of anomalous bodies or aberrant desires. Certainly, some examples of the "noble poor" seemed to exist. But as photographers searched for subjects who could purport to represent Madonna or Mrs. America, they found far more stories that contradicted the happy family farmer narrative than those that supported it. These alternative narratives depicted poverty that was caused by structural inequality and could not be solved through rehabilitation alone: stories about centuries of racial inequality, decades of capitalist exploitation, and the consequences of disability, illness, and aging for people who lived without the social safety net of a "traditional" family. Yet stories that contradicted the potential for the happy, healthy white heterosexual farm family did not often circulate prominently and remain largely hidden within the vast FSA archive.

As FSA photography attempted to redeem rural white families, those families—as Lee's encounter with Hale illustrates—resisted and resented being the subjects of social reform photography, which they felt to be beneath them, associated with people of color and moral transgression. In the late 1930s, a poor farm laborer defended his family to Lange in explicitly racialized terms. Demonstrating a possessive investment in whiteness, the man proclaimed, "We ain't no paupers. We hold ourselves to be white folks."[18] Navigating his family's class status by appealing to their racial privilege, Lange's subject named what was implicit in documentary photography of the 1930s: that rural white families, regardless of how poor they were, did not belong to the racialized and morally questionable category of "paupers." As rural white poverty became more culturally visible, it highlighted white families' deviation from white middle-class gender norms—men failing as breadwinners, their haggard wives worn down from labor unbefitting them. Simultaneously, it provided poor white families with gendered economic narratives that allowed them to defend their moral honor, claim that their poverty was temporary, and insist on their belonging to the privileged category of "white folks."

The project of culturally rehabilitating rural whiteness was never easy or complete. If white photographic subjects were defensive about their racialized moral belonging, then photographers and editors surely considered such worries as well. Yet, in search of iconic figures who represented the need for and achievement of rural rehabilitation, FSA photographs continually documented disabled, sick, and aging white women and men who lived with nonnormative families.

OF LUMBERJACKS AND ENTERTAINERS: TRACING QUEER & DISABLED FIGURES IN THE FSA ARCHIVE

Despite the FSA's public emphasis on Madonnas and Mrs. Americas, queer and crip figures pervade the archive. Yet, as anti-idyllic understandings of rural life were being rehabilitated, these figures were relegated to the private realm of letters and personal journals and kept out of the public record of state photography and its captions. Sometimes photographers went to great lengths to conceal disability or nonnormative family structures; other times, they allowed disability or gender nonconformity to be visible but emphasized a subject's normativity in other ways. In the context of rural poverty, making pictures of "sissies" or "gimps" might raise the anti-idyllic specter of peculiar places that were beyond the bounds of rehabilitation.

Disabilities, particularly among men, were often concealed because they disrupted the heteronormative economic ideal that a rural family could be rehabilitated through a husband's physical capacity to labor and provide for his family. This is exemplified by comments made by Wolcott on a trip to Tennessee in 1940. Wolcott's assignment, which she found quite trying, was to take photographs of two families receiving welfare relief, one white and one Black. This type of assignment was typical, and from the outset it excluded kinship groups that did not look like a healthy, abled "family" should.[19] And indeed, nonnormative families and sick and disabled men were the primary source of her trouble. Finding families who were on public assistance was easy enough, as Wolcott traveled with a social worker.[20] What was "practically impossible," however, was finding "a man for the pix." Even when she found men to pose as part of a welfare-relief family, they were in bad shape: the white man she found was "a half cripple," and both he and the Black man were so ill that they had to go to the hospital before her session was over. If suitable men were so scarce—because they were disabled or in poor health, working out of town with the Works Progress Administration, or considered "chronic-transient" types who simply refused to stick around—this surely contributed to the poverty experienced by single women with large families.[21] Yet representing the true family situations of women on relief would not seem to evoke the same public compassion.

Even when a photographer like Lange centered a man's disability, the photo's composition and abridged official caption visually rehabilitated him by emphasizing his virility and continued capacity to labor.[22] Lange, who had polio as a child, self-identified as "physically disabled" and suggested that her experiences as a "semi-cripple" were integral to her life and work.[23] As Sally Stein contends, even though Lange sometimes distanced herself from those who were "conspicuously crippled," her body of work is filled with "footprints" that demonstrate how her embodiment shaped her photographic perspective: men stooping, squatting, and arranging their bodies to seek comfort; pictures made from angles that render people's bodies "stunted, crumpled, condensed to grotesquely foreshortened shapes"; and the recurring motif of the "body that leans," that depends on physical support.[24]

A 1939 photo from North Carolina combines all of these visual elements, even naming the subject as ill (fig. 2.2). In the center of a yard, a white man of about thirty sits on a wooden chair, clasping his hands loosely over a wooden cane. His family is arranged in the yard around him. Two children hunker on either side, restless, their legs drawn angularly into themselves. In the background, a woman rests her body against a tree, as a third child, in turn, rests upon her. The man's disability and its relationship to his labor capacity are made plain in both the photograph and its official caption, which reads "Father crippled with rheumatism. When well he works in a chair making factory." As the photo and caption make the man's disability visible, however, they appeal to white masculine independence and heteronormativity to rehabilitate him.[25] The caption identifies the man through familial relations—he is a "father," not a husband or farmer or factory worker—and the photograph's composition depicts him as able to sup-

2.2 A white family of five is pictured in a yard. At the center, the father sits in a wooden chair, hands resting on a stick or cane. Behind him, the mother leans against a tree, as one of the children leans against her. The official FSA caption read "Father crippled with rheumatism. When well he works in a chair making factory. Orange County, North Carolina." Library of Congress, FSA/OWI Collection, LC-DIG-fsa-8b34221.

port his family. The wooden chair that he sits on evokes his work at a chair factory and suggests that when in need, he can depend on himself. Since his wife stands a few paces behind him, her husband appears tall through perspective. She does not threaten to overtake him as head of the household, though she is positioned as simultaneously dependent and dependable: she is supported by the tree she leans against, while she supports the child who leans against her.

Yet Lange would have noticed what casual viewers might not: no one in the family sits or stands comfortably. Her longer General Caption heightened the photograph's ambiguity. FSA photographers used General Captions to provide context for a group of photos, but Lange's General Captions, crafted to generate "layers of meaning" through image and text, provided much more than context.[26] The abbreviated caption that the FSA officially paired with the photo is drawn from the "Family" section of the General Caption that Lange wrote with sociologist Margaret Jarman Hagood. In the full "Family" section of the caption, Lange and Hagood wrote:

> This mother had four children in three years; the oldest girl is seven, there are twin boys of six and the baby is five. The father works in a chair factory in Hillsboro, he has not worked for a month because he has been crippled with rheumatism. His tonsils were removed yesterday and he hopes he will be able to go to work again soon. The family have always lived in the country.
> The farm was once used to raise tobacco but none of it is cultivated now.[27]

With these five sentences, the story is much more nuanced. While the image centers the man, the text begins with the woman's perspective, and her crisis began earlier, when they became parents of four in three years. Now her recession into the back of the frame and her use of the tree for support might be read as a sign that she wishes to have less family responsibility, that she might be ready for her husband to take a more pivotal role. The full caption also complicates the temporality of the scene, raising hope that the man's illness might be temporary, then juxtaposing that hopeful futurity with a sense of how things have always been ("The family have always lived in the country") and how they used to be ("The farm was once used to raise tobacco but none of it is cultivated now"). Yet, if one were simply browsing the photo file at the FSA office, the ambiguity of the General Caption would be absent.

Likewise, gender nonconforming subjects were interpreted variously, sometimes kept off camera and sometimes captured on film, depending on the labor and disability associations. Ablebodied women who were perceived as masculine were often photographed laboring but were not named as gender or sexually nonconforming. In contrast, men who were perceived as feminine were labeled as such, but only as curiosities in private writing; such men rarely made it into the silver nitrate of the FSA archive. Wolcott, for example, wrote to Stryker that a mixed-race Louisiana man that she met seemed to be a "pansy," adding that "he certainly has some of the earmarks," although she did not elaborate what those were.[28] In 1942, photographer John Vachon wrote in his travel journal that he found it "strange" that a "hill farmer" in the Missouri Ozarks "should have a 20 year old effeminate son," but he neither photographed the man nor mentioned him in one of the numerous letters he wrote during that trip.[29] Gender nonconforming women appeared in FSA photographs as long as they were working outside, as typified by an onion worker photographed by Rothstein, who wore pants with a men's shirt and short haircut (fig. 2.3). The attire that women like her wore was not simply practical, but was often decidedly stylized and masculine. This is evident in a 1937 Lee photograph that depicts a woman wearing a wide men's tie with a collared, button-down shirt, plaid trousers, and dress shoes as she fills a watering can for the camera (fig. 2.4). As the disabled North Carolina man could be redeemed as a father and part-time chair-maker, these women could be visually rehabilitated—in this case, due to their ablebodied economic independence.

Every now and then, however, an FSA photographer framed not just an odd person, but a downright peculiar scene. The Pioneers' Home and Alamo Bar series stand out as curious examples of the relationships between sexual and gender difference, political economy, and disability and aging. Whether out of discretion or ignorance of nonheterosexuality among poor people, photographers rarely remarked upon the nonnormative lifestyles evident in a home for disabled bachelor lumberjacks or the gaze of a saloon singer protective of her intimate companion. Perhaps their unmarried lifestyles and intimate same-sex bonds were simply expected for people in their occupations. Lumberjacks and entertainers, among others, were not only disadvantaged by their wages, but by the fact that their vocations made marriage difficult. Freedom from marriage may have been the appeal, but not having a spouse and children meant less household income and a smaller safety net as one aged or if one became disabled. Not all poor rural folks were abled farmers with families, capable (and desiring) of rehabilitation.

By considering the social and economic contexts of these photographs, as well as the photographic encounters themselves, I analyze the ways that gender and sexual difference were bound to economic marginality and disability, and how those relationships were disavowed. FSA photography emphasized the potential of poor white rural families to be rehabilitated, and in doing so, publicly minimized connections between poverty, disability, and nonnormative family structures (even as eugenics remained an "absent presence" in FSA photography).[30] Yet those associations, as sensationalized as they were by eugenics, were never only prurient. Since the FSA raised the question of rural poverty, it was often on the cusp of depicting the reasons why people with disabilities and nonnormative family structures were more likely to be poor: not just social and economic demands for transient male and female labor that were publicly abjured, but the role of social welfare programs that strongly favored those understood to be

2.3 A woman with short curly hair prepares to pour a large basket of onions into a burlap sack held by a young man in pinstriped overalls and a fedora. The woman wears heavy work pants and a collared shirt, tucked into her pants, sleeves rolled up neatly around her biceps. Library of Congress, FSA/OWI Collection, LC-USF33-003309-M4.

2.4 A white woman fills a water can from a well. She wears plaid trousers, a collared button-down shirt, and a wide tie. Library of Congress, FSA/OWI Collection, LC-USF3301-011342-M3.

capable of rehabilitation. Bachelor lumberjacks may have been perceived as "queer" and saloon singers with intimate female friends as "odd," but their locations on the social fringe and economic margins were reinforced by the very welfare programs that reluctantly captured their photographs.

LOGGING BACHELORS:
QUEERCRIP DOMESTICITY IN THE NORTH WOODS

In Northern Minnesota, Vachon appeared to find Mrs. America. In his 1939 photograph from Lake of the Woods County, a light-complexioned woman stands in a kitchen, her handy homemaking evident in the neat stacks of dishes and name-brand products—Arm & Hammer baking soda, Quaker Oats—that occupy the cabinets and counter behind her (fig. 2.5). Perhaps fifty or sixty years old, the woman does not share the lined, prematurely aged face of so many "Madonnas of the fields," nor is she posed with children in tow. Yet, like so many Madonna figures, her situation was not quite what it seemed: Vachon's apparent "Mrs. America" was not managing this household as a wife and mother, but as a paid nurse or housekeeper for a group of eight elderly and disabled bachelors. Vachon had found the counterpart to Wolcott's manless Tennessee town: a community of retired bachelor lumberjacks, living together in a former hospital building. These

2.5 A white woman of about sixty stands in a kitchen, wearing a neat apron. Behind her are kitchen cabinets holding dishes and name-brand products like Arm & Hammer Baking Soda. Library of Congress, FSA/OWI Collection, LC-USF33-T01-001468-M3.

men, six of whom are depicted in the other thirteen photographs that Vachon took that day, were residents of the Northern Minnesota Pioneers' Home (fig. 2.6). The Pioneers' Home was a cooperative retirement home that the unmarried men had founded by pooling their newly gotten Old Age Assistance (OAA)[31] and by petitioning for aid from the county, state, and federal resettlement agencies associated with the Beltrami Island Project.[32] As local, state, and federal agencies attempted, without much success, to rehabilitate the public image of nonheteronormative men on the Minnesota cutover, the private worries of state officials told a different story.

Lumberjacks were understood as rowdy, unruly, and itinerant, much closer to the anti-idyll than the Madonna or Mrs. America of rural rehabilitation. New Deal programs that were perceived to support people on a "nonfamilial" basis, according to Margot Canaday, were disparaged and subordinated to those that specifically focused on supporting breadwinners and mothers in need.[33] As Shah contends, the "queer sociality attendant on transient labor" was typically occluded—in this case, by New Deal programs—in favor of the "intimacy cultivated within families and with familiars."[34] This was perhaps even truer for the queercrip socialities left behind by those who could no longer physically or mentally perform such labor: disabled, retired lumberjacks who were more impoverished than their younger, abled peers and did not even have the structure of the logging camp to "contain" them.

The northern Minnesota men's lone claim to rehabilitation was their status as white settlers on Anishinaabe (Ojibwe) land. This claim was inscribed in the name of their cooperative retirement home, the "Northern Minnesota Pioneers' Home," an explicit appeal to their racialized frontier virility over their elderly, crippled bachelorhood. The Pioneers' Home was situated on land that had belonged to the Red Lake Band of Ojibwe only twenty-five years earlier. Red Lake Ojibwe had successfully protected their land from allotment by holding all of their land communally, rather than parceling it out to individual family units.[35] The Red Lake Indian Reservation remains the only such "closed" reservation in the state, but in 1904 the state of Minnesota took thousands of acres of land from the Red Lake Indian Reservation, asking land companies to sell it to white homesteaders.[36] Among these homesteaders was at least one of the men who resided in the Pioneers' Home, Anton Parieda.[37] Even if the other men had been

2.6 Six elderly white men are posed together in a bedroom. Three stand and three sit together on a bed. All look directly into the camera except one, who does not seem to be oriented to the camera's location. His hands are clasped loosely on his lap. Some of the men seem to have impairments and have created adaptations. Library of Congress, FSA/OWI Collection, LC-DIG-ds-13168.

squatters rather than homesteaders—which may or may not have been the case—they were occupying land that had been coercively taken from Red Lake Ojibwe, whether by squatting or by maintaining the Pioneers' Home in Spooner, Minnesota. Further, as they received FSA and other state resources to provide meager funds for their retirement, the very same FSA project that benefited them—a project that ultimately resulted in the creation of a national forest and a national wildlife reserve—was used as a pretext to try to further dispossess Red Lake Ojibwe of their right to freely inhabit their land.[38]

To address long-term economic problems facing white settlers in the cutover and five other "problem areas" across the United States, the Resettlement Administration (RA) and related agencies attended to poor farmers through a program of rural rehabilitation that sought to forge more "normal" social and economic conditions in rural problem areas. Vachon was sent to photograph the Pioneers' Home in 1939 because it belonged to the Beltrami Island Project, one of the RA's earliest resettlement programs. As part of the cutover region constituted by northern Minnesota, Wisconsin, and Michigan, Beltrami Island—which is not an island but an inland geological formation—was determined to be a land-use "problem area," marred by the stump-strewn ground left behind by lumber companies after they extracted all of the valuable timber in the 1910s and 1920s. Designating the area a problem of land use obscured the fact that the state knew the land was not suitable for farming but created complicated environmental schemes to encourage poor white people to make homestead claims and dispossess Red Lake Ojibwe.

The circumstances depicted in the Pioneers' Home photographs demonstrated that not all white men could be rehabilitated, and that the conditions that caused poverty in the North Woods fostered the very family formations and bodyminds that were deemed outside the bounds of rehabilitation. Successful rehabilitation, according to the Minnesota agency tasked with rehabilitating the settlers and squatters who lived in the vicinity of what would become the Pioneers' Home, would create "self-sustaining human beings by enabling them to secure subsistence and gainful employment . . . in accordance with economic and social standards of good citizenship."[39] In practice, the resettlement agencies did not expect individuals to be self-sustaining, but to belong to family units that combined women's, men's, and children's labor to sustain themselves. It was considerably more difficult for men and women who were old, disabled, and unpartnered to become "rehabilitated" and survive without public assistance as the charter mandated. Authorities even noted a former lumberjack who had married a younger woman primarily to "have the security of a home since he is no longer young."[40]

2.7 Three old men, former lumberjacks, sit on a bed at the Northern Minnesota Pioneers' Home. The two on the right support each other: one leans tenderly toward the other, who sits primly beside him. Library of Congress, FSA/OWI Collection, LC-DIG-ds-13170.

Many ex-lumberjacks never married and thus were considered incapable of rehabilitation, meaning that those who could not be rehabilitated made up a significant percentage of the population. The social and economic conditions of the North Woods, which were structured by the homosocial workforces and transnational movements of the lumber industry, left behind large numbers of unmarried men without children who were old or disabled and had already traveled great distances from their families of origin. Yet successful rural rehabilitation required normative, abled families, thereby excluding those who were economically vulnerable—precisely because they could not rely on their physical abilities and the social safety net of a family through blood or marriage.

Vachon's Pioneers' Home series evocatively renders the social problems that stranded lumberjacks represented to resettlement agents; the social needs that retired lumberjacks experienced; and the queer, interdependent households that men formed to answer those needs. In "Ex-lumberjacks living in Northern Minnesota Pioneers' Home," three elderly men sit on a bed in a building that had once been the Spooner Hospital (fig. 2.7). The two on the right literally support one other, as one man leans tenderly to-ward the smaller man who sits primly beside him. Throughout Vachon's series, we find these two men together, one of them with a gaze that is al-ways slightly off—perhaps a sign that he had had a stroke, was experienc-ing dementia, or had a visual impairment—and the other always seeming mentally alert, but perhaps lacking the dexterity necessary to repair his clothes or fasten his buttons, as his clothing (oversized shirtsleeves, held up at his wrists with a band or cuff) appears adaptive. The photographs reveal the intimacy, care, and companionship that the men were able to offer one another, which they combined with the paid household labor of a local woman. By reading the gaps and absences in the Pioneers' Home series, we can understand the structural forces and personal desires that joined together to create this queercrip retirement home—forces of state, economy, settler colonialism, and intimacy that were typically disavowed by New Deal agencies.

The Minnesota Pioneers' Home might be understood as a form of queercrip domesticity rooted neither in the independence of individuals, nor in the dependence that characterized state and charitable institutions, but in the interdependence of eight men who were not related through blood or law. The Pioneers' Home, like the Chinese bachelor societies that Shah figures as an example of "queer domesticity," countered normative expectations that a household would be organized around a white married couple and its pursuit of reproduction. Even if the Pioneers' Home had only been founded out of mutual caretaking, it included "emotional relations between men and women that upset normative heterosexual marriage, as well as homosocial and homoerotic relations" like those Shah describes.[41] It also transgressed health-based domestic norms, since the idealized home of the early twenty-first century required not only white middle-class heterosexuality, but abledness.[42] Disability in the 1930s was understood not necessarily as a form of physical impairment, but as the "limitation in socio-economic function" that someone might experience as a result of physical or intellectual disabilities, illness, or old age.[43] By forging an inter-dependent and homosocial domesticity, the men of the Pioneers' Home would have disrupted gender and sexual norms even if they had no sexual or romantic relationships with one another.

Loving and erotic relationships between lumberjacks were not at all unusual, and the fact that the Pioneers' Home men were disabled and elderly does not preclude the possibility that their tenderness for one an-other was born out of the "love of a man for a man," in the words of one lumberjack-poet. If it were several decades earlier, eight cohabitating lum-berjacks almost certainly would have shared more with one another than their occupation. Sex between men who worked in logging, mining, and other extractive industries was well documented, but it was often chronicled by public health, vice, and criminal investigations that drummed up fears about sex between white men and nonwhite immigrants, sex between men and boys, and sex between people who took on different gender roles.[44] While immigrant men of color were commonly arrested, considered sexual perverts, and charged with sex crimes, white boys and men were represented as innocent of any intentional wrongdoing. Imagined to be "ordinary Americans," white migrant laborers who had sex with each other were characterized either as the victims of sexual assault or as so-called "situational homosexuals" who only had sex with one another because, for example, the logging camp lacked sufficient blankets and they became chilled at night.[45] Lumberjacks who wished to have intercourse with women could easily do so, particularly with sex workers in logging towns. Still, most outside observers groundlessly insisted that sex between lumberjacks came of convenience in the bunk room and would be abandoned in favor of heterosexual marriage once a man retired from logging.[46] One Minnesota missionary suggested that lumberjacks had sex with both men and women, but that neither came of love. They "have known the companionship of swine in the form of men and vampires who resembled women," the chaplain wrote, but "they have wanted love and known only vice."[47] Yet many ex-lumberjacks never found the kind of long-term heterosexual love that churchmen wished for them. Instead, they often continued to live with or otherwise depend on one another, deepening the bonds that they had forged as logging camp bunkmates (fig. 2.8).

A 1917 lumberjack ballad depicted the sex and romance that lumberjacks could share with one another—romance that the narrator suggests a woman could never provide. "The love of a woman is sweet," the narrator insists to open the poem, "In life I have fondled a few." Alluding to the biblical story of David and Jonathan, the ballad evokes warm feelings toward women before questioning whether one might desire more than a woman's love could provide. "But what is the nectar you drink," the poem asks, "The love of a man for a man?" The final two stanzas relate that love:

> For when she has thrown you aside,
> Has passed from embraces and sight,
> And all of the noonday has died
> And left but the stars and the night,
> You feel on your shoulder a hand,
> For comfort you come where you can,
> And deep in your heart understand
> The love of a man for a man.
>
> He'll go with you over the trail,
> The trail that is lonesome and long;

2.8 In a logging camp bunk room, three middle-aged white men sit together on a wooden bench, seemingly amused. One wears a mustache and a hat tipped to the side of his bald head. Several bunk beds, pushed together and holding thin mattresses, are visible in the background. On a few of the beds, men lie reading. Library of Congress, FSA/OWI Collection, LC-DIG-fsa-8b19967.

> His faith will not falter nor fail,
> Nor falter the lilt of his song.
> He knows both your soul and your sins,
> And does not too carefully scan.
> The highway to Heaven begins
> With the love of a man for a man.[48]

The love of a man for a man begins, the poem suggests, with the simple touch of a hand to a shoulder, and a desire for immediate "comfort" in the form of "com[ing] where you can." This experience is felt deeply, beyond its mere convenience. The language of "comfort" and "love" is a stark contrast to the language that vice investigators used to refer to same-sex activities in male migrant worker communities. Logging camp sexuality, like prison sexuality, to which it was frequently compared, challenged the modern division of heterosexuality from homosexuality, and further challenged the category of "situational homosexuality" that emerged to contain that which transgressed such neat distinctions.[49] Lumberjacks enjoyed each other's company in sexual, romantic, and social ways. Sometimes they enjoyed women's sexual and romantic company, and other times they did not seek it out. Either way, men in logging camps formed deep emotional attachments with one another that went far beyond the mere convenience of bunk-room sex.

The history of white lumberjack intimacy and sexuality is not celebratory, however. The figure of the lumberjack shares much in common with the figures of the sailor, soldier, and cowboy that constitute what Hiram Pérez terms the "rough trade of U.S. imperialism."[50] Through their colonial and imperial proximity to an exoticized "brownness," Pérez contends, these figures became archetypal icons of American masculinity and gay male desire.[51] By 1938, the lumberjacks of the Pioneers' Home were not the mythologized ideal of the strapping young "timber beast," but they nonetheless benefited from the settler mobilities that logging provided in North America.

From their intimate posture to their demand that resettlement agencies allow them to live together, the retired lumberjacks of the Pioneers' Home lived lives that were indelibly shaped by the social opportunities and the economic constraints of homesteading, logging, agricultural, and resettlement policies. Yet the photographs of the Pioneers' Home series contained the men within the sterile domestic environment of the former Spooner Hospital. Vachon's lumberjack photographs define them not through work or family, but through mundane sociality. Rather than centering their "productive labor" and "masculine independence," as photos of disabled men typically did, the men of the Pioneers' Home were depicted playing cards, reading the newspaper, and sitting together to pose for the camera.[52]

In one photo, this domestic containment is more ambiguous. In it, a single man—the man who shared intimacy with another on the bed—stands in the center, flanked on one side by signs of a well-cared-for domestic residence and on the other by familiar iconography: a framed and matted painting of a Madonna-and-child figure (fig. 2.9). In the painting, a young white woman holds a child to her chest. As the child grasps at the woman's long dark hair, the woman casts her gaze away from the viewers and the crook of her arm promises to protect the cherubic toddler from the world. Yet, in the context of the Pioneers' Home, this Madonna-and-child figure does not evoke the "familial and social stability" that it might otherwise.[53] The mass-produced religious iconography, placed in the background of a scene centering an elderly, unmarried man, evokes the tremendous social distance between the two.

The Pioneers' Home series hints at histories that were disavowed by public officials, who strained to clean up the ignoble history of poor Beltrami Island residents who were single or disabled, and the even more

2.9 An elderly white man stands, alone, in front of a painting done in the style of the Madonna and child. His pants are unfastened but held up by suspenders, and his oversized shirtsleeves are held up at the wrists by a band or cuff. Library of Congress, FSA/OWI Collection, LC-USF33-T01-001469-M2.

ignoble history of economic and state forces that constrained their lives. In doing so, officials obscured the material history of the lumberjacks and their relationship to the idealized home. Yet archival documents indexed significant fears about the questionable character of these men without families: lumberjacks' unmarried status led to fears that they were too individualistic, but their association with communistic agitation led to fears that they were not individualistic enough. R. I. Nowell, the FSA regional director for the area including Minnesota, Wisconsin, and Michigan, contended that the Beltrami Island Project was a challenge "primarily because of the characteristics of the families, because submarginal men are often closely associated with submarginal land. Many heads of family were former lumberjacks."[54] Nowell made explicit what was often thinly veiled. First, language like "submarginal," while ostensibly used to describe land, soil, or farms, was often about the individuals associated with it. Second, lumberjacks were seen as submarginal not because they lacked farming skills—which could have been rectified through extension service outreach—but because of the "characteristics of their families." The defining characteristic of lumberjacks' "families" was that they did not exist, at least not in any traditional sense. Despite the insistent use of the term "family" in published materials on rural rehabilitation, unpublished reports acknowledged that a plurality of households in Beltrami were just one person and the median household size was merely three.[55] Without a wife or children to assist with the incredibly labor-intensive work of farming on the cutover, unmarried former lumberjacks and bachelor farmers faced dire economic need and were often homeless, squatting in the forest. Yet, precisely for the reasons they needed assistance, "unattached persons" were less than ideal candidates for it.[56]

Though unmarried, the men of the Pioneers' Home did have supportive labor from a woman—the housekeeper who was pictured, Mrs.-America-like, in the neat kitchen with the name-brand products. Since she did not appear in any of the textual records and was not photographed in her own home, it is not clear what kind of family support she herself had—just that her labor was necessary for the lumberjacks' queercrip domesticity. Perhaps she was part of the Works Progress Administration's housekeeper program to employ poor women for families who needed support in the home.[57] Or maybe she had trained as a Delano Red Cross nurse, part of a public health program for rural communities that were impoverished and "peculiarly isolated."[58]

Resettlement officials who dissembled about the number of bachelors in the Beltrami Island area also downplayed the number of elderly and disabled people who needed relief. Nowell noted that every project in the cutover area had a "surprisingly large" number of people who were considered "chronic relief cases," arguing that widows with small children, "persons with physical handicaps," and "old couples" should instead be institutionalized.[59] There was no obvious institution to send them to, though. In a county where every township had been dissolved due to indebtedness, and where nearly 90% of farmers had lost their land for the same reason, there was no tax base to provide even a basic almshouse.[60] Even so, state and federal resettlement officials became involved with such cases reluctantly, acting on fears that squatters would cause forest fires and disrupt their efforts to create a state forest in an area not suited for farming.[61] Approximately 10% of the 300 "families" who were resettled were considered chronic relief cases; "old age" and "permanent disability" were the most commonly cited reasons for their need.[62]

Lumberjacks longed for the nonheteronormative life of being single, even though it made their economic struggles more difficult, concentrating the onus of farm labor on their weary bodies rather than sharing the burden with a wife and children. They expressed a melancholy longing to "hit the trail for an old fashioned bunk house, where single blessedness was the order of the day," desiring a singleness nonetheless surrounded by bunkmates.[63] Lumberjacks made more normative claims when they went on strike and sought to garner public support, insisting that a living wage would allow them to "maintain a home and raise a family which is the right of every man."[64] But many former lumberjacks, including Pioneers' Home resident Arthur Cooley, eschewed heterosexual families, establishing farms and cohabitating with other men. According to the 1920 census, the Michigan-born Cooley, then forty-eight years old, lived with a thirty-four-year-old German immigrant, described not as a hired man or a boarder but as a "partner."[65] Yet without a "family" in the traditional sense, even a younger farming partner could not provide a man like Cooley with enough assistance to weather disabilities and aging.

Although published reports rarely said so, the logging industry was the great cause of disability and poor health in northern Minnesota. Logging was a dangerous profession with a high accident rate, yet in 1917, at the peak of logging operations in Minnesota, not a single logging camp had a first-aid facility.[66] Disabilities and injuries are evident in numerous FSA photographs in logging areas. In one of the Pioneers' Home photos, an elderly man lies in repose on a bed, a pillow stuffed between his head and the window frame (fig. 2.10). In his burled right hand and his typical left hand, he holds a *Railroad Magazine*. In addition to industrial accidents, lumberjacks could become ill or disabled when routine health concerns were overlooked and became dangerous. Foremen faced so much pressure to be productive that when lumberjacks were sick—particularly on bitterly cold days, when managers feared that men were malingering—they were

2.10 An elderly white man lies on a bed reading *Railroad Magazine*. He holds the magazine in both hands; one hand has typical digits, while the other is burled. Library of Congress, FSA/OWI Collection, LC-DIG-ds-13169.

treated with laxatives to discourage them from claiming illness in the future.[67] Of course, injuries were not limited to workplace accidents or illnesses. A Lee photograph reveals that bar fights were another vocational hazard for the men who spent months at a time in logging camps between short, wild visits to towns (fig. 2.11).

When lumberjacks became disabled or too ill to work anymore, they were simply left behind. Social critics were very concerned about the problem of the so-called "stranded lumberjack," which they imagined to be a community full of abled lumberjacks left behind when a logging camp moved to a new locale. This was not typically the case. When the Crookston Lumber Company crossed national borders and moved to Blind River, Ontario, after closing their Beltrami County logging operations in 1925, they did not "strand" all of their lumberjacks in Minnesota but brought hundreds of mill hands and woodsmen with them. Those whom they left behind were one specific demographic: the "disabled and inefficient workers."[68] In the Wisconsin North Woods, the RA even responded to the preponderance of elders who were unable to farm independently by creating specific resettlement communities just for "aged persons."[69] Yet, with the exception of the Pioneers' Home, most FSA photographs of the cutover

2.11 Three middle-aged lumberjacks strike a hammy pose in a doorway. One slouches and smokes, wearing a bandage around his eye due to an injury in a drunken brawl. The other two playfully act out the fistfight. Library of Congress, FSA/OWI Collection, LC-USF33-011352-M2.

emphasized the vigor and physical capacities of the young and middle-aged men and women who lived there, obscuring the disproportionate old age and disability of the population.

The Pioneers' Home evoked a North Woods history of militant radicalism and organizing—not just for workers' rights, but for welfare rights. Although Vachon represented the mutual aid of the Pioneers' Home as a part of the Beltrami Island Project like any other, the men who resided there had petitioned the state to allow them to live co-operatively rather than individually, as resettlement agents initially intended.[70] Building their plans around the notion that the aged and infirm lived with traditional families, the State Emergency Relief Administration (SERA) of Minnesota—in contrast to Wisconsin—allotted a maximum of $600 to purchase a small home for each family that could not support itself.[71] As the local newspaper confirmed, however, "Some of the older or infirm men are without families and cannot well continue to live alone in single homes."[72] Eight men, described as "six old age assistance clients and two general relief clients," petitioned the county commissioners, SERA, and the FSA to "acquire for them, in lieu of separate homes," the Spooner Hospital, "that they might live together there and operate it on a co-operative basis."[73] Offered state assistance that did not meet their needs, the disabled and unmarried men of the Pioneers' Home requested alternative arrangements.

The lumberjacks' welfare board request would have been dismissed out of hand had they not been white settlers. "General relief" programs in counties like Beltrami were limited to "non-enrolled Indians and white persons," leaving only programs like Aid to Dependent Children (ADC) available to enrolled Ojibwe.[74] As welfare authorities responded to the demands of disreputable white retired lumberjacks, they not only denied aid to Ojibwe families in need but accused them of welfare fraud. Historian Brenda Child, a member of the Red Lake Band of Ojibwe, describes her mother, Jeanette Jones, being turned down by the Beltrami County Welfare Board for "lack of funds" in 1939—the same year the Pioneers' Home was created, just one county away.[75] In the 1940s, Jones and her family were accused of welfare fraud and forced to reimburse the county for an ADC grant they had received. Jones and her husband were both ill, and with their two oldest sons away from home, in the US Army, they needed some kind of assistance to get by.[76] In contrast to how Jones and her family were treated, white residents in Lake of the Woods County were aided by a county relief worker who personally reached out to every single general relief client—by definition, white or non-enrolled—who was eligible for old-age assistance in order to help them fill out the application.[77]

Demands for better living conditions were part of the immigrant, settler culture among the white communities of northern Minnesota. As white settlers in a white settler state, the law was written to their advantage, entitling them to everything from land to welfare. Yet, as immigrants whose designation as "white" was relatively recent, authorities often feared them to be disruptive foreigners.[78] Although the lumberjacks of the Pioneers' Home were eligible for welfare programs that Ojibwe people were largely excluded from, resettlement agents were initially hesitant to offer assistance. They were concerned about the region's recent history of welfare agitation, and, to a lesser extent, labor agitation. When the Industrial Workers of the World (IWW) had offered their support in 1917, the lumberjacks' effort to unionize was brutally suppressed by local government officials. Further, lumberjacks were rejected by more mainstream organized labor like the American Federation of Labor (AFL) because they were single, unskilled, transient, and worked in a dangerous industry.[79] Although the timber strikes were more inclusive than many labor actions—they actively included both full-time farmers and part-time farmers who worked part-time in the timber industry—the strikes could not address the needs of many of the men exploited by the timber industry, particularly elderly lumberjacks who were forced to spend "their last days in state-run shelters and transient camps."[80]

Even without union support, many northern Minnesota communities organized action for better living conditions. RA researchers expressed concern in 1934 that Beltrami County was home to first- and second-generation Finnish, Russian, and Danish immigrants who declared support for communism and demonstrated a willingness to organize across ethnic lines.[81] The Beltrami County relief office informed researchers that they were facing "extreme demands for relief, unwillingness to work, threatened hanging of the local relief director, brawls and riots, communistic agitation," and "impolite and even intimidating action toward the relief worker."[82] County officials believed they needed to respond by "treat[ing] them rough," by using relief as a "whip to make them behave, make them work, make them disist [*sic*] from demanding." Despite being more than a decade into a deep economic depression, local elites were upset that poor residents might organize to demand better conditions. Such elites insisted that "giving adequate relief" would not solve the problem but prolong it.[83] While relief workers blamed widespread poverty on the character of poor people themselves, they were even more upset when poor people dared to organize to change their living conditions. Lumberjacks, farmers, and other people who lived on the cutover were structurally disadvantaged by family formation, disability, and poverty. Yet, when they organized for state relief or for better labor conditions, they were characterized as lazy good-for-nothings.

The white people living on the cutover, regardless of poverty and disability, benefited from the state's desire to settle white homesteaders on Red Lake Ojibwe land at any cost. Over two-thirds of farms in the Beltrami Island Project area had been taken from Red Lake Ojibwe through white homestead claims.[84] Unlike most reservations in the United States, which were divided into individually owned parcels by the 1887 General Allotment Act, the Red Lake Reservation was (and is) held in common. Allotment profoundly transformed Native social organization, impelling Indians to "own" land as individual family units rather than larger kinship collectives. It was, as Mark Rifkin contends, profoundly heteronormative, erasing "native forms of kinship and the collective geographies established and maintained through webs of attachment and obligation."[85] To refuse allotment and keep their remaining land and water held in common, however, the Red Lake Reservation was forced to cede 2.9 million acres through the 1889 Nelson Allotment Act.[86] As Child asserts, although the negotiations leading to the Nelson Act helped Red Lake "maintain land and sovereignty," for the people of Red Lake, the "arrival of new settlers on their former hunting, farming, and gather lands" represented "greater poverty and less freedom."[87] And later government programs, including the New Deal Works Progress Administration and Civilian Conservation Corps, would deploy other "workings of domesticity" to assimilate Red Lake Ojibwe into white settler gender and sexual norms.[88]

Policies of heteronormative dispossession and environmental degradation were also omitted from the FSA's assessment of the causes of poverty in northern Minnesota. A wetlands draining and ditching program—designed to encourage white homesteading on swampy peat land—claimed even more Ojibwe land, despite white settlers' concerns about staking claims to farm in a swamp.[89] Officials contested what they characterized as the lumbermen's "strange" claim that the land had "little or no agriculture value," insisting the land would be productive once drained.[90] The program ultimately did what the state intended, taking land and sovereignty from the nearby Red Lake Indian Reservation, but it had many negative consequences for Ojibwe people and even the white settlers.[91] As Red Lake leaders had predicted, the drainage project increased forest fires and flooded low-lying wild rice beds, which significantly affected the Red Lake Reservation's livelihood.[92] The program also left white settlers impoverished and unable to make a living on poor soil, bankrupting small white towns and counties.

The Pioneers' Home series told a story about northern Minnesota poverty that resonated with exclusionary official public reports, yet Vachon's photographs depicted a social formation that resettlement agents explicitly downplayed. The Pioneers' Home series ultimately told the wrong kind of story to become iconic in the 1930s: elderly, disabled bachelors and the woman who was employed to provide care for them did not fit the ideal gendered stories of the Madonna or Mrs. America. Tied to a specific government project, the Pioneers' Home left a small paper trail scattered across government archives. As we will soon see, FSA photographs about unmarried women who shared intimate relationships are equally evocative but even more difficult to trace.

GAZING AT MILDRED IRWIN

In a 1938 photograph, saloon singer Mildred Irwin stares coldly at photographer Vachon, her fingers held still on the keys of a piano, her back leaned protectively toward the woman standing behind her (fig. 2.12). That woman, wearing a silk cravat and a long blazer, makes a small smile for the camera as her hand rests subtly on Irwin's shoulder. The image is provocative, sparking questions about the two women and the intimacy they share, as well as their relationship to the photographer who made such an inexplicable mistake in framing the photo: as Irwin fixes her eyes on Vachon, her companion's gaze is unavailable to us, as her eyes are cut out of the frame. Since Irwin, unlike the retired lumberjacks of the Pioneers' Home, was not part of a government program, knowledge about her life is limited to one questionable source: Vachon's inebriated, lascivious gaze. Yet even a dubious source offers the potential for alternate readings. In spite of Vachon's single-minded interest and narrative about Irwin, some of his photographs hint at other intimacies that her life may have held.

2.12 Mildred Irwin sits at the piano, unsmiling, leaning protectively toward a young woman who stands behind her, one hand touching Irwin's shoulder. The top of the young woman's head is out of frame, cut off by the photographer. Library of Congress, FSA/OWI Collection, LC-USF34-008753-D.

Over a long weekend in 1938, Vachon took a series of photographs that could, at first glance, evoke the idealized small town where Mrs. America was to be found. Instead, the images document a philandering photographer's flirtatious pursuit of a middle-aged saloon singer, inadvertently registering the apparently unmarried singer's precarious social, sexual, and economic situation—as well as her intimacy with the dark-haired woman in the blazer. The saloon singer called herself Mildred Irwin, and Vachon reported that she told him she had worked as a prostitute in Omaha before retiring to this saloon in North Platte, Nebraska. Irwin's vocation and her flirtatious glances toward Vachon's camera might lead one to conclude that she contradicts the iconic gendered figures of FSA photography through another tired image: that of the "whore" who completes the Madonna/whore pairing. This photo series and Vachon's correspondence about it reveal the economic demand for railroad-town sex workers that existed: it was not only lumberjacks and other working-class men who crisscrossed the rural United States seeking pleasure along the way, but middle-class men like photographers and journalists. Yet Irwin's pretty smile for Vachon is only a small part of why her image transgresses the small-town domestic idyll. It is Irwin's sweetly protective posture toward the other woman in the saloon that disrupts both the idyllic Mrs. America and the anti-idyllic sex worker trope.

On a long trip through Nebraska, Vachon ventured into the Alamo Bar one evening for personal recreation but quickly returned with his camera. Vachon spent the next day taking exterior shots of North Platte's small downtown. These photographs resembled classic FSA small-town imagery, replete with charming storefronts and rows of cars parked diagonally on well-maintained brick-paved roads, with a small exception: the "Palace Hotel Café" sign in the foreground and the "Liquors" sign toward the far end of the street.[93] The morning after his time at the Alamo Bar, Vachon woke up to recall that he had taken photos of Irwin "at the piano, of the leering boys at the bar listening to nasty songs, of old broken-down cow punchers in the booths . . ."[94] Slipping his mind were two photographs of an unnamed woman who appeared to be a close acquaintance of Irwin's. Vachon's Alamo Bar series documented the ogling gaze of an intoxicated photographer and leering bar patrons, but also, inadvertently, the gazes the women cast back at the photographer and toward one another.

When Vachon stumbled upon the Alamo Bar, he was bored by the gendered dream of the happy farmer. He had had a very routine, "dull" week full of idealized stories about the successful domestic programs run by the FSA and other rural social work agencies.[95] On Monday he met with "two home supervisors, nice homey women, in homes," he wrote playfully, expressing his boredom watching such women "showing ladies how to can, how to sew, etc." Later that week, he ventured out for a drink, where he found "a corner saloon, a saloon in the grand tradition." Enticed by the romance of a Western saloon, Vachon had a few beers and seemed to find the perfect counterpart to the Madonna and Mrs. America stories: Irwin, "an ex-Omaha prostitute, and very proud of it." Newly enthused about his photography, he wrote to Stryker that although he was drunk and "probably a little off focus" in some of his shots from that evening, "out of the whole I think we've got something."[96]

What excited Vachon most about his Alamo Bar photo series was the potential to make it a story about Irwin and how she lived. Vachon wrote to his wife Millicent (Penny) that he intended to return to the bar the next evening, to "get more facts from Mildred, go up into her room—(she lives in the hotel next door) photograph her there, get pictures of her wardrobe, her bureau drawers, etc." Then, he thought, he would have a full story to tell, "something I could sell."[97] Vachon may have sought an excuse to enter Irwin's bedroom; he had pressured and deceived Irwin in other ways, and he sought more than photos from her.[98] Yet he may have also been partly driven by a professional interest in juxtaposing a saloon singer's hotel domesticity against the more idealized "homeyness" of the farm wives whom he had met all week. Since he did not return to take interior photographs of Irwin's hotel room, we are left only with his images from the bar that evening and Main Street the next day.

If the Alamo Bar photos are transgressive in any way, it is not that Irwin is shown to be different from or opposed to the rural domestic ideal. Irwin was not the idealized farm wife, but Vachon identified her with another romanticized category of womanhood: the frontier prostitute.[99] Although the RA itself contended that "OUR FRONTIERS ARE GONE," FSA photographers were often enticed by the romance of the white US West and nostalgia for frontier days.[100] Vachon wrote to Penny that North Platte was "getting into genuine West," and that he would be "a cowboy story addict" when he returned home.[101] Vachon's romantic attraction to the West went hand in hand with his romanticized attraction to sex workers. Later in his life, when he tried his hand at fiction—unsuccessfully submitting short stories to magazines like *Esquire* and *Playboy*—Vachon's tales would often begin with a traveling man sitting in a hotel or at a bar and proclaiming, "I would like to go to a whorehouse."[102] Vachon was enchanted by the imagery of a charming entertainer at a bona fide Western saloon situated in a rough-and-tumble railroad town.

With a few important exceptions, the silver-and-gelatin Irwin seems to inhabit the social role Vachon desired of her, singing cheerfully and flirting with his camera as she no doubt did for dozens of out-of-towners and local men each evening. Her happiness to perform for him was surely augmented by the fact that he lied and told her he was a Broadway scout. Yet as a professional entertainer—whether as a musician or as a sex worker—Irwin would have known how to work men regardless of their credentials.[103] Vachon indicated as much, describing the way "customers fed her kitty, and requested nasty songs that she knew," including one "about a girl who wanted to be a prostitute" and another "about her mom—pretty double entendre and dirty."[104] In many of Vachon's photographs of Irwin at the piano, she makes direct eye contact with the camera, smiling at him mischievously, belting out a note with purpose, or singing sweetly to him (fig. 2.13). She wears her chin-length blonde hair down with a curl, held out of her face with a barrette, and she accessorizes her dark-colored sleeveless dress with a gauzy shrug, a white flower pinned to her chest, and a chunky ring on her pinky finger. Vachon, attracted to Irwin, described her as a "big huge large fat blonde woman of 45 to 50 yrs," with "beautiful red smeary red make up on her puss."[105] Irwin captured the attention of the other men in the bar as well. Although some of the men in Vachon's photographs stare at him, most level their gazes in the direction of the piano player, sometimes smiling or taking a drink, other times hollering at her from booths or staring lasciviously from barstools behind the piano.

2.13 Mildred Irwin sings and plays piano at the Alamo Bar. In the background, two men at the bar slouch and leer at her. Library of Congress, FSA/OWI Collection, LC-DIG-fsa-8b14115.

Within the full Alamo Bar series, the photograph of Irwin and her female companion is startling, disrupting the mood that Vachon evoked in his writing and in the other photographs. When Irwin is with the other woman, she is romancing neither the camera nor the patrons of the saloon. Gone is her jovial expression, replaced with one of stony defiance. A Pabst sign lights the background, and viewers might make out the shadowy shoulder of a man sitting at the bar. Yet the heart of the photo is in the foreground, where Irwin's female companion is cut out of the frame from the eyes up. Irwin seems unhappy that Vachon has cast his gaze upon her and her friend together. Whether Vachon noticed this or realized that he was cutting the other woman's eyes out of frame is unclear, but presumably the photo was an inebriated mistake. Vachon may have been so singularly focused on Irwin that he lost track of her companion. Maybe he was distracted, put off by Irwin's chilly demeanor toward him. Or perhaps there was something in how the younger woman cast her eyes at Irwin, in how their expressions changed when they were together, that upset Vachon on some level. The effect of the image is that viewers are privy to a rare on-record glare from Irwin toward a man, left only to imagine the gaze of the woman who stands fast behind her.

Irwin and her companion share an easy familiarity, though the character of their intimacy is ambiguous. If Irwin was a sex worker, her companion may have been as well. Sex workers in the western United States typically had friendly and loving relationships with one another, despite the false but widespread belief that women were constantly competing over men.[106] From Montana to Nevada to California, sex workers in the western United States forged sexual and romantic relationships with one another and other gender- and sexually nonconforming women who were not sex workers.[107] Accounts of "sexual and/or loving relationships" between sex workers, according to Ruth Rosen, appeared in nearly all accounts of sex work written by women; madams considered "lesbian relationships among prostitutes" to be a "rather natural and common occurrence," only worrying about it when it threatened to disrupt their work.[108] The association of lesbianism with prostitution was not limited to the US West.[109] Lesbian writers like Joan Nestle recalled that in late 1950s and early 1960s New York, lesbians and "whores" "sat on bar stools next to each other, we partied together, and we made love together."[110] Irwin's companion's blazer and cravat even call to mind the subcultural styles popular in East Coast lesbian communities in the mid-century United States, like those Nestle was a part of.[111]

The conditions of small-town sex work may have encouraged relationships between women. Saloons typically employed one to three women per night, and their "cooperation if not friendship" was essential to the success of the business.[112] Women in the West often traveled from boomtown to boomtown in pairs, protecting one another in times of crisis and sharing the same rooms and beds along the way.[113] North Platte was a railroad town, not a mining boomtown, but it was still considered a "rough and wide-open town."[114] Sex work was common in small towns across western Nebraska in the 1930s, and men recalled the social bonds between North Platte's "painted women of the evening," who would go out to the drugstore together for cherry Cokes.[115]

If Irwin and her friend were sex workers, they may have found themselves in North Platte in search of better working conditions than they experienced in Omaha. Studies from the late 1930s noted that "criminality" in Omaha was rising more among white women than any other group.[116] If we trust Vachon that Irwin had been a sex worker in Omaha for nineteen years, then Irwin would not have been among this group of women new to sex work.[117] Still, she may have left Omaha for related reasons, as thirty-five-year-olds were considered middle-aged among saloon sex workers and increased competition for jobs may have pushed the forty-something Irwin out of her long-term booking in Omaha.[118] Or vice raids could have encouraged Irwin to leave town; Vachon mentioned a week later that he was having trouble finding willing photographic subjects in Omaha because the *Omaha World-Herald* had been "carrying on a vice crusade, exposing gambling and prostitution etc. with photographs."[119]

2.14 A man sits at a bar next to Irwin's companion, both swiveled around to watch a performance. The woman laughs easily. The man holds a cigar. Library of Congress, FSA/OWI Collection, LC-USF34-008772-D.

It is also possible that the woman pictured with Irwin was a new acquaintance. Perhaps Irwin's companion—who appears to be the only other woman in the saloon—was, like Vachon, visiting from a distant city in an act of frontier "slumming" akin to the better-documented "slumming" in poor urban neighborhoods. Historical and literary accounts of early twentieth-century slumming focus on major urban centers like New York and Chicago, but Chad Heap argues that the slumming phenomenon "materialized in every major US urban center and many smaller ones."[120] Vachon's romanticized desire to spend time in a real Western saloon was certainly a form of slumming, if far removed from the racialized desires motivating white slummers in Harlem. If Irwin's companion was new to Nebraska, however, she may have been attracted to the saloon singer in some of the same romanticized ways that Vachon was: the allure of breaking social, class, and sexual norms in the US West.

Regardless of what brought the two women together, their photographed intimacy is intriguing, particularly when compared to Vachon's other photograph of Irwin's companion from that evening (fig. 2.14). The stylish, dark-haired woman sits on a barstool, swiveled in the direction of Irwin's piano, which is off camera. An older man, wearing black Western-style duds and holding a cigar in his hand, is seated on a barstool beside her. Although he is swiveled in the same direction she is, their body language and facial expressions do not suggest that they are close. The woman, likely responding to Irwin's performance antics, is laughing, wearing a bigger and more natural smile than she does in the posed photograph with Irwin. The expression on the face of the man next to her is out of sync with her easy laughter. She is swiveled away from him, and her closed posture and body language suggest that she is not on a date with the man, either for free or for pay—at least not on this evening. Since we can see her full face this time, we know that her jovial gaze is trained in Irwin's direction.

Despite the companionship and adoration of the dark-haired woman in the blazer, the contingencies of Irwin's life meant that her companion was not the only person with whom she shared her time. Vachon reported that he and Irwin shared a few kisses.[121] If true, and if consensual, Irwin may have had a range of motivations: a desire to be "discovered" by a man who claimed he was a Broadway scout, a need to get paid more than bar earnings, or potentially a reciprocal desire. Vachon sought to depict Irwin as a cheerful small-town entertainer. Yet this attempted rehabilitation was interrupted by intrusions and unexpected gazes, from leering cowboys and Vachon himself, to an adoring companion and Irwin's protective stance toward her.

Even as FSA photography attempted to rehabilitate images of rural whiteness and turn the lens away from anti-idyllic scenes, peculiar formations persisted and found their way into the FSA archive. Figured as, at worst, the downtrodden-yet-sympathetic "before" of a "before and after" rehabilitation success story, rural white poverty was distanced from the anti-idyll. Without spouses and children, however, women like Irwin and men like those of the Pioneers' Home were not ideal subjects for public rehabilitation, nor did they have the requisite resources—a heteronormative family and a youthful, abled vitality—to materially benefit from rehabilitation programs. Irwin and the Pioneers' Home men deployed queercrip forms of mutual aid and interdependency to survive, combined with white appeals to welfare and settler respectability. Still, the public would not discern the "dream of the happy farmer" in the protective posture of Irwin, nor in the mutual care of the Pioneers' Home.

Decades later, loosed from their contemporary context, FSA photos began to function as free-floating signifiers of rural white poverty, called upon to represent the extremes of both the idyll and the anti-idyll. Looking back, old-timey black-and-white New Deal photographs could be used to summon a traditional sense of small-town values or to conjure the scene of an incestuous gay "sex gone bad" murder (discussed in chapter six).[122] As the most extensive photographic representation of rural white poverty in the

United States, FSA photographs did not have to linger on the purported moral and corporeal aspects of poverty in order to be associated with them.

After World War II, a suburban ideal superseded the "dream of the happy farmer" in national importance. A metropolitan desire to romanticize white country life persisted, however, even in media responses to nearly unthinkable circumstances. This was the case in 1957, when police arrested Ed Gein just a few counties away from where Lee met Hale. When police arrived at Gein's farm, they found his home filled with remains and relics from disinterred women's corpses. As I discuss in chapter three, national periodicals and big-city newspapers from Chicago and Milwaukee struggled to place Gein's violence. Instead of viewing central Wisconsin through an anti-idyllic lens, they rendered Gein an aberrational figure, running with elaborate theories about schizophrenia and a "feminine complex" to make sense of Gein's behavior. Newspaper editors from nearby small towns, however, had no trouble placing Gein's behavior, immediately telling anti-idyllic tales of a "dead heart" region of Wisconsin.

3: MADNESS IN THE DEAD HEART

Ed Gein and the Fabrication
of the Transgender Heartland
"Psycho" Killer Myth

On November 16, 1957, a sheriff stepped into a ghastly scene in rural Plainfield, Wisconsin. A missing woman's mutilated corpse had been found on the farm of a fifty-one-year-old white bachelor named Ed Gein. What investigators discovered inside the home sent shockwaves through the local community and the entire nation: body parts from the corpses of ten different women, a heart in a sack on an unused stove, and household items upholstered with human skin. Several days later, the story became even more sensational when Gein allegedly confessed that his crimes were motivated by a desire to be a woman. Gein's legend inspired films from *Psycho* to *Silence of the Lambs*, precipitating the genre of the slasher film and the trope of the "psychopathic transvestite" while reinvigorating the archetype of the "homicidal maniac."[1] Despite the tremendous influence that Gein's legend eventually had on the anti-idyll, primarily through horror films of the 1970s (the subject of chapter five), the anti-idyll was curiously absent from metropolitan 1950s press coverage of Gein. This is particularly true when compared to the frank, vivid conversations about deviance that appeared in regional newspapers at the same time. As rural white Wisconsin papers plumbed the pathologies of the place that Gein called home and created grist for the national anti-idyll that would emerge in the 1970s, urban newspapers and popular magazines focused on individualized psychological pathologies that constituted the false emerging archetype of the deranged, gender nonnormative mass murderer.

Most Americans learned about both mental illness and gender nonconformity through the media.[2] Press coverage of the gender-deviant psychopath in the 1950s was contradictory, varying significantly depending on

3.1 Ed Gein is escorted to the Wisconsin State Crime Lab. Another photographer is visible in the background. Wisconsin Historical Society, WHS-2021.

the publication and its "imagined 'general public.'"[3] As Emily Skidmore contends, the "dissonance between local and national" newspaper narratives reveals how region and scale shape the "logics regulating social membership."[4] The stories told about Gein took shape at three scales: big-city newspapers and national magazines that Wisconsin weeklies referred to as the "metropolitan press," newspapers and rumors in Plainfield itself, and newspapers and rumors from the rural region surrounding Plainfield.

The metropolitan press focused on Gein's purported pathologies, but not those of his hometown.[5] The metropolitan press probed elaborate theories about his psychological state: his relationship with his mother, gender and sexuality, relationship to consensus reality, and disposition toward macabre violence from corpse-stealing to murder. But to the metropolitan press, Plainfield, right down to its name, seemed "American, Midwestern, humble," a generic white small-town foil to a horrific crime.[6] In central Wisconsin, *psy* fields—psychology, psychiatry, psychoanalysis, and the like—were of little to no interest, and Plainfield was not an abstraction but a real place.[7] In Plainfield newspapers, Gein's neighbors were concerned less with his mental state than with his crude performance of everyday white masculinity: the quality of his craftsmanship, how he maintained his home, and his racialized choice of reading materials. Gein's oddities, while offensive, did not signal potential psychopathy but marked him as a familiar local figure. Just beyond the bounds of Plainfield, rural white Wisconsinites located Gein's aberrance not in his psyche or in his behavior, but in the sandy, swampy, unfruitful soil of an area known as the "dead heart region." Small-town newspapers from the region surrounding Plainfield drew on the racialized language of the "dead heart" to compare the area in which Gein resided to wild, uncultivated, and "uncivilized" colonial outposts. In the metropolitan press of the 1950s, Gein was considered a madman, but his home was an idealized, universalized place; in the regional Wisconsin press of the 1950s, Gein was considered an ordinary white neighbor, but his home was rendered a mad place.

UNTANGLING MADNESS, GENDER DISSONANCE, AND VIOLENCE

"Madness," according to Margaret Price, is not a trait inherent in a murderer, but a rhetorical mechanism that places killers in a "space of unrecoverable deviance" apart from the space of sanity and safety. Gein was located in the space of "unrecoverable deviance" through interrelated concerns about mental disability and gender dysphoria.

I use "mental disability" and "gender dysphoria" as less sensational, less clinical ways of naming the motley assortment of *psy* and gender rumors that swirled around Gein. "Mental disability," as used by disability studies scholars, includes "mental illness" as well as cognitive and intellectual disabilities.[8] The capaciousness of "mental disability" is consistent with lay understandings of mental difference in the 1950s, when "mental illnesses" and cognitive or developmental disabilities were not yet consistently distinguished from one another. In the 1950s and 1960s, Gein was typically described as a "psychopath," "psycho," "schizophrenic," or person with a "split personality," yet also as "simple-minded" or "foolish."[9] "Gender dysphoria" will seem more clinical to some, but it need not necessarily. Since the mid-twentieth century, "gender dysphoria" has been used to describe a feeling of distress or discomfort that a person may have about their assigned gender and morphological body. Yet trans and queer writers have understood gender dysphoria as a dispassionate way of describing a feeling of gendered "body dissonance," refusing to cede the term to medical authorities or even limit it to trans identity.[10] In the 1950s and 1960s, magazines and urban newspapers typically referred to Gein's rumored gender dysphoria as "transvestism," a "feminine complex," "sex aberration," "desire to be a woman," or, less frequently, "sexual psychopathy." As John Phillips contends, the "psycho-trans" genre that Gein inspired does not require that the subject "really" be trans, as long as they demonstrate a dysphoric "state of uncertainty" or confusion about their gender identity.[11] When the metropolitan press identified Gein as a "psychopath" and "transvestite," they sensationalized mental disability and gender dysphoria, fusing the two together.

The myth that serial murderers are motivated by "insanity" and "gender distress" originated from Gein and his fictionalized manifestations.[12] Before the 1950s, it was much less common for Americans to associate mental illness with violence.[13] Gein's arrest in 1957 seemed to justify a growing Cold War moral panic about the so-called "sexual psychopath": a white man whose gender and sexual aberrance implied an innate amorality that would result in sadistic violence against women and children.[14] With the release of Alfred Hitchcock's *Psycho* in 1960, Gein—via his fictionalized counterpart, Norman Bates—formed a new stock character (the homicidal white maniac) and inaugurated a new genre of film (the slasher).[15] But one need not be unwell to commit murder, sexual assault, or other violent crimes; indeed, the vast majority of serial murders are committed by "sane" people who "do not suffer from a profound mental disorder."[16] The myth of the psycho killer has been protecting white Americans from a much scarier story: most danger comes from trusted friends, family members, acquaintances, and expressions of dominant culture.[17]

During the 1950s, middle-class white people could understand their communities as safe by projecting all white threats of violence onto the singular figure of the sexual psychopath. By attributing white violence and nonconformity to this scapegoat, whiteness and white people writ large were exculpated from responsibility.[18] Inherent in the notion of sexual psychopathy was a theory of white racial superiority, which held that because of the effects of civilization,[19] more stringent community mores,[20] and more advanced psychosexual development, "white abnormality" was equivalent to "blacks' normal state of being."[21] Black Americans were still diagnosed with psychopathy—perhaps overdiagnosed—but the public face of the sexual psychopath remained white.[22] This verified pre-existing white convictions that white men who committed violence did so for reasons beyond their control, while Black men were "guilty of willful violence."[23]

As the bearer of all crime and deviance in white communities, the figure of the psychopath conflated the "most benign and the most dangerous forms of sexual nonconformity," from sex between consenting adults to the sadistic rape and murder of an infant.[24] During the 1950s, federal immigration law explicitly barred "psychopathic personalities" in order to exclude homosexuals, and states passed laws calling for the "indefinite civil commitment" of sexual psychopaths.[25] Homosexuals, lawmakers believed, demonstrated a "refusal to accommodate to social conventions" that could be a warning sign of psychopathy, making it necessary to examine and institutionalize sexual and gender nonconformists long before they could commit a crime or behave in a dangerous way.[26] In Sioux City, Iowa, to take just one example, police responded to the murders of two young children in 1954 by pre-emptively arresting and institutionalizing twenty gay men who had nothing to do with the murders; Sioux City police did so again in 1958.[27]

Revisiting Gein risks reifying the myth of the "mad trans killer" that has circulated so widely and done so much damage to trans women and people with mental disabilities since 1957. For decades, trans studies and trans activism have sought to take transgender experiences back from the clinicians who labeled us as sick and aberrant in order to construct our own social and political senses of self.[28] Early trans studies scholars were not just driven by the stigma of mental disabilities or medicalization: they critiqued the rehabilitation regime and the technologies of control that gender clinics enacted on trans people's embodiments and identifications, and the inordinate power that a small number of surgeons had over the bodies and words of trans people who sought gender confirmation surgeries.[29] Still, fear of being associated with "the mentally ill" has been part of trans critiques of medicalization, doing a particular disservice to those who both are trans and have mental disabilities. As Eli Clare contends, rather than claiming that trans people "aren't really 'crazy'; unlike the 'crazies' over there"—in other words, rather than trying to remove ourselves from a stigmatized category while leaving the stigma intact for others—we must understand how *psy* diagnoses wield power over many different people.[30]

Yet, as trans scholars have sought to rhetorically separate "transgender" from "homicidal psychosis" (in Phillips's words), they have implied that people who experience psychosis really *ought* to be rhetorically positioned with murderers.[31] The shorthand "psycho" conflates the notion of psychosis (the experience of losing contact with consensus reality) with that of psychopathy (a historically contingent diagnosis) and with utterly amoral, sadistic violence.[32] People who experience psychosis, particularly those with diagnoses like schizophrenia, have been considered the "most reviled of the disabled."[33] These associations are due partly to representations in slasher films and partly to the myth of the violent schizophrenic Black man that emerged during the Civil Rights movement.[34] Such myths are dangerous for people with schizophrenia and for Black people with all kinds of mental illnesses. People with mental illnesses, including people with schizophrenia, are significantly more likely to be victims of violence than to commit violence.[35]

Losing touch with consensus reality is disruptive, but it is not inherently dangerous. Writer Esmé Weijun Wang says that her experience of Cotard's delusion—a sense that she was dead, because the "normal emotion" she expected to feel for a loved one was "absent"—felt deeply distressing. Yet she notes it did not make her dangerous to others—to the contrary.

It made her kinder to those around her, as she was temporarily "buoyant" with the belief that she had received "a second chance in some kind of after-life."[36] Community responses to a person's hallucinations or delusions also matter deeply. This is illustrated by a case related by anthropologist Karen Nakamura: a man hallucinating a UFO wished to fly it but was dissuaded by acquaintances who reminded him that he did not have the necessary UFO operator's license.[37] As anthropologist Sue Estroff argues, when the temporary experience of "psychosis" is transformed into the diagnostic category of "the psychotic," a period of illness is transformed into a *type* of person, one so feared and devalued as to seem inherently homicidal.[38]

Attributing Gein's violence to a psychiatric disability obscures the reality that many men in their "right minds" do murder people, particularly women. Yet diagnoses of mental disability are often spectacularized, while actual injury to women, like domestic violence and sexual harassment, is not. What if we were to treat mental disabilities and gender dysphoria as mundane and unspectacular—what would stand out then? It is possible to simultaneously recognize Gein's violence as reprehensible and understand other aspects of his life—including mental disability and gender dysphoria, to the extent that he experienced either—as mundane. This approach draws from Clare's "disability politics of transness," which compels us to treat "bodily difference" as "profoundly *familiar*," and Cameron Awkward-Rich's method of reading "like a depressed transsexual,"[39] which compels us to take "feeling bad" as a "mundane fact" that need not be denied for a depressed trans person's life to be livable.[40] Trans disability critique need not only be applied to the lives of disabled trans people but also to the discourses that shape public perceptions of us. As a lens for analyzing 1950s Gein discourse, trans disability critique urges us to question which "drab difficulties"—as psychiatrists of the past often classified domestic violence, for example—were quietly normalized in order to spotlight tall tales about gender dysphoria and mental disability.[41]

Stories about Gein's mental state and gender dysphoria originated from his two-day interrogation by Madison police after his arrest. Public interest in psychiatry and mental illness had grown after World War II,[42] and Gein, "one of psychiatry's most extraordinary case histories," according to *Time* magazine, was subjected to popular *psy* analysis.[43] Before Gein was questioned, his police interrogators had already formed a lay theory of the gender and mental pathologies that they imagined to explain his macabre violence, and they foisted those narratives onto the notoriously suggestible Gein.[44] When stories about Gein's confession leaked to the *Chicago Tribune* and then circulated more widely, metropolitan media outlets sought comments from *psy* professionals with no personal knowledge of Gein. The psychiatrists and psychologists who actually treated Gein, by contrast, were careful not to claim a complete understanding of Gein or his motivations. Since most Americans learned about Gein through the metropolitan press, they were taught to understand Gein's behavior in the lay *psy* language of oedipal complexes, split personalities, and sex aberrations.

Psy languages of social difference, despite their popularity in the late 1950s, had not permeated the nation evenly. In regional newspapers and interviews with larger media outlets, people from central Wisconsin consistently critiqued psychiatry's power to explain social nonconformity. As the editor of the *Plainfield Sun* wrote in the *Milwaukee Journal*, "no amount of psychiatric explanations of mother fixations or the like is going to completely answer the mystery of Ed Gein."[45] It was not merely that Plainfield, like so many communities forced to confront the existence of violence in their midst, found themselves defending their past judgment, or that there was a disjuncture between national and local media narratives.[46] Small towns around the nation, social scientists in the 1950s lamented, were overly accepting of their "nonconforming types," their "cranks, psychotics and 'odd' personalities."[47] After his crimes were revealed, Plainfield reevaluated Gein's social belonging and deemed his actions appalling but nonetheless resisted *psy* explanations of them.

While urban newspapers became increasingly homogenized during the 1950s, weekly small-town papers remained fiercely idiosyncratic, led by strong editorial personalities.[48] This was evident in central Wisconsin, where the Gein case provoked petty squabbles that were routine between small towns. With a few notable exceptions, urban Midwestern newspapers like the *Milwaukee Journal* and the *Minneapolis Tribune* approached the Gein matter with a social distance and ethnographic curiosity reminiscent of their peers at newspapers and magazines in larger, more distant cities. There was, of course, no single "metropolitan" or "regional" story, but these categorizations, as broad as they are, help us name and counter the metropolitan press story that would otherwise masquerade as universal. Fundamentally, small-town Wisconsin newspapers asked and answered different kinds of questions than their big-city peers, revealing that a *psy*-inflected worldview was not universal.

Wisconsin communities used different rhetorical maneuvers to locate Gein in a space of "unrecoverable deviance" and thereby deepen the moat around the "sanctuary of reason" that protects "normal" people from violent offenders like Gein.[49] Rural Wisconsin may have rejected the *psy* language of mental illness, but they found Gein "mad" by questioning his belonging to white civilization. Madness exists in an "oppositional relationship" with reason and with Enlightenment virtue rooted in "antiblack, misogynist, colonialist, and other pernicious ideologies."[50] Since psychiatrists "identified mental health with a form of civilized rationality," the white

3.2 Law enforcement escort Gein to the door of the Wisconsin State Crime Lab, where he was interrogated. Wisconsin Historical Society, WHS-41775.

"madman" has often been understood through "highly racial terms" such as "savage" or "primitive."[51] To his most proximate neighbors in central Wisconsin, Gein's madness took the form not of insanity, but of apparent primitiveness: primitive tastes in reading materials and perhaps flesh, primitive habits of accumulation, and rudimentary craftsmanship. In contrast, to Gein's more distant neighbors, those who lived more than a few miles or a county line away, Gein's madness was rooted in the land itself, a "dead heart" of soil and civilization that purportedly explained Gein as well as the criminal farmers whose land adjoined his.

By the 1970s, nationalized anti-idyllic representations of the Gein myth drew heavily from the latter interpretation—the notion of a mad landscape—as well as the disjuncture between modern social science and a community that insisted on old-fashioned ways of determining social belonging. Plainfield itself became suspect, no longer a "blank" location for crime but a suspicious landscape that bred crime. Anti-idyllic optics were first trained on Gein and Plainfield in subcultural media, such as horror magazines. Out of these emerged an anti-idyllic Heartland gothic in the form of books like *Wisconsin Death Trip* and films like Werner Herzog's *Stroszek*. In the 1950s, the Gein story provided ingredients for the formation of anti-idyllic optics, though it was not until the 1970s that the *psy* focus on deviance joined with concerns about a "culture of poverty" to articulate a national anti-idyll.

THE MADNESS IN THE MAN: THE CREATION OF THE "PSYCHO-TRANS" MYTH

Hours after killing Bernice Worden at the family hardware store she operated, Gein was arrested. Worden's son Frank had suspected Gein immediately, as Gein had been pressuring Bernice to go on a date with him. Three days later, on November 19, 1957, Gein was interrogated at the Wisconsin Crime Laboratory in Madison. He was feeling woozy after being physically beaten by the sheriff, medicated heavily, and given "electrical treatment."[52] Interrogator Joseph Wilimovsky of the Crime Lab acted friendly toward Gein, but he had a preconceived theory about Gein's psychological motivations. Over a thirty-hour interrogation, Wilimovsky asked dozens of variations of the same question: Have you ever tried to "inject yourself into believing that you were a woman"? Did you feel that you would have "preferred to have been born a woman or girl"? Have you ever wished to "remove or cut off your penis" and have it "in the shape of the sexual organs of a woman" instead?[53] On November 21, the *Chicago Tribune* reported that Gein's crimes—two murders and ten stolen corpses—were motivated by the fact that he "wanted to be [a] woman." This "compulsion," purportedly driven by an unnatural love for his mother, had "prompted him to kill women and steal other bodies from graves to get parts to wear upon his own body."[54] The *Tribune* article was reprinted and described in newspapers around the world, and thus began the myth that Gein was a "psycho-trans" killer.[55]

Rural Wisconsin newspapers ran these stories as well but quickly moved on to other theories, more concerned about the soil that had produced Gein and his violent neighbors. The metropolitan media remained fixated on a constellation of mental pathologies, locating "madness" entirely within Gein as an individual. *Newsweek*, for example, attributed the horrific events to the "deep recesses of a mind so twisted that it passes human understanding," then located this warped mind on a "farm outside the little town of Plainfield in the Wisconsin lake country," a rather flattering description of a struggling farm town.[56] *Psycho*, the film that cemented the Gein myth, located its "psychopath" in the country rather than the city, challenging the very idea of "where crime can occur," but it did not represent the country as anti-idyllic or suspect. Not until horror films of the 1970s did the country become a mad place in the national imagination.[57]

Lay *psy* theorizing about Gein's motives and actions—from his interrogators to the media—deployed popular notions about oedipal complexes, sexual psychopathy, and transvestism to try to make sense of the unthinkable scene that police found at Gein's farm. When police arrived, they found Worden's corpse dressed out like a deer in the summer kitchen adjoining the house. Inside the home, they found an even more morbid scene: chairs upholstered with human skin, half a skull used as a bowl, long strips of skin, a sheet of skin from a torso, and a box of "vaginas."[58] From these findings, the myth that Gein loved his mother so much that he desired to become her—by removing and wearing parts of women's corpses—circulated rapidly.[59] It hardly need be said: the desire to skin a corpse in order to take possession of another woman's body is not and has never been part of being transgender, transsexual, or transvestite.

The myth of Gein's "feminine complex" has been tremendously influential. It inspired novelists such as Robert Bloch, the Wisconsinite who wrote the novel *Psycho* was based on; countless filmmakers, from Hitchcock to Tobe Hooper to Jonathan Demme; and even film scholars who, in analyzing films with the "psycho-trans" myth, have inadvertently reproduced the pernicious implication that wearing skin from a corpse could conceivably be part of being trans.[60] Most injuriously, however, the myth found its way into a particularly virulent strain of anti-trans bigotry heralded by Janice Raymond and Mary Daly. Raymond's and Daly's purported feminism defined trans women's very existence as an act of violence against non-transgender women. Raymond infamously declared that transsexual women "reduc[e] the real female form to an artifact"—into "fetishized parts of the female torso" and "'things' to be acquired."[61] Whether Raymond was consciously influenced by Gein mythology or not, her language was almost indistinguishable from 1950s newspaper articles about him. Likewise, Mary Daly's description of transsexuals as "ghoulish gynecologists" and a "necrophilic [sic] invasion" clearly drew on *Frankenstein* but harkened back to Gein as well.[62] In the twenty-first century, communities whose purportedly "feminist" politics have been influenced by Raymond and Daly continue to invoke Gein's name and mythos to justify hatred and violence toward trans women.[63]

Ironically, the "psycho-trans" myth emerged from a deeply misogynistic *psy* discourse that blamed every social ill imaginable on mothers. "Eddie Gein (rhymes with wean)," *Time* reported, was a "mamma's boy," and this was the cause of his deviance.[64] Valorization of white motherhood notwithstanding, throughout the 1940s and 1950s, moms were under attack for being domineering and overprotective, emasculating the men in their lives, and raising passive sons who became sexually deviant, criminal, or politically radical. This crisis of "momism," as best-selling author Philip Wylie termed it, seemed to be the perfect explanation for Gein's aberrance: "frail" and "slightly-built," Gein embodied fears of enfeebled masculinity.[65] Initially, in spite of Gein's small frame, news stories did not identify his mom or family as the root of the problem, but instead drew upon the "awesome picture of a once wholesome family," complete with a hardworking father and appropriately devoted mother, to dramatize how far he had deviated.[66] This idealized white family was not the truth either, though Gein reportedly wished for it to be. Hospital social workers documented that Gein's father was a "heavy drinker, easily angered, and abusive," and that it was known that the elder Gein "didn't like to work."[67] This report was made public during Gein's sanity hearing, but by then the metropolitan press was already fixated on the "mother-love" story.[68] The reality was less sensational. Gein had loved and cared for his mother. Her death, which immediately followed his brother's death, left him with no living family and triggered a period of deep depression, during which he began to imagine a reality in which she had not passed.[69] Feeling intense grief for the loss of his mother may have been perverse by 1950s standards, but men's grief need not necessarily be construed as pathological.

Claims that Gein had an "unnatural attachment" to his mother—that he suffered from a perverse form of "mother-love" that "grew to obsessions with sex"—were rooted in the care that he provided to his elderly parent after she was paralyzed from a series of strokes.[70] As Wilimovsky interrogated Gein, he imposed his ideas of mother-love and gender dysphoria onto Gein, often merging them together. "Did you ever consider Eddie," he asked, "that the love that your mother expressed for you and the way that you mothered your own mother when she was ill, that you felt that you should have been a woman, or that you would of [*sic*] preferred to have been born a woman or girl?" Gein responded, "It doesn't seem to come clear, you know?"[71] The idea that Gein "mothered" his mom when she was seriously ill required that caring labor be so feminized that any family care by a man was pathological—even for a disabled and dying parent, even by a man who was that parent's lone living relative. Even given that kind of ideology around gender and care, Wilimovsky's question still made an enormous logical leap between a man caring for a disabled parent and that man feeling that he "should have been a woman." But the popular ideology of momism was more than capacious enough to turn Wilimovsky's rambling question into a coherent narrative for newspapers: Gein's close relationship with his mother, strengthened by nursing her after two strokes, led to a "feminine complex."[72] It was apparently that simple.

The ease of this narrative relied on ambiguous, polyvalent phrases like "feminine complex" and "sex obsessions," which could refer to anything from wishing for a "sex change operation" to having a frail build, from not dating women to collecting "vaginas" from corpses in a cardboard box. During the 1950s, transsexuality, crossdressing, homosexuality, and other forms of gender and sexual nonconformity were frequently understood as a "singular category of deviance."[73] This was not universally true, of course. Gender and sexually nonconforming people had more precise understandings of each term, as did the psychiatrists who studied them. Since 1910, "transvestism," coined by sexologist Magnus Hirschfeld, had described a range of cross-gender phenomena; in the 1950s, the distinction between "transvestism" and "transsexualism" was just emerging.[74] As psychiatrists like Harry Benjamin began using "transsexual" to name those who sought surgical or other morphological interventions, activists like Virginia Prince were winnowing the meanings of "transvestite" to refer only to heterosexual male crossdressing.[75] Yet, as Emily Skidmore contends, most Americans did not learn about transsexuality through medicine, but through media discourses.[76] In 1952, American former GI Christine Jorgensen became the "first global transsexual celebrity," and began to distinguish the disreputable "sex deviant" from the more respectable "transsexual."[77] Wisconsinites were familiar with Jorgensen, and wire stories about other notable trans women even shared pages with newspaper stories about Gein.[78] Journalists, police interrogators, and most members of the public had just enough familiarity with the language of gender and sexual deviance to elaborate their own mixed-up theories through Gein.

Inchoate ideas of gender and sexual deviance allowed reporters and readers to freely associate gender dysphoria, transsexualism, and transvestism with a dramatic range of other conditions and behaviors. Psychiatrists publicly interviewed about Gein described his apparent condition as a "common form of homosexuality known as transvestism" or "an extreme form of fetishism that involved dressing himself in a vestlike garment made from . . . skin."[79] In the *Diagnostic and Statistical Manual (DSM)*, the diagnostic handbook used by American psychologists and psychiatrists, homosexuality and transvestism shared the label of "sexual deviations" with fetishism, voyeurism, and pedophilia. Clare has eloquently described the harm wrought by this taxonomy, which, through the proximity of "pedophilia" to "transvestism," renders child molestation equivalent to a girl wearing blue jeans.[80] Informed by the *DSM*'s twisted taxonomy of sexual deviation, observers from 1957 through the twenty-first century have described Gein as though the act of wearing parts of corpses was a perfectly logical extension of a man wearing a dress. It is not. Because it seems this must be said, I will say it directly: wearing skin flayed from an embalmed corpse is not "carrying transvestism a step further," nor does transsexualism involve stealing corpses in order to procure a "woman's skin." These are absurd insinuations that cause real harm to trans women.[81]

Media narratives shaped and shared gender myths about Gein, but those ideas were first imposed on Gein during his police interrogation. Wil-

3.3 A police officer instructs Ed Gein how to sign paperwork inside the Wisconsin State Crime Lab or a local city jail. Wisconsin Historical Society, WHS-11803.

imovsky questioned Gein doggedly, in crude terms, about gender identity, gender dysphoria, and the body parts that Gein had removed from corpses. He framed these questions in nearly every way imaginable, asking if Gein had ever wished that he could "give birth or carry a child" or if he wished he had been born a woman, if Gein had considered "cutting [his] penis and testicles off," and even if he had ever witnessed an animal castration.[82] Rather than asking Gein open-ended questions about what he had done with the body parts found in his home, Wilimovsky pressured Gein, dozens of times, to confess that he had used the body parts he took from corpses as clothing or as reconstructed genitals. Many of Wilimovsky's ostensible questions were in fact very vivid scenarios with no basis in evidence: perhaps, Wilimovsky proposed, Gein had worn the genitalia he collected, used the genitalia to "cover the penis so you couldn't see the penis, and just see the vagina of a woman," or "put on a pair of women's panties" with one of the "vaginas" inside.[83] Wilimovsky's suggestions reveal an emerging, popular interpretation of *psy* theory that attempted to link violence with embodied sexual deviance.

Gein was uncommonly suggestible, eager to please his interrogators, and doubtful of his own memory, but he did not confirm Wilimovsky's *psy*-inflected hunches that his actions stemmed from gender dysphoria.[84] Gein denied most of the feelings and behaviors Wilimovsky pressed him about, saying "No," "that doesn't come clear," or "I don't remember it that way."

Occasionally, he replied with a more ambiguous and amiably Midwestern "That could be."[85] At other times, he responded in contradictory ways, going along with Wilimovsky's suggestions at first, then backtracking when he realized he could not complete the picture that Wilimovsky began for him. Every now and then, however, Gein managed to proffer a motive that was not dictated to him. Toward the end of the interrogation, Wilimovsky queried Gein about two pieces of breast tissue turned inside out:

WILIMOVSKY: For what reason did you possess them? Did you ever place them beneath a corset or brassiere?
GEIN: No, I don't believe I did—they wasn't really finished yet. I was—
WILIMOVSKY: Was it your intention—
GEIN: Well, kind of a remembrance, I believe—to remind me of her.
WILIMOVSKY: A remembranc [sic] of her. What were your intentions on completing—I mean what did you plan on putting some decorations on 'em or something?
GEIN: Yes, something like that.[86]

As Wilimovsky began to impart an intention to Gein, Gein took his opening as a sincere inquiry, interrupting his interrogator to disclose that he kept the breast tissue as a remembrance of the woman he killed. He later told his *psy* clinicians that he kept "sexually significant parts" because, in his words, "they seemed like living things," and he feared that if he buried them, "the worms" would eat them.[87] Gein's stated intention to craft a "remembrance" briefly revealed his own motivations in the midst of Wilimovsky's shoddy interrogation work. But the tale Wilimovsky wove for Gein resonated with people because it fit into existing narratives of sexual deviance. And so, the metropolitan media ran with the notion of an unhinged mass killer wearing a suit of women's skin.

The evocative myth that Gein put the literal "vest" in "transvestite" proved enduring. Before Gein's interrogation, Sheriff Herbert Wanserski told the *Chicago Tribune* that among the items found at Gein's home was a "vest-like garment fashioned from the torso of a woman."[88] Wanserski, who spoke frequently and hyperbolically to the media, dramatically transformed what the *Milwaukee Journal* originally described as "sheets of human hide" into a garment, a vest, something created with the intent to be worn.[89] If the skin that Gein removed from disinterred corpses resembled the shapes of vests and leg wraps, as newspapers began to report, it was because the skin was taken from human bodies, which clothing is shaped to cover. Wanserski's statement is the only available evidence that alleges Gein intended to wear these sheets of skin. With the exception of a few items that Gein set aside—notably, noses and "vaginas"—he used most of the body parts that he took from corpses to make or repair household items, such as chairs, knife sheaths, and bowls. Wanserski's "vest" of human skin functioned as an imaginary pivot point between the transvestite and the transsexual.

The false notion that Gein sought to make a human vest for himself quickly became a key part of his mythology. Just one day after Wanserski's statement, Gein was reported to "slip into the torso skin vest" and "parade around by himself in his lonely farm house."[90] In a 1979 study, Wisconsin folklorist Roger Mitchell recalled that he started his project with a "hazy image" of someone in a "vest of female skin."[91] The mythic vest changed with each iteration: Gein had a full suit, including a vest and a coat; he had a full "human body suit, neatly sewn together";[92] he wore the vest under his clothes; he wore the vest only at night; or he wore the vest while staring at himself "in a prism of mirrors," howling "like a wolfhound."[93] In each telling, the story strayed further and further from the women he harmed.

There was a much simpler explanation for Gein's gendered and sexualized violence: deep hostility toward women. This was partly—but only partly—attributable to his frustrated sexual interest in women. As his clinicians attested, Gein strongly desired heterosexual relationships with women but struggled to form a satisfying one.[94] That affected his social relationships with other men, who teased him about his dating difficulties.[95] Even Wilimovsky participated in this heteromasculine social ritual, embarrassing Gein during the interrogation by describing the process of ejaculation to him in condescending detail.[96] Yet in spite of reports that Gein "did no courting" and had "associated little with girls," he did ask women on dates, and he pressured them to go out with him.[97] Many men routinely assumed that Gein's awkwardness and inability to "relate to women in a usual heterosexual manner" meant that his entreaties to women were jokes, insisting they never knew Gein to have "pestered any women."[98] But bashful, uneasy men can harass women just as any other kind of man can, and when Gein badgered a man's own loved ones, he began to appreciate that.[99]

Gein's hostility toward women extended far beyond the realms of dating and sex. His frequent disputes with neighbors were conspicuously gendered, his rage directed at women even when his quarrels were with men. When Gein was asked why he robbed his first grave and disinterred the corpse of Mrs. Adams, he named a petty gripe with her son over $10.[100] Despite being "prudishly critical" of women, Gein's conflicts with women were rarely driven by concerns about sexual morality.[101] When Gein was asked about his first murder victim, tavern owner Mary Hogan, he denied Wilimovsky's suggestion that she was a "wicked woman" who "sold her body." Instead, he said, he had heard that Hogan was a "tough woman."[102]

Gein had several complaints about Bernice Worden, including a decades-long grievance based on a rumor that she had allegedly broken up a man's relationship with a woman who then committed suicide. More recently, she had turned him down for a date, and he was upset with her because her son Frank had gone hunting without him.[103] Gein held grudges against neighbors who refused to loan wagons, friends who failed to repay him, and acquaintances who were "crooked" and cheated the government.[104] Gein's bitterness and sense of mistreatment applied to both women and men, but women always suffered the consequences of his rancor. Yet Gein's freely offered explanations for his violence—petty grudges and a propensity to take those grudges out on women—were disregarded in favor of stories about novel psychosexual disturbances.

If an aggrieved farmer was not sensational enough for the media, stories about a Midwestern madman were. In newspapers across the nation, psychiatrists were called upon to diagnose Gein from a distance. In addition to showing readers how a case like Gein could be diagnosed from afar, these stories educated readers on schizophrenia and related diagnoses during a period when their meanings were in flux. *Time* magazine consulted with Dr. Edward Kelleher, the head of Chicago's Municipal Court Psychiatric Institute, who "flatly called Gein a schizophrenic."[105] In a *Minneapolis Tribune* interview, University of Minnesota psychology professor Dr. Starke Hathaway concurred with Kelleher, explaining that schizophrenia was the "only medical entity" that could possibly cause "behavior so strange."[106] Still, schizophrenia was much less stigmatized in the 1950s than it would become a decade later, not yet associated with being "crazy in particular ways." As Jonathan Metzl contends, in the 1960s and 1970s, schizophrenia was transformed from a disease that "connoted white American neurosis" to a violent condition used to pathologize and institutionalize Black male activists.[107] Interpretations of what schizophrenia meant for Gein varied: although it was commonly described as a "split personality," Hathaway informed the *Tribune*, it was better understood as a "withdrawal from reality."[108] This seemed to fit with Gein's initial claims that he could not recall killing Worden, and that he must have done so in a "dazelike" state.[109] Other experts did consider schizophrenia a "split personality," one that could explain Gein's rumored gender dysphoria or his love/hate relationship with women.[110]

While *psy* professionals in the media focused on diagnoses, the providers who treated, observed, or spoke with Gein were more interested in what his mental disability meant for him at a practical level. These clinicians diagnosed him with depression and chronic schizophrenia; they did not ever suggest the idea of "split personalities," nor did they do more than mention the rumors of "transvestism."[111] Dr. Edward Schubert testified that the diagnosis of schizophrenia was not a statement on whether Gein was legally "insane" or not, as most schizophrenics could "operate in society" and live outside an institution.[112] Gein, he told the court, in contrast to most people with schizophrenia, was "handicapped tremendously" by his "mental disorder."[113] Although there were reports that Gein dug up graves because "something inside [him] told [him] to do it," or because he felt he was "an agent of God and implementing His will," the psychiatrists who treated him most consistently said that he was usually in contact with consensus reality.[114] This took concerted effort and could be disrupted by stress, but "at no time" since 1957 had he been known to be "substantially out of contact with reality."[115] Gein denied that he heard voices or orders.[116]

Gein's diagnoses and mental life, whatever they might be, do not explain actions like murder, corpse-stealing, and human taxidermy. In 1957, just one psychiatrist was responsible enough to make such a disclaimer. Dr. George Armour insisted that even if Gein had a mental illness and committed murder, "You cannot equate criminal acts, such as murder, with mental illness." He further instructed readers that people with mental illnesses were no more likely than "normal populations" to behave criminally.[117] In spite of this, other psychiatrists commenced with the assumption that they were looking at "an obviously psychotic series of crimes."[118] Gein's local community, however, disagreed. "Almost unanimously," residents of the greater Plainfield area believed Gein to be "clearly sane."[119] In part, this was because they wanted Gein to stand trial and face his crimes and feared that being found insane would not be sufficient punishment. Yet it was also because Gein simply did not meet central Wisconsin understandings of what it meant to be "handicapped tremendously," as psychologist Schubert attested he was.[120] Gein seemed as capable of economically providing for himself as anyone else, and the things he did privately had no bearing on that capacity.

The metropolitan media, in order to locate the space of deviance within Gein himself, rendered Plainfield as an idealized small town reminiscent of late FSA photography. This was most evident in an eight-page photo spread in *Life* magazine that juxtaposed the turmoil of Gein's mind with generic small-town details. The first pages escorted readers to Gein's home and asked them to peer into his window, as a photograph taken inside his home gazed out at the onlookers. On the next two-page spread, readers were introduced to Gein's apparently chaotic mind. Two photographs of his jumbled, dirty, disorganized kitchen and living room were contrasted with the room he had kept locked for years: his parents' bedroom, neatly arranged and free from clutter. Having peeked into the split, tumultuous interior of Gein's home and mind, *Life* readers were driven to his otherwise ordinary town. Stretched across the top of the next two pages, a familiar Main Street scene centered on a corner store whose sign read "WORDEN'S." At the bottom of the spread, an array of small profiles—photos and quotations—of area men and women reinforced the notion that Plainfield could be any small town. Each profile was labeled with a gendered role, with men categorized by vocation (storekeeper, barber, farmer, editor) and women categorized by personal relationship (parent, housewife, friend). *Life* rendered Plainfield two-dimensionally, categorizing its citizens into gendered small-town social types. Gein, the outlier, was alone in his space of unrecoverable deviance.

An editorial in a nearby town's newspaper named this rhetorical maneuver, declaring that it was difficult to believe that terrible acts like Gein's could "occur at home among our loved ones," and imagining that they must always occur "at more distant places."[121] If something terrible did happen *here*, in this place called home, then there must be another explanation for how that person was distanced from us.

THE MADNESS IN THE MUNDANE:
GEIN'S PRIMITIVE WORK, HOME, AND HOBBIES

Just a day after Gein's arrest, two men at a filling station near Plainfield complained bitterly about how major newspapers were psychologizing Gein and thereby diminishing rural ways of knowing. If only journalists would "talk to people in the small towns, where you really get to know your neighbors," one of the men insisted, "maybe they'd possibly learn something."[122] The irony, of course, was that Gein's small-town neighbors did not know him as well as they imagined. As his community began to reconcile that fact, they retraced the contours of his belonging, examining details that perhaps should have troubled them. The "space of unrecoverable deviance" in which Gein's neighbors ultimately located him was not that of mother-love, gender dysphoria, or psychiatric conditions. Rather, in Plainfield, Gein's "madness"—his separation from the world of "reason"— was rooted in his quotidian failure to set himself apart from a racialized notion of the "primitive." In hindsight, his neighbors were troubled by his rude craftsmanship, rundown home, and perverse identification with non-Western characters in his favorite adventure stories. Even Gein, however, was ultimately "folded back into whiteness" as "mad white subjects" typically are, according to Rachel Gorman.[123] Gein's "mad" departure from racialized norms of modern, civilized rural life was countered by strong appeals to whiteness: his nonthreatening embodiment of the small-town "odd bachelor" figure, his innate racial status as "belonging" in a majority-white town, and his proximity to the managerial whiteness that his brother had obtained by overseeing Jamaican farmworkers. Plainfield's examination of Gein rejected *psy* theories, marking his aberrance instead through racialized assessments of the mundane.

Gein was able to live freely in Plainfield while stealing corpses and getting away with the 1954 murder of neighbor Hogan because of local roots, whiteness, and a culture that shunned women for speaking out about discomfort. When a local grocer expressed surprise at Gein's arrest, because he had "never heard of any of the Geins having been in trouble before," he articulated a small-town expectation that residents know multiple generations of a neighbor's family, and that the reputation of extended family has bearing on one's own reputation.[124] The idea that belonging was shaped by whether a person's family had stayed in that place for generations was implicitly racialized and excluded most of the people of color in the area, whose recent histories were more migratory. Ho-Chunk people, who returned to their indigenous home in Wisconsin after forced removals in the early 1800s, followed a "tradition of mobility," wherein they would camp and move from place to place during the year.[125] Tejano, Mexican, and Jamaican migrant workers might return each summer but did not stay year-round,[126] and two Black families with cabins in the area visited them only in the summer.[127] Whiteness was integral to local belonging beyond family history. "Suddenly," the League of Women Voters reported, two full decades after Tejano and Mexican workers began migrating to Plainfield's Waushara County to pick beets and cucumbers, white residents began to notice "these people who were in the community several months of the year but never of the community."[128] To be of the community—to be even *noticed* after two decades of life in an area—required a stationary white family.

Gein's belonging was contingent on gender as well—the ways that women's fears and concerns about him were minimized by men. After Gein's arrest, several women mentioned to newspapers that they had worried about their safety with him. Doris Diggles explained that she always locked her door when he was outside, even though "he was just a harmless goof, we thought."[129] Georgia Foster recalled making a joke to Gein about the skulls in his home but regretted the joke after getting chastising looks from both her husband and Gein.[130] In each case, a woman who felt uncomfortable around Gein tried to diminish her own concerns because she knew that "we"—the male-dominated community around her—were supposed to consider him a harmless goof.

Unlike city papers, which described the grotesque findings at Gein's farmhouse in distanced, ethnographic language, regional papers invited readers in as though they were entering Gein's home for a visit. While magazines and metropolitan newspapers aimed to shock their readers with the amount of items found in Gein's home, regional papers juxtaposed the mundane with the macabre. By inviting readers into Gein's home, central Wisconsin contrasted the ordinary nature of Gein's life with the extraordinary depravity he was accused of. "You step through the kitchen door," the *Wisconsin Rapids Daily Tribune* began, "and there is an ordinary kitchen chair, except that its seat is upholstered with human skin. There is what appears to be a small bowl on the table, but it is not a bowl. It is the top half of a human skull."[131]

To make sense of the chasm between Gein's self-evident local belonging and the distressing crimes he had committed, Gein's hometown *Plainfield Sun* began its coverage with a rhetorical distancing, avowing that the "civilized mind" could "scarcely comprehend" what had transpired at their neighbor's farm.[132] Since readers from Plainfield were so proximate to Gein, local newspapers used the idea that he was "savage," while everyone else was civilized, to create an imagined cultural distance that would allow his neighbors to feel a new sense of separation from him. Civilized white men could enjoy adventure stories of imperialist violence or collections of what appeared to be human relics precisely because they were "civilized" and had the capacity to temper that violence with white European values. During the 1910s, when Gein was coming of age, Theodore Roosevelt and other US leaders believed that American frontiersmen had to embrace the violent masculinity necessary to "outsavage the savages"— both long-standing Indigenous colonial subjects in North America, and more recent ones in the Philippines and Cuba. Yet, a white American man could embrace that masculine, racialized violence only temporarily, and would combine it with "manly civilized morality" harkening back to the Victorian era.[133]

Before Gein was arrested, then, even his "mad collections" of skulls and other human relics had a potentially conventional explanation. Gein had told friends and neighbors that he had a collection of "shrunken heads" sent to him by a cousin in the Philippines; presumably, the cousin would have been part of the US occupying force in the Philippines, and therefore a "legitimate" possessor of violent, imperialist masculinity. Even if a friend did not believe that particular story, Gein's collections might not seem suspect because commercialized white masculine enjoyment of human relics purportedly sourced from Indigenous peoples was ubiquitous. Replicas marketed as shrunken heads were sold at traveling carnivals, for example.[134] In the 1940s and 1950s, white Americans could encounter "headhunters" in the pages of *National Geographic,* in a display of Jivaro "shrunken heads" at the Smithsonian Institution, or at an exhibit representing Igorot people of the Philippines at the St. Louis World's Fair.[135] In each of these contexts, the racialized use of human relics symbolized the "primitive" or "savage" colonial other and reminded white Americans what their modern "civilization" was defined against.

Gein and his friends attributed his fantasies about collecting human relics to his voracious appetite for reading, a working-class alternative to museum-going that brought him folktales from around the world.[136] News reports cited his inspirations as supposed Indigenous practices in the Philippines and South America, as well as adventure stories about "lions and tigers and Africa and India."[137] This conflation of different peoples, continents, and even species is characteristic of how Orientalism denies specificity to the "Other." Less frequently mentioned in the news were Gein's many European inspirations, from an English "exhumation club" to Norwegian skullcaps for drinking mead.[138] Of his European influences, however, only Gein's interest in Nazi atrocities was routinely cited—likely because, as Lawrence Douglas contends, Nazi atrocities were figured as atavistic and exceptional to European civilization.[139]

Gein's racialized fantasies of pulp adventure and detective stories were not unusual; he shared them with many working-class white men in the postwar United States.[140] Where Gein differed was in failing to recognize that the pleasure white men were meant to take in shrunken-head souvenirs was rooted in a sense of orientalist superiority over the people and cultures that created such artifacts. Gein lacked the understanding that the anthropologist was considered a rational white man with the capacity for "self-reflective knowledge" that differentiated him from the "primitive" he purported to study.[141] He also lacked the "rational self-reflection" to understand that the corpses he stole belonged to white people, rather than colonial subjects. What, after all, was so different about a white man's "mad collection" of exhumed skulls and a white man's "museum collection" of exhumed skulls?[142]

Gein's alleged cannibalism deepened local perceptions of his "savagery." The rumor that Gein ate human flesh was soon debunked,[143] but the mere possibility of cannibalism had embedded itself in his neighbors' minds, and they began to develop psychosomatic gastrointestinal disease.[144] In certain instances, "cannibalism" came to stand in for a larger group of "extracurricular activities" with parts of corpses that had no other name.[145] Robert Gollmar, the judge who presided over Gein's 1968 criminal trial, described the ineffability of this category in a 1982 interview: Gein was a cannibal, a grave robber, "and I don't know the term, but he took the skin of his victims and manufactured chairs and other things."[146] In rural Wisconsin, dressing out a deer, tanning a hide, and butchering livestock were unremarkable tasks. But for someone to fail to distinguish between a human and nonhuman animal for any of those tasks—that there might even need to be a category for "human leatherwork" akin to "cannibalism"—was deeply unsettling. An editorial in the northern Wisconsin *Antigo Daily Journal* reasoned that since animals kill only in order to eat or defend themselves from attacks, Gein's behavior placed him "lower than an animal, and certainly lower than the savage who resorts to cannibalism."[147]

The rudimentary techniques that Gein used to preserve bodies indicated that he had not earned the white masculine social status associated with being a competent farmer. Rumors spread that Gein practiced taxidermy or embalming on his victims,[148] and according to *Life* magazine, these skills suggested that Gein was a "meticulous worker" in his own "demented way."[149] Unlike the national press, Wisconsinites knew that Gein's work was crude at best. Gein had put his victims' skin in a salt brine and rubbed it with oil[150]—rather unsophisticated, "traditional methods of dealing with rawhide."[151] A local investigator registered his disgust with Gein's poor (human) upholstery chairs. The chair seats were "crudely made," explained Captain Lloyd Schoephoerster. Underneath the chairs, "you could see strips of fat. It wasn't a good job."[152] Even Gein's interrogator pointed out Gein's poor knife work as he documented the different techniques Gein had used to remove flesh from the skull.[153] Confronted with one of the most shocking scenes in state and US history, white Wisconsin residents made sense of it through the familiar category of modern craftsmanship.

Issues of sex were also charged with unease about Gein's coarse workmanship. Gein's official psychiatric reports noted that although "sexual excitement" was part of Gein's behavior, there had been no "sexual behavior" with the bodies, partly because they "smelled offensively."[154] Though Gein's Madison-based interrogators and *psy* clinicians believed his behavior to be motivated by *psy* phenomena, they, too, were Midwestern men who looked down on his crude abilities with masculine handiwork. At least one of the sexual organs that Gein saved had begun to turn green and mold, despite ostensibly having been embalmed before he stole the body from its grave. When asking Gein why he had applied aluminum paint to that body part, Wilimovsky uncharacteristically accepted Gein's practical explanation that he had painted it to preserve it and stop it from decaying.[155] On the sexual organs that were better preserved, the means of preservation was then the problem. Asked whether he had attempted to have intercourse with Worden after "salting" her "vagina," Gein replied that he tried "without success."[156] Gein's lack of skill made his actions more disturbing to many.

As Gein's neighbors attributed his "unrecoverable deviance" to his perverse inability to distinguish himself from "the primitive," they explained why they had not suspected him sooner: Gein fit a familiar figure of small-town whiteness, the odd bachelor. In contrast to metropolitan accounts that viewed Gein's oddness as a sign of psychopathy, local accounts rendered Gein's status as an odd bachelor reassuring—a justification for why they had *not* suspected him sooner. Gein was no more "eccentric" than "any of dozens of other people they knew," his neighbors explained to the *Milwaukee Journal*.[157] Gein's whiteness and decades of living in Plainfield mitigated any suspicions his neighbors might have had. His bachelorhood was desexualized and judged nonthreatening, blunted with moderating adjectives: he was a "kindly" bachelor[158] or "shy little bachelor recluse."[159] Gein's estrangement from family and occupation was interpreted as an ability to provide flexible caring and manual labor to his community. He drove elderly neighbors to the hospital, was a good babysitter, and helped a farmer whose wife was ill; he baled hay, cleaned debris from county ditches, and worked a portable sawmill.[160] His flexible social and economic role was important, if low-status. His neighbors accepted that an "old bachelor living alone," without company or the "civilizing" effect of a wife, would be a "little peculiar,"[161] spurning the *psy* framework of the "drifter," which suggested that an odd bachelor who was unbound by family and occupation was inherently dangerous.[162]

Although an odd bachelor with local roots might be accepted, the same was not true for a mysterious spinster. In Plainfield, as in many small communities, belonging was determined by family roots, vocational value, and respectability—traits that were racialized, gendered, and sexualized. This partly explains why Gein was not suspected after the 1954 disappearance of tavern owner Hogan, despite repeatedly telling friends that he had killed her.[163] Hogan was unmarried and had lived in the Plainfield area for only five years. After her death, confusion about whether she was a spinster or two-time divorcée highlighted her shallow community ties and the "blank spots" in her life history.[164] In describing Hogan's vocation and her ability to "handle herself" with drunk customers, local newspapers suggested that her toughness and self-sufficiency were aberrant.[165] Her physicality, described as "dark" and "heavyset," deepened the sense that she did not belong.[166] Although Hogan was white and ethnically German, her outsider status was compounded by the racialized company she kept, as her tavern was a "favorite gathering place for Jamaican and Mexican migrant farm workers" during the summer. Even if Hogan was close to the farmworkers who patronized her tavern, she did not matter to those whose opinions were esteemed.[167] The gendered, racialized forms of small-town belonging that initially protected an odd bachelor like Gein did the opposite for a tough single woman like Hogan.

Serving drinks to migrants of color would not ingratiate a white person to her rural Wisconsin community, but managing migrant workers of color could. Managerial whiteness over Black farmworkers solidified the Gein family's reputation, counteracting the family's reputed indolence. Gein took great pride, his clinicians reported, in his late brother Henry's ability to "control a crew of Jamaican farm workers."[168] During World War II, the

United States contracted with the Jamaican government to send thousands of men to work on US farms.[169] The "well-learned" Jamaican farmworkers were dismayed by the racism and abuse that they faced in the United States, including intense police scrutiny, low pay, and poor housing.[170] In Wisconsin, twenty-six Jamaican men refused to work after telling authorities they were "afraid for their lives," forced to work for a foreman who carried a pistol and physically threatened them.[171] An overseer who surely used brutality to "handle" the men working for him, Henry remade his social status through a possessive investment in whiteness.[172] Gein claimed this status for himself, finding it necessary to combat rumors that he could be a "mite shiftless"[173] or that he only "worked when he felt like it,"[174] as well as gossip that his father was lazy and that his family was "queer because they did not work on Sunday."[175] Henry's brutal subordination of Black Jamaican workers gave the family access to a higher status of whiteness.

Plainfield's racial hierarchies went unchallenged, but its refusal to understand Gein's deviance through *psy* fields did not. Eighteen months after Gein's arrest, Plainfield found itself on the "psychoanalytic couch," in a 1959 *Menninger Clinic* bulletin analyzing the community's reaction to Gein.[176] The bulletin did not scrutinize Plainfield's parochial sense of belonging or its protection of violent white men. Rather, psychiatrists reported that Gein's former neighbors had responded to the discovery of his crimes in an "exhibitionistic and narcissistic manner," deriving pleasure from jokes about cannibalism and sexual perversion. One of Gein's psychiatrists argued that the "Gein humor" phenomenon was a community-wide psychic defense mechanism that allowed his neighbors to "forestall criticism of themselves for unknowingly tolerating such a criminal in their midst."[177]

Plainfield's tolerance for Gein ended the moment his crimes and "primitive" lifestyle were revealed. For the village, Gein's "unrecoverable deviance" was located not just in his crimes but in his mundane inability to distinguish himself from a disturbing racialized "primitiveness." His neighbors rejected him immediately, reacting with talk of mob violence and threats to bomb the jail where he was held.[178] When Gein's home mysteriously burned down a few months later, newspapers across Wisconsin took an atypical pro-arson stance, another reaction that would later be regarded as a pathological inability to reckon with shame.[179] In spite of Plainfield's disavowal of Gein, many people across the nation blamed the Wisconsin town for refusing *psy* interventions and failing to be "alert to indications of abnormality" that could have stopped him sooner.[180] Plainfield's failure to find Gein's oddities suspicious, combined with their failure to face the shock of his crimes head-on, made Plainfield itself suspect.

When Gein told a reporter in 1968 that "locality has an awful lot to do with a person's life," he articulated multiple spatial understandings of his crimes. For Gein, the statement meant that his neighbors had been unfriendly and perhaps caused his deviance. For *psy* practitioners and the metropolitan media, it meant that an overly friendly rural community had allowed an odd white bachelor to blossom, unchecked, into a maniac. For small-town media from a little farther out—say, fifty miles from Plainfield—it meant that Gein's behavior could be attributed to the soil and wildness of the landscape itself. In contrast to metropolitan media that claimed Plainfield was an idealized representative of any small town, regional weeklies from nearby small towns made it clear that the area where Gein lived was not generic at all, but was a distinctive, foreboding province known as the "dead heart." When Gein's story re-emerged in the 1970s, the anti-idyllic horror films that he inspired drew on the trope of a dangerously insular small town that refused to suspect its own, as well as the trope of a wild, savage landscape with atavistic powers.

THE MADNESS IN THE SOIL: WISCONSIN'S GREAT DEAD HEART

While the metropolitan press rendered Gein "mad" through intricate theories of sex complexes and psychopathy, small-town Wisconsin media located Gein's madness in metaphorical proximity to the primitive. Weeklies from Plainfield were careful to limit implications of the primitive to Gein as an individual, finding ways to fold him back into whiteness and largely absolve their broader community from responsibility.[181] Papers from a bit farther away, however, contended that the perverse "space of unrecoverable deviance" that Gein inhabited was not in his head or his home but the landscape: the "great dead heart," a large swath of central Wisconsin defined by social and ecological wildness that defied both civilization and cultivation.[182] The anti-idyllic dead-heart discourse scrutinized central Wisconsin from the perspective of proximate outsiders: small-town elites who lived in the greater region, about an hour's drive from Gein's farm. Defined by "wildness," this regional anti-idyll called into question the myth of the white settler family that functioned as an emblem of the Midwestern Heartland and the white nation writ large. The mythologized white settler family was imagined to domesticate the frontier, taming the "hostile wilderness," transforming it into farmland, and dispossessing Indigenous peoples of land and ways of life.[183] The "dead heart" of Wisconsin rooted the moral and mental status of the landscape's inhabitants in the quality of the landscape's soil. The region was imagined as "sparsely settled," a suspended frontier of infertile soil that resisted settler domestication, yet was "empty" of Indigenous people, despite centuries of dispossession and Indigenous resistance to dispossession.[184] Newspapers from the area surrounding Plainfield attributed Gein's madness to this landscape. When the

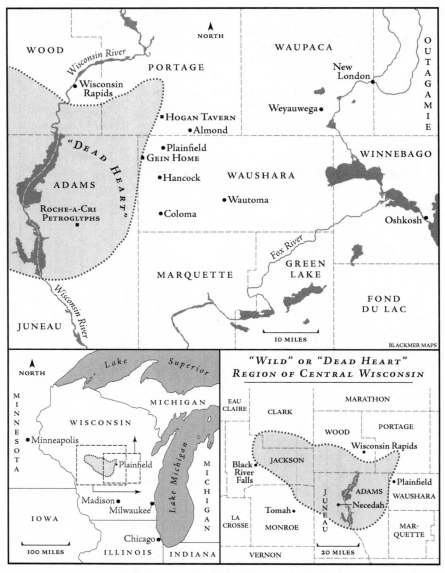

3.4 Maps of Central Wisconsin: Plainfield area (top) and "dead heart" region per descriptions in the *New London Press* c. 1957. Cartography: Kate Blackmer.

national anti-idyll re-emerged years later, the idea of a mad white land-scape fused with the idea of the psychopath and the "savage" home in the 1970s national anti-idyll.

Gein's murders, corpse-stealing, and rumored cannibalism occurred, according to *New London Press* editor Gordon Culver, when Gein was in a "spell of wildness."[185] This spell was not part of a *psy* disorder, but was characteristic of the wild, almost supernaturally "primitive" landscape that Gein and his neighbors inhabited.[186] Although Culver spurred the "dead heart" debate after Gein's arrest, the idea that parts of central Wisconsin were perversely poor and borderline amoral had existed for some time. The debate took place in at least four regional newspapers, and many other people shared similar views even if they did not use the same language. Culver's editorial about the dead heart was printed in the *New London Press*, then reprinted by the *Weyauwega Chronicle*, where, according to the *Plainfield Sun*, Plainfield residents read it and began "passing [it] around in resentment."[187] Five years earlier, in 1952, a similar description of the "wild" area near the border of Adams County and Waushara County had been printed in the *Waushara Argus*, and years later, judges, attorneys, and vacationers would describe that region of central Wisconsin in strikingly similar terms.[188] Local business owners who lived within the town limits of Plainfield were the town's main defenders, disputing the existence of the dead heart, or at least its boundaries, in both the *New London Press* and the *Plainfield Sun*.

Gein's farm, Culver wrote, was on the edge of the "great dead heart" of Wisconsin, an area that stretched across six counties to the west and north:

> It is sort of like a half-wolf, half-dog area where the wolf takes over here, the dog takes over there. But always coming out of the "dead heart" area is the everlasting mood of wildness and mystery. And we suspect the lonely 51-year-old bachelor now being held in the Waushara county jail at Wautoma was held to that spell of wildness. Where he was alone. Would be left alone. Where the laws of man were obliterated by the con-stant and encroaching frontier of wilderness. Where a man would kill a person and clean it like he would a deer.

Culver's dead heart was a lawless, isolated, and feral frontier, not a folksy farm town. If Gein was in a "dazelike" state when he stole corpses and murdered middle-aged women, it was because the landscape itself im-paired his mental and moral capacity. The dead heart was not ultimately bound by municipal markers, but by a "mood" of mystery and a "peculiar, lonely, wild feeling."[189] That wildness seemingly led to crime, from chicken thieves to high murder rates.[190] The dead-heart imagery was powerful and evoked the unfulfilled moral promises of the white Heartland.

The dead-heart area was imagined as desolate and "throbbingly poor," but it was primarily defined by the sense that it was beyond the boundaries of "civilization." The phrase "dead heart," echoing Joseph Conrad's "heart of darkness," conjured a remote, Indigenous area that resisted colonization and adherence to European values. One of the first times "dead heart" appeared in print, in a 1906 book about wells, the phrase was used to describe the arid interior of the Australian continent.[191] Australia's "dead heart" interior remained wild, or uncultivated—unfarmable, and relatedly, "untamed" and "uncultured." With the power of wells, the book sought to demonstrate, the white race would persevere in colonizing and cultivating the region. The white settler, as Eve Tuck and K. Wayne Yang explain, saw himself as "holding dominion over the earth and its flora and fauna," considering himself to be "more developed, more human, more deserving" than any other species.[192] Culver typified this, lamenting that although a "handful of good farms" brought "an aura of civilization to this area," the region's inherent "wildness" just refused to allow civilization to "permeate."[193] The dead-heart discourse erased Indigenous peoples from the landscape of central Wisconsin while asserting white dominion over it.

White Wisconsinites' role in conquering and expropriating the area from Indigenous peoples was referenced only obliquely, as a specter of a distant past, even as words like "territory" and "settlements" suggested that the "settling" was not complete. White settlers colonized central Wisconsin, dispossessing Ho-Chunk, Menominee, Ojibwe, Potawatomie, and other peoples through farm-based policies like the Homestead Act and Lever Act.[194] After white settlers and miners forced them out, some Ho-Chunks returned to central Wisconsin in the late nineteenth century and now "maintain a strong presence and political voice in the state."[195] Ho-Chunks were active and visible during the mid-century, as well, seeking and obtaining federal recognition, gathering with a quarter million Indigenous people at the Standing Rock Indian Ceremonial, and renewing pow-wow traditions to commemorate decorated Ho-Chunk veteran Mitchell Red Cloud Jr.[196] To white settlers, however, Ho-Chunk people were apparitions, present only through place names and petroglyphs.[197]

The "dead heart" brought racialized notions of civilization together with earthy metaphors of soil and wood. If the white family farm was supposed to cultivate civilization, its material was soil. Soil is "in good heart" or "good texture" when it is fertile and capable of producing good crops.[198] The soil in central Wisconsin was not arid, as in Australia, but overly marshy, a condition made worse by the stumps left behind when logging companies "cut over" the area. Or, as Culver put it, off the main roads, there was "nothing but marsh and cutover lands and more wilderness and desolation."[199] Decades later, Gollmar theorized that "something in the soil" might explain the four murderers from Gein's area.[200] If the soil could not or would not be cultivated, then perhaps the people were fundamentally prone to violence and incapable of improvement as well. The dead heart of Wisconsin mattered as an agricultural area and as part of the "Heartland," a prism for national ideals.[201] Yet, despite the moral promise of the Heartland, central Wisconsin was rotting from the inside out, like the dead heart of a tree whose inner heartwood had been attacked by pests.

Poverty was a consequence of soil that could not be compelled to grow enough hay even for a handful of cows.[202] Culver used florid language and hyperbole to emphasize how poor and rundown the dead-heart region was, particularly off the main highways: in the dead heart, the landscape itself evoked the "feeling of people struggling just for subsistence."[203] Plainfield residents were among the first to acknowledge that the land was "not the best farming country in the world," and that some of the "people, farms, and surrounds" in the area were "unfavorable."[204] But for people from other parts of Wisconsin who visited during fishing or hunting season, the area's poverty implied mental instability. A woman from Waushara, a town near Plainfield, recalled hearing rumors about people who vacationed in central Wisconsin: Gein was "loony," yes, but the area's rundown homes suggested that "*all* the people up around there" were "the same way!"[205]

Through the anti-idyllic optics of the dead heart, Culver used vernacular language to name the constellation of mental and moral deviance that accompanied white economic struggle and the ostensible failure of settler colonialism. Plainfield residents, Culver contended, were more likely than others to accept something "strange and odd," because their "own struggles are sufficient for their capacities."[206] Decades later, Wisconsin writer David Schreiner interpreted Culver's claims to mean that "self-hermitic, self-employed, poverty-stricken people" demonstrated "little real meddling in other people's business."[207] Yet Plainfield immediately assumed Culver was implying mental disability: the "remark about the capacities of the people," Plainfield resident Carl J. Alverson retorted, was "of course about the mental capacities."[208] Gollmar had the same impression as Culver, using language reminiscent of early twentieth-century eugenicists to describe one of the murderers from Gein's part of the county as a girl with a "pretty weak mind," prone to "epileptic fits" and auditory hallucinations like bells ringing.[209] Combined with poor morality, as manifested in "shacky dance halls," moonshining, fistfights, and chicken thieves, Plainfield's supposedly diminished mental capacity confirmed the idea that the dead-heart area was a cognitively impairing landscape of degeneracy. The virtue of the idealized Jeffersonian farmer was imagined to inhere in his hard work, morality, and unique democratic abilities. But since "cognitive capacity" had been a key democratic virtue since the days of John Locke,[210] mental and moral disabilities were a threat to the very idea of democratic self-governance. In the dead heart, "mental capacity" was shorthand for the "wilderness" outside of reason, virtue, and civic capacity.

Plainfield's civic defenders, such as restaurant and grocery-store owner Franklin Otto, appealed to agriculture and civic improvement to locate Plainfield within civilization and distance it from the image of untouched "wilderness." When contrasted with a wild "dead heart," agriculture represented the modern: improving the land, taming it, taking it from a wild state of nature to one of human progress. To defend Plainfield, Otto described every good farm in the region, detailing the modern machinery used to cultivate the uncooperative land so it might feed top-rated Holstein herds and yield large oat harvests. As for the troublesome citizenry, Otto named numerous local "advancement associations" and their efforts to host supervised dances for teenagers and provide Christmas gifts to needy children.[211] *Plainfield Sun* editor and owner Ed Marolla similarly commanded attention to the "little civic things"—cooperation between different Christian denominations, for example, or tolerance between different European ethnic groups—that make a town a "pleasant place to live."[212] Yet, Marolla's claim reinforced the existence of racial and religious distinctions, erasing—perhaps intentionally—the presence of non-Europeans and non-Christians. Otto and Marolla defended Plainfield through appeals to white, Christian, American values of tolerance and improvement and whitewashed visions of the town's population.[213] Gein himself was tossed in with the wilderness, labeled a "thorn" among his people, a man who "didn't improve nor care to."[214]

Otto's praise for Plainfield's farmers belied the tension between the town of Plainfield and its country neighbors. Properly, "Plainfield" referred to a small village, a few hundred people who lived in the vicinity of the crossroads marked by Worden's hardware store; colloquially, it could connote the farmers and would-be farmers who lived miles away but gathered in the village to "shop and swap small talk."[215] To the extent that the dead-heart discourse referred to Plainfield, it was specific to people who lived in the country, not those who resided in town. It was in the country, at the edge of Adams County, that the "dead heart" flourished, Otto insisted, defending the village itself. In 1977, Gollmar described Gein's neighbors across the road as being "backwoods people," "very rural" people who had a dirt floor and "didn't care about the other people."[216] In a separate interview, Gollmar reminded a researcher that Gein "lived out in the country," as though that itself explained his behavior.[217] As Otto defended his community, he insisted that Plainfield depended on the area's farmers, and that Plainfield businessmen would not "be in service to this community for very long" if farmers were truly struggling.[218] Yet Otto's point was undermined in the next six months, when two prominent community leaders—Otto himself and Marolla—moved away after buying a Madison hotel and suburban Milwaukee newspaper, respectively.[219]

Despite Culver's cutting accusations about the dead-heart area and the charged regional conversation that followed, the metropolitan media remained focused on *psy* explanations for Gein's behavior that viewed Plainfield as a generic, idealized small town—with one exception. One paragraph toward the end of a November 20, 1957, *Chicago Tribune* article hinted that anti-idyllic ways of understanding rural white communities persisted in the metropolitan media of the 1950s, even as they were subordinated to images of idealized small-town life. When reporter Paul Holmes made his way to Gein's farm on the outskirts of Plainfield, he observed the same disquieting sights as regional elites: rundown buildings, "untamed" natural landscapes, and questionable agricultural productivity. Unlike Wisconsin purveyors of the dead-heart discourse, Holmes treated readers like colonial outsiders venturing into a wild unknown. "On approaching the murder house," he wrote, presaging the formula of 1970s horror films, travelers crossed a "rickety bridge" reaching over an undammed creek. Perched precariously over the creek was a "grotesque" abandoned mill, a "physical premonition" of what was to greet the traveler at Gein's farm. "Crazily distorted," Holmes continued, the mill was an unsound building—cracked and frail, it was an edifice on the verge of "insanity."[220]

In the immediate aftermath of Gein's arrest, as people were to make sense of the senseless facts, metropolitan, local, and regional media debated whether Gein's madness was located in his mind, his mundane habits, or the landscape. During the 1950s, the key question was whether insanity inhered in the person or the place. In the 1960s, the War on Poverty represented poverty as deeply embodied, linking psychological depression with economic depression and physical illness. By the 1970s, debate was unnecessary: "Schizophrenia is the word for Wisconsin," local horror writer Schreiner contended, "if a region and its people can be thus classified."[221] The anti-idyll, an optic focusing on rural white landscapes of psychiatric disability, physical disability, poverty, and sexuality, had come together.

4: "MAIMED IN BODY AND SPIRIT"

The Spectacle of White Appalachian Poverty Tours during the 1960s

In the 1960s, Americans "rediscovered" poverty. With this rediscovery, which imagined poverty to be largely hidden and isolated within particular "depressed" regions, came a new manifestation of the rural white anti-idyll: tours to teach outsiders about poverty in majority-white communities of the central and southern Appalachian Mountains. These 1960s Appalachian poverty tours, together with the larger poverty discourse they contributed to, revived eugenic conceptions of poverty as deeply embodied, recalled the visual language of white rural poverty forged during the Great Depression, and located them in a region that was coming to be known as "Appalachia."[1] They were part of a larger movement that sought to bring public attention to the communities that Michael Harrington famously called the "other America" in 1962. Outsider interest in white Appalachia was piqued during John F. Kennedy's 1960 presidential primary campaign in West Virginia and proliferated in the years that followed. Writers like Harry Caudill, author of *Night Comes to the Cumberlands*, beckoned reporters and politicians to visit rural white mountain communities, promising glimpses of the sensational poverty, disability, and nonheteronormativity that purportedly accompanied economic exploitation.

Poverty tourists did not "find" the anti-idyll in mountain communities, of course. They journeyed to Appalachia and brought to bear anti-idyllic expectations and ways of looking that they had learned of in other regions, from the iron range of Minnesota to the turnip farms of Erskine Caldwell's Georgia. In 1960, a man named Claude Hooton pretended to be a telephone-company worker in order to look in on a family who lived in a hillside cottage that appeared idyllic but was locally notorious for being otherwise. Hooton was in West Virginia working on the Kennedy primary campaign, a momentous victory that propelled Kennedy to the nomination and then the presidency. Yet Hooton was not on the clock when he visited this home. He was there to indulge a personal curiosity, seeking to verify what seemed to be an anti-idyllic folktale told to him by a local hotel owner. The gossip in Hooton's story circulated in much the same way as in earlier anti-idyllic encounters, such as the eugenic family studies of chapter one: local community leaders (the hotel owner and the "county Kennedy man") gossiped with an interloper from out of town (Hooton), using their local knowledge about where and how aberrant families live. They did so in order to tell a tall tale about depravity, while distinguishing themselves from the poorer and less normative members of their community. When the interloper visited, he looked for what he had been instructed to see, saw it, and came to insist that it was "typical of a great many."[2]

This is the kind of interaction that Hooton recounted with zeal in a 1966 oral history, drawing on the same imagery that horror films would use a decade later—imagery that was surely a stark contrast to how any family that he intruded upon would understand their own bodyminds, social circumstances, and interactions with supposed telephone-company workers. Hooton claimed that as he drove up to the cottage, he saw two disabled people who "really did look like one-eyes," who were "just kind of slobbering," and who were certain to portend worse to come: inside, he witnessed "a boy and girl . . . making love." These circumstances led Hooton to make an extraordinary logical leap, taking this as confirmation of the most horrifying rumor: that the father of the family had sexually assaulted and impregnated two of his daughters. Of course, what Hooton witnessed—disabled people, some rubbish, and two young people having sex inside a home that *he* had forced his way into—was by no means proof of such abhorrent familial violence. And surely, if the father had assaulted his daughters as rumored, the solution was not for strange men to coerce their way into the family's home.[3] Further, one might hope, in spite of the period's norms, that a girl being sexually assaulted by her father would be taken seriously for the sake of her own well-being—not because her family was poor, not because she might potentially bear a child with a disability, and not because she and her violator were melded into interchangeable symbols of an anti-idyllic spectacle. But that was not to be. Hooton had been trained to understand sex, disability, violence, and poverty as interchangeable elements of a rural white anti-idyll. He had "read the stories and heard the reports" about rural poverty, and when the opportunity presented itself, he wanted to be able to tell such a tale himself, to regale later interviewers with proof that such scenes could be real.[4]

The dominant mode of the anti-idyllic gaze in the 1960s was not voyeuristic like Hooton's, but paternalistic in its liberalism. Writers like Harrington and Caudill developed a more precise narrative about the relationship between gender, sexuality, disability, and class: poverty, the theory went, indelibly shaped every facet of a person's life, from physical injuries and depressed spirits to missing teeth and nonnormative love lives. This contributed to a so-called "culture of poverty." The notion of a culture of poverty did not originate in white communities, nor is it predominantly associated with them. But for a brief moment in the early 1960s, the "culture of poverty" could conjure one of several groups: rural Mexicans and Puerto Rican migrants, whom anthropologist Oscar Lewis first described with the term in the 1950s; Black urban communities that Daniel Patrick Moynihan would infamously pathologize in 1965; rural white Appalachians; or even "the elderly" (a subject of *The Other America*). This moment was to be short-lived, as the racialization of poverty—and with it, the perceived deservingness of the poor—changed substantially during the mid-1960s.

This shift in the racialization of poverty also transformed policy and media coverage. Before the mid-1960s, the national media "overwhelmingly" understood poverty to be a "white problem."[5] After the Watts uprising of 1965, followed by Black urban uprisings in the summers of 1966 and 1967, federal programs and national media turned their focus to Black urban poverty—which, unlike white poverty, was overwhelmingly perceived as "undeserving."[6] Today, the Economic Opportunity Act (EOA)—the major legislation that came out of the publicly declared "War on Poverty"—is typically associated with poor Black communities in major cities, federal programs such as Head Start, local programs such as New York's Mobilization for Youth, and grassroots advocacy by poor people from a variety of backgrounds.[7] Yet in 1964, when President Lyndon B. Johnson first declared a "War on Poverty," he deliberately focused on "poor white Americans of the rural backwash."[8]

To represent poor white people in Appalachia as "deserving poor" required an investment in mythologized histories of mountain whiteness and white racial superiority. Beginning in the late nineteenth century, missionaries and writers of "local color" literature imagined the poor white folks of West Virginia to be "our contemporary ancestors": white Americans who were a bit "behind" in cultural and economic development but had perfect credentials for "racial betterment."[9] First, they were the "purest Anglo-Saxon stock in all the United States," a claim attributed to their purported isolation from both immigrants and Black Americans.[10] Second, they had a reputation as "pioneers" (colonizers) who had "outlasted" (dispossessed) Indigenous peoples.[11] More than sixty years later, presidential aides and journalists directly appealed to these older claims, branding the region the "descendants of pioneer American Families" to represent them as deserving of federal aid.[12] In doing so, they erased the dispossession of Indigenous peoples, and the history of thousands of Black families who migrated to areas such as eastern Kentucky in the early 1900s.[13]

In this chapter, I examine how disability, gender, and sexuality were intertwined in Appalachian culture-of-poverty discourse and elaborate how a queercrip analysis informed by Black feminist and queer of color critique might reimagine such purported "deficiencies." I then analyze a controversial presidential visit to a poor white "Appalachian" family who became fodder for gossip when the expected rehabilitation narrative was disrupted by the complexities of being poor and disabled. Third, in analyzing a social worker's account of the anxiety that poor white West Virginia men faced in navigating poverty bureaucracy, I consider how mental disabilities such as depression combine with labyrinthine bureaucracies to make poor people feel estranged. The chapter concludes by analyzing how politics and media functioned to whitewash both the start of the War on Poverty and poverty in Appalachia.

"MAIMED IN BODY AND SPIRIT":
QUEERCRIP ANALYSIS AND THE CULTURE
OF POVERTY IN WHITE APPALACHIA

Narratives about Appalachian poverty in the 1960s were saturated with references to disability, both material and metaphorical. For the most part, these narratives did not center industrial illnesses and physical injuries—black lung disease, back injuries, amputated limbs, etc.—that could testify to the heteromasculine labor of coal mining, nor the agency of disability activism.[14] What instead rose to prominence in the 1960s as part of the idea of a "culture of poverty" were anti-idyllic views of "culture-bound" mental disabilities, such as "nerves" or a depressed malaise, which were, in turn, frequently associated with male "passivity." Consequently, popular understandings of disability in poor white Appalachia were deeply enmeshed with nonheteronormativity, from gender presentation to erotic expression to family formation. Appalachians and Appalachian studies have become practiced critics of pathologizing the idea of a culture of poverty, adept at turning attention back to the structural inequality that shapes the health and lives of poor people everywhere.[15] Yet nonheteronormative and nonablenormative modes of life need not be disavowed as mere symptoms of exploitation; they might be understood as unremarkable, if not, in some cases, desirable.

The idea of a culture of poverty that was marked by insufficient sexual regulation, inadequate adherence to gender norms, and bodymind aberrations did not begin in Appalachia, nor even in the United States. Lewis coined the phrase in 1959 to characterize nonheteronormative families in rural Mexico.[16] In his 1962 book *The Other America*, Harrington expanded and departed from Lewis's theory by examining poor communities from the elderly to migrant farmworkers in Florida and California to white Appalachians. Three years later, Moynihan permanently transformed culture-of-poverty theory in a report in which he infamously proclaimed Black family life to be a "tangle of pathology" caused by a pathological culture of poverty in "urban ghettoes." Since Moynihan's usage, "culture of poverty" has most notoriously been used to disparage Black women for nonnormative kinship arrangements and to denigrate Black men for "improperly" embodying masculinity (a concern that was shaped, as Kevin Mumford asserts, by concerns about homosexuality).[17] Moynihan's claims about Black women's nonheteronormativity shaped public policy and public discourse for decades, establishing the "moral grammar and the political practices" that were used in the 1980s and 1990s to dismantle the US welfare state.[18] As Moynihan's ideology pervaded liberal, neoconservative, and even Black nationalist ways of thinking, it was vigorously contested by Black women involved with the welfare rights movement and by Black lesbian feminists.[19]

For most Americans, then, poor white folks in Appalachia are not the first community conjured by the phrase "culture of poverty." Yet the culture of poverty is also how many Americans come to know Appalachia, regardless of whether they think of it in those terms. In 2016, J. D. Vance, best-selling author of *Hillbilly Elegy*, capitalized on the disjuncture between readers' expectations that the culture of poverty was distinctly Black and their simultaneous awareness of a white "poverty culture" located in the mountains: "I have known many welfare queens," Vance wrote, "and all were white."[20] Every few decades, when poverty in the southern Appalachian Mountains is "rediscovered" by outsiders, the region's struggles are once again attributed to supposedly deficient cultural values. Sometimes the poster children of those struggles are characterized as malingering, unemployed, disabled men, depicted as emasculated shadows of once-virile white coal miners or white settler-colonizers.[21] Sometimes the poster children are more absurdly sensational, like children with so-called "Mountain Dew mouth."[22]

This notion of a white Appalachian culture of poverty—and what would soon become the hallmarks of a distinctly perverse kind of white Appalachian depression—was established by 1962 with the publication of *The Other America, Night Comes to the Cumberlands*, and Thomas Ford's *The Southern Appalachian Region: A Survey*, and it soon pervaded the language used by politicians, administrators, and academics. In *The Other America*, Harrington famously described the poor as "maimed in body and spirit."[23] Everything about the poor, he claimed, "from the condition of their teeth to the way in which they love, is suffused and permeated by the fact of their poverty."[24] Poor people's "depression" was therefore both economic and affective: they lacked material things but were also limited in their outlook on life, access to healthcare, and inability to form heteronormative family units.[25] As Harrington made claims about poverty writ large, others grounded depression in the specific topography of mountain life. In the Ford survey, Rupert Vance contended that Appalachians' apathy resulted from the physical isolation of "distance and rugged terrain" in the mountains, which had created "mental and cultural isolation."[26] In the years that followed, as the urban Black "culture of poverty" was transformed into a psychologized notion of Black "cultural deprivation," psychiatrists working in Appalachia likewise transformed poverty from a "culture" to a "syndrome" characterized by a "chronic psychological depression."[27]

"Poverty syndrome," according to psychiatrist David Loof, was a consequence of how poor Appalachian men's depression or household absence affected their sons, resulting in boys with "anxious-dependent, somewhat effeminate personalities."[28] Loof contended that the sons of female-headed households or fathers who were "generally apathetic, resigned, passive" would become passive and effeminate. For some boys this manifested in "psychosexual confusion," inducing them to pursue "various forms of passive, receptive sexuality" with other boys or young men; for others, this anxious passivity simply meant that they interacted with other people "like petulant little old ladies."[29] Harrington's much less clinical aim had been to engender compassion for the poor and thereby to generate the will to make political and economic change. To induce compassion, though, Harrington imagined that when poor people were unmarried or lived intergenerationally, they did so because structural oppression did not allow them the capacity to envision a more normative life for themselves. He could not allow for the possibility that they might not wish to be legally married or might enjoy the sustenance of living with an extended family. Nor could he or Loof imagine that a young man might simply enjoy receptive intercourse, regardless of whether his father was poor or depressed.

Frequently, even among politicians, culture-of-poverty theory—which was ostensibly distinct from eugenic ideas of poverty—lapsed into descriptions of poverty as "vicious" and "hereditary," as "an inherited disease," the problem of the "hereditary poor, the born poor," or even, on occasion, through direct comparisons to the Kallikak family.[30] This was especially evident in *Night Comes to the Cumberlands* by Kentucky attorney and state representative Caudill. Caudill combined liberal critiques of structural economic problems with an insistence that nonmarital sexuality, gender nonconformity, and disability were individual moral failings. "The sexual mores of the mountaineer were never strict," Caudill wrote, lamenting that welfare had worsened the morals of "slatterns," "pathetic mountaineer women," and "fertile and amoral females" who "resided in every camp and on every creek."[31] Caudill was quite explicit about his racist, colonialist vision: he wished for white Kentucky men to regain the purported virility of their violent grandfathers who "fought the Indian as a beast" and who sexually assaulted Native women.[32] He claimed contemporary white Kentucky men were "welfare malingerers" who peddled a "wide range of ailments," from sore backs to shortness of breath to nervousness. "Nerves," he insisted, foreshadowing Loof, were so tied to malingering that they were being referred to by local doctors as a "chronic, passive dependency-syndrome."[33]

But complaints of "nerves" in eastern Kentucky and West Virginia had long predated the War on Poverty, and the idiom functioned much differently than Caudill assumed. "Nerves" did not name a psychosomatic illness—that is, the physical manifestations of a psychological condition— but the inverse: psychological manifestations of the pain, fatigue, and "various queer bodily sensations" caused by physical conditions such as hunger or arthritis.[34] In other words, as a folk idiom, "nerves" evidenced poor mountaineers' intelligence and implicitly critiqued the false separation between "physical" illness and "mental" illness.

Appalachian culture-of-poverty discourse indexed forms of white rural nonconformity—gender unorthodoxy, sexual dissidence, vernacular epistemologies of pain, fatigue, and worry—that are denied in normative appeals to the idealized mountaineer family. Heterogeneous bodyminds, genders, and sexualities need not be understood as inherently pathological. As Roderick Ferguson contends, the damage done by the Moynihan Report was not just that it called Black culture "pathological," but that in doing so, it tried to "transform" that "presumably 'pathological' culture into one that was suitable for gender and sexual conformity and compliant with heteropatriarchal regulation."[35] Ferguson's critique builds on a long tradition of Black feminists—beginning with Black women welfare activists, like Johnnie Tilmon, and Black lesbians—who contested the notion that nonheteronormative family formations like single motherhood functioned as a "sign of cultural deficiency."[36] Black welfare rights activists in places like Detroit and Morgantown, West Virginia, fought back against the mundane but dehumanizing ways that welfare authorities asserted state power: impossible bureaucratic hoops, invasive home inspections, and unwarranted denial of welfare checks.[37] In other words, rather than complying with heteropatriarchal regulation, poor Black women insisted on complex personhood.

Analysis of disability in poor communities likewise demands complexity. "Nerves" might describe a poor man's back injury, as well as his anxiety about his back injury, as well as his reliance on alcohol, as well as his apprehension about whether his issues are causing his sons to be "effeminate." Or it might name a poor woman's weariness and impatience with her lot in life, plus the labor it takes to look after her husband and children while working in a textile mill, plus the toll that drinking is taking on her, plus her worries about gossipmongers. As Avery Gordon and Patricia Williams theorize, "life is complicated," and it need not be arbitrarily simplified in order to render marginalized people as victims or "superhuman agents"—or as "deserving" versus "undeserving" poor.[38]

In 1960, as poor disabled white coal miners called for their fellows to join them on the picket line, they sought to tell a simple story of exploitation with a clear moral arc. That story stated that disabled miners were "victims" of corporate greed, poor because of an unambiguous physical injury acquired through a masculine vocation, and capable of being restored to full white manhood. The narrative's simplicity required acceding to heteropatriarchal regulation. As disabled miners called upon others to join them on the picket line, they insisted that they wanted "no sissies or jelly fish backboners," just "men with guts, who are not afraid to stand up for what is right, on behalf of their disabled brothers."[39] Coming together under the banner of disability, they felt the need to distance themselves from masculinity deemed insufficiently heteronormative or "weak." But disability and gender are not so easily separated, as their own rhetoric demonstrates. To publicly emphasize their masculine ability to fight required embodied metaphors—backbone, guts, standing up—that reinscribed ablenormativity.

As I turn to poverty visits by presidents and social workers, the stories I examine are notably less tidy. These case studies are centered on people who are not paragons of virtue—people who risk confirming stereotypes of malingering or strangeness, who might be considered "undeserving" because they experience addiction or seemingly lack motivation.

GOSSIP ABOUNDS: BEHIND THE PUBLIC FACE OF THE PRESIDENTIAL POVERTY TOURS

Three months after announcing an "unconditional war on poverty" during his first State of the Union address, Johnson set out on two poverty tours. Most of the families on these tours were white and seemed to live in Appalachia, conflating the issue of "poverty" with "white Appalachia."[40] The families Johnson met in April and May 1964 were photographed and reported on by news outlets around the nation. For the few months that the face of poverty was white and rural, families like the Fletchers in Kentucky became those faces for the War on Poverty, and remained visual touchstones of white Appalachian poverty for decades. Just months after

4.1 The Marlow family huddles on their front porch looking out at Marine One, which has just landed in their yard near Rocky Mount, North Carolina. As her mother and siblings stare at Marine One, fourteen-year-old Mary Elizabeth Marlow looks back over her shoulder, staring at the camera taking their photograph. Photographer: Cecil Stoughton. Lyndon B. Johnson Library, 225-43-WH64.

the Appalachian poverty tours, however, the Johnson administration had a problem with one of their poster families. In May, Johnson had spent a whirlwind few hours in Rocky Mount, North Carolina (a town not in Appalachia, incidentally, but on the border of the piedmont and coastal plain). There, Johnson met William and Doris Mills Marlow, the latter of whom would soon become persistent about requesting assistance. In the margins of a September 20 letter from Doris to Johnson aide Bill Moyers, someone—perhaps Moyers—evidenced his frustration by scrawling "Marlow again!!"[41] The Marlow "problem," which had begun a month earlier, was passed back and forth between presidential aides, and between the presidential administration and the gubernatorial administration of North Carolina's Terry Sanford. Doris wrote to the president out of desperation after the North Carolina media began to cast her as the malingering, mooching, criminal, substance-abusing, "undeserving poor" of the anti-idyll. Her family's struggles reveal the impossible, contradictory demands made of poor families and how poverty tours disrupted their lives.

The Marlow family was chosen for a presidential visit—in spite of concerns from state officials—because they appeared to have the requisite elements to tell a particular story about poverty and rehabilitation. On paper, they seemed to fit the bill. William, a veteran who had been recently hospitalized, qualified as a "father at least partially disabled."[42] The oldest of his seven children, Billie, had dropped out of school years earlier, meeting another requirement. William's apparently improving health implied he would be able to qualify for jobs programs, which by and large excluded the disabled. With that, the Marlow family seemed tailor-made for a story of rehabilitation and redemption: government assistance would help William find employment, which would in turn allow Billie to return to school and redeem the state's investment in the family.

There was one last requirement, however, that had made the selection committee's choice more difficult: "a white family was preferred." Before that, the selection committee had "easily found a number of families" who met the requirements, they later told the *Rocky Mount Evening Telegram*. There was an "abundance of rural poverty" in the two-county area around Rocky Mount, and many families in the area subsisted on less than $3,000 per year because they were Black and in "perpetual debt to some white, rich landowner."[43] Being forced to choose a white family, the selection committee claimed, narrowed their long list down to a single, questionable family.[44] Johnson did visit one Black family on his May 1964 poverty tour, on a stop in Gainesville, Georgia. But when Johnson visited Black general-store owners Mr. and Mrs. A. J. Butler, he emphasized small-town "urban renewal" programs rather than rural poverty programs.[45] Since the administration insisted on painting the poverty programs as white, the selection committee had to choose the Marlows to be the face of the "deserving poor." Unlike those on the ground, the Johnson administration did not seem to consider the social and economic head start provided by whiteness and what it took for a white family to be poor in spite of possessing the property of whiteness itself even though many Southerners, both white and Black, were practiced in making moral judgments about the category of "poor whites."[46] If the administration had considered visiting a Black family in Rocky Mount, they would not have been relegated to choosing a family with the history of lawbreaking and substance abuse that made the Marlows risky faces for a new government program.

The circumstances of the Marlow family, and of poverty and disability more generally, were more complex than a prefabricated story of "deserving" poverty could accommodate. Months later, the *Telegram* reported obliquely that the "area abounds with gossip about the reputation of the Marlows."[47] Conservative media commentator and future Senator Jesse Helms reported that a "persistent round of rumors" was swirling around the Marlows just weeks after the president's visit—rumors that were obscured though "only kindness perhaps, prevent[ed] a full discussion of the specific circumstances of the family."[48]

The rehabilitation story imagined for a family with a disabled head of household did not consider the different courses that disabilities can take: some improve, some are chronic, some are better until they aren't again, but nearly all defy the neat, normative expectation of "curative time."[49] William's qualifying disability was back trouble—his doctor had told him that he had "arthritis and a soft, crumbling spine"—but in different tellings, "nerves," addiction, and illness were also part of his family's story.[50] The requirements for the Rocky Mount family scarcely conceived the poor father's wife to exist at all, outside of bearing him numerous children. Yet Doris not only raised the children and worked outside the home, she managed a home and family that was in constant crisis, from her husband's hospitalization to eviction to the debts that accumulated throughout. The stipulations engineered to guarantee the picture of the "deserving poor" ultimately demonstrated what an impossibility that was. An article in the *Telegram* reminded readers that "often forgotten in the avalanche of gossip is the fact that the family was not chosen to be a paragon of morality, but was selected as an example of a family troubled by some of the problems" of poverty.[51]

The Marlows' public fall from grace stung all the more because of the rosy portrait of respectability and uplift that both politicians and the media had painted during Johnson's poverty tours. Newspapers appealed to the folksiness of middle-class white farm life even when describing families with dramatically different socioeconomic conditions, and they diminished the tremendous power differentials between the president and the poor families who were briefly in the spotlight. Reporters frequently used banal gendered descriptions of brief cross-class affinities to invite readers to relate, describing the president's daughter and Doris talking "like two women talk when they get together," or recounting the president and William discussing farming, "as men will."[52]

Yet claims to neighborliness could only go so far. A poor family's neighbor would not typically visit by helicopter, invite a flock of reporters to accompany him, and announce to the entire nation that this family, right here, was the very face of poverty, as Johnson had done a week earlier in Inez, Kentucky, where he anointed Tom Fletcher the face of poverty. Photographs of Johnson's visit with Fletcher belie the textual claims that Johnson "visit[ed] like a next door neighbor," highlighting the disparities between the two men.[53] Walter Bennet's iconic *Time Magazine* photograph framed the fundamentally paternalistic relationship between the men, drawing on stark differences in the men's physicality and how they held themselves. In Bennet's photograph, Fletcher hunkers on his porch, knees pulled tight to his small chest; Johnson, though squatting, towers over him. Bennet captured an important dynamic of the poverty visits, depicting Fletcher as burdened by the weight of his circumstances and Johnson as wielding the influence to potentially lift some of Fletcher's weight.

Fletcher's actual next-door neighbors, Noah Bowen and his family, met Johnson at Fletcher's home that same day, but they were not on even terms with the president either: later, Mrs. Bowen, like Doris Marlow, would write to the president with requests for assistance.[54] Nor was Johnson meeting with Fletcher and Bowen under anything approximating "ordinary" circumstances. With the president came a flock of federal, state, and local officials, and a large assembly of press. A color photograph by White House photographer Cecil Stoughton complicates the power dynamics of Johnson's poverty visit, which was not ultimately about an interaction between two men. Stoughton's photograph, reversing the perspective of Bennet's, reveals what was occluded by it: as Stoughton looks out over Fletcher's shoulder, toward the road, dozens of men with cameras wend their way toward his home (fig. 4.2). From this vantage point, Fletcher stands taller than Johnson, even as the cameras march toward him.

As Johnson made his way through the hollows, towns, and small cities of Appalachia, he regularly made unplanned stops to introduce himself to disabled white men, even though War on Poverty programs typically excluded the disabled. In Knoxville, Tennessee, Johnson "unexpectedly" stopped to greet a disabled man sitting on his porch with neighbors.[55] Earlier that day, in Cumberland, Maryland, Johnson had stopped at the State Unemployment Office and spoken with a "49-year-old one-legged former miner."[56] This focus on the disabled was undermined by the policy of War on Poverty programs: its architects, framing their choices as "alleviating poverty for the elderly and disabled" or trying to "eliminate poverty for those who still had a chance," consciously chose the latter.[57] Decision-makers repeatedly determined disability and "immorality" to be beyond the limits of rehabilitation. In Michigan, a welfare official expressed concern that half of those whom he was expected to help were not suitable for Title V job training programs due to "extreme health problems," including alcoholism, obesity, "defective vision," and "mental health problems."[58] The Job Corps, a program created for sixteen-to-twenty-one-year-old boys who had dropped out of high school, explicitly excluded young people with "physical defects" such as blindness, limb loss, "severe epilepsy," and "total deafness," as well as "character defects" such as homosexuality (though that did not inoculate the Job Corps from scandals about homosexuality).[59] A report on job opportunities for people with disabilities noted that "OEO [Office of Economic Opportunity] money" writ large was not available for "mental health programs."[60] Disability made for a useful narrative about "deserving poverty," but in practice, the needs of people with a wide range of disabilities and illnesses were considered beyond the boundaries of state assistance.

4.2 The Fletcher family meets the president and first lady. From this vantage point, standing on the wooden porch alongside Tom Fletcher, viewers are looking out at dozens of men with cameras who wend their way down the road toward his home. Since Johnson is on the ground, Fletcher appears taller than the president, who was practiced in using his 6-foot-3-1/2-inch frame to loom over others. Photographer: Cecil Stoughton. Lyndon B. Johnson Library, C293-4-WH64.

A spontaneous greeting with a paralyzed man in Inez, Kentucky, highlighted contradictions between the poverty rhetoric that leaned on disability and the poverty programs that excluded the "seriously disabled" who did not have "high public appeal."[61] Near his helicopter's landing strip, after Johnson left the Fletcher and Bowen families, he introduced himself to J. C. Blankenship, a white man lying on a gurney who had reportedly been paralyzed below the waist for six years.[62] In the photograph, taken by Stoughton, Blankenship lies on a gurney that has been rolled outside. His pale pink hospital blanket is a bright contrast to the green lawn around him (fig. 4.3). Even aside from the man at the center of the photograph, the image was markedly distinct from the poverty visit photographs that became symbols of Appalachian poverty. The homes in the background look

4.3 President Lyndon B. Johnson makes an impromptu stop to meet a disabled man, J. C. Blankenship, in his yard near Inez, Kentucky. The disabled man appears to be in his twenties, and his expression is difficult to read. He lies on a hospital gurney with a blanket laid over him, as Johnson shakes the hand of another man directly above him. A crowd of onlookers takes photographs of Johnson. Photographer: Cecil Stoughton. Lyndon B. Johnson Library, 224-43-WH64.

modern and well maintained, a stark contrast with the humble Fletcher home. The people surrounding Blankenship are not meeting Johnson because they were chosen as a symbol of American misfortune, but, it seems, because they were excited by the chance of meeting the president. To Blankenship's left is a young family wearing coordinated red outfits; to his right, behind the president, is a stylish woman in a green gingham dress who appears to be mid-gesture in a conversation with the first lady; and behind him—all around him, really—are young men in plaid shirts aiming Brownie cameras at Johnson. Blankenship himself appears young, perhaps in his twenties. He has flex-straws, an assistive technology, laid across his legs. But it is difficult to read his expression. Blankenship lies positioned to watch a handshake occurring above him, between Johnson and another man, perhaps a sheriff, who wears a cowboy hat. The photograph's vantage point, well suited for the faces of those standing, is not ideal for the man at the center. Although Blankenship's body is in the visual center of the photograph, he is not its central subject.

William Marlow, a white man who was seen to have the "right kind" of disability, a "simple" injury that could seemingly be rehabilitated, illustrates the intertwining complexity of disability, poverty, and demands for moral purity. Months before the *Telegram* article noted gossip abounding, state and local officials had worried about the Marlows becoming the face of the program.[63] Johnson's aides were aware of the fact that Billie, the ostensible hope of the family, had an arrest record for check forgery and stealing a bike—news that would leak within a few months of the visit.[64] The local selection committee knew that William was on probation for making moonshine, and that both William and Doris, as the *Telegram* diplomatically phrased it, were "not teetotalers."[65] One of the men who arranged Johnson's visit privately expressed concerns that the visit "easily could have been embarrassing to the family as well as to the community and the State" and hinted to a *Charlotte Observer* editor that the White House may have been unwise in choosing to visit a tenant farmer "in that particular area."[66]

Before these concerns became public, media and neighborly scrutiny was already upending the Marlows' lives, presenting them as fakers and bums. Some of the suspicion was fed by their neighbors, one of whom began to make "some very cynical noises" that spurred an *Observer* investigation and then a politically motivated editorial in a Virginia newspaper that circulated nationally. But as the Marlows defended their pride, they insisted that the state had "tried to make us look poorer than we are"—a defense that was then twisted into evidence that they had been faking their poverty.[67] Simultaneously, hundreds of onlookers a day began driving by their home—and then came the letters, gossip, and threats. More neighbors became disgruntled.[68] The family began to receive anonymous hate mail, "crackpot letters." The Marlows' association with Johnson provoked the wrath of white supremacists who blamed the family for Johnson's policies on integration and civil rights, raising the specter of violence from organizations like the Ku Klux Klan.[69]

The logistics of the visit itself had compounded the Marlow family's daily stresses. William's sixty-nine-year-old mother, Mary Griggs, was stunned and frightened when she returned home from a trip to visit a relative to find her quiet country road full of Secret Service, police, and journalists. "I was scared to death," she told a reporter for the *Winston-Salem*

Journal. "I didn't know what to think when I rode up."[70] When Johnson mentioned Griggs in his official remarks, he and his speechwriters may not have realized that the president had not met her.[71] The Marlows did not have a telephone line, and the event was organized hastily, while she was out of town; there had been no way to warn Griggs about what to expect when she returned home.[72] Reporters from Rocky Mount and the nearby town of Spring Hope, both women, also noticed the dust and sand whipped up by Marine One and understood that even if it did not ruin the Marlows' patch of potatoes and collards, it had certainly dirtied the clean clothes that Doris had been instructed to leave out on the line, adding to the labor of a mother of seven who did not have running water.[73] Weeks after the May visit, William "suffered a nervous breakdown."[74] By July, the oldest son Billie, who had dropped out of school to help his father, and who was imagined to lend the family the promise of rehabilitation and respectability, had been arrested for "repeated incidents of driving without a license." He had completed a thirty-day jail sentence but was living and working on his own, apart from his parents and siblings.[75]

The aggravation of poverty—even poverty that was white, rural, and imagined to be "respectable"—complicated life in ways that made it that much more difficult to scramble up to a more secure socioeconomic condition. These further complications led to Doris's persistent correspondence with the Johnson administration. After Johnson's visit, their landlord evicted them. As tenant farmers, moving to a house in town took away their primary source of income and brought new expenses by way of water and gas bills. Doris was employed full-time in a sewing room, but it was not possible to support her family of ten. (The cotton dust of the textile mill also predisposed her to byssinosis, better known as "brown lung," which has many similarities to the better-known "black lung" disease caused by coal mining.)[76] In her letters to the president, Doris spoke of her struggles to pay rent, buy and pay for a heater, buy groceries, make lunch for her kids, and then go to work without lunch for herself. Her family's debt, she explained, dated back to her husband's "illness," for which he had been hospitalized on and off for four years. Regardless, the debt meant her family could not get credit; her full-time job meant her family could not get welfare; her husband had a job for a day and a half before he "had to quit" since his disability prevented him from doing "heavy work" and his education prevented from doing "office work." The Veterans Administration in the Rocky Mount Employment Office was "trying to locate him a handicap job" but had not yet found one.[77] As a result of Doris's perseverance, however, the Johnson and Sanford administrations made significant efforts to help, deploying men and agencies to help her husband find permanent work, and even discreetly sending the family $200 cash—a situation that surely would have unfolded differently had the Marlows not been white.[78]

4.4 As the sun sets, all seven Marlow children—ranging in age from seven to eighteen—pose casually on their front porch. The younger boys ham it up for the camera: the smallest boy smiles widely and stands tall with his hand in his pocket; the boy on the far left leans on a post and hangs his toes off the edge of the porch; and the boy beside him smiles widely, showing his dimples, as he dangles his wrist over the shoulder of another brother and cocks his hip slightly to the side. Photographer: Cecil Stoughton. Lyndon B. Johnson Library, C333-11-WH64.

For the bureaucrat who impatiently scribbled "Marlow again!!" on her letter, it was frustrating to have "trouble" appear on the horizon again: to receive yet another letter from a persistent woman with a questionable reputation, making demands on the president in the throes of election season; to perhaps regret the hasty choices that brought this family to the public's attention at all; to question the decision to ignore the red flags—arrest records, rumors of alcoholism—and visit the Marlow family anyway, since, of the many poor families in the region, they were the only whites who met the political criteria, and the War on Poverty could not appear to be a "Black" bill. But for Doris, regardless of the "morality" she and her family did or did not evince, her family was hungry. She feared that her family, on the cusp not of election season but of winter, was at risk of freezing. Being troublesome, even to the president and governor, was the least of her worries. She may not have been operating the bureaucratic machinery as intended, but she was provoking a reaction. So far, it had gotten her kids new clothes for school. It is no wonder she felt it might not hurt to try again.

When reporters checked in with the Marlows in 1973, William was recovering from a heart attack, and the family was still struggling economically. Doris bore Johnson no ill will, however. "A lot more families are living better because of him," she affirmed, even if her family was not.[79] Then again, perhaps she was unsurprised. She had never fully embraced curative temporality and the hope that accompanied it. When Johnson visited in 1964 and William expressed optimism that things would "start getting better now," Doris was more pragmatic. "Even if it don't," she said, "we have something to remember."[80]

"NONE TOO STOUT": NAVIGATING THE WELFARE BUREAUCRACY WITH MENTAL DISABILITY

If Doris Marlow had not been able to appeal directly to the president, she would have had a difficult time working with the municipal, county, state, and federal bureaucracies necessary to receive social welfare benefits. Poverty agencies knew that it was difficult for "rural clients to manipulate the bureaucratic machinery" of the social welfare system.[81] For any poor person, welfare bureaucracies could seem overwhelming, opaque, and capricious. This was compounded for those who had a mental disability. I now rewind a few months, to late 1963, and travel from the edge of the North Carolina piedmont to the mountains of West Virginia. I analyze an account by a social worker, Mary Wright, that grapples with the overdetermined "type" of the "passive" former coal miner with "worn out nerves." Wright offered keen insight into navigating the poverty bureaucracy with a mental disability, even as her attempt to understand that "type" risked further estranging the experiences of poverty, mountain life, and disability.

Wright penned her case report about the pseudonymous "Buddy Banks" while working for Action for Appalachian Youth (AAY). AAY was one of sixteen original "demonstration programs" devised as models for what would become the War on Poverty, but from the start, AAY was an odd fit.[82] Founded in Charleston, West Virginia, it was funded by a grant from Kennedy's Office of Juvenile Delinquency (OJD), which strictly focused on "inner city youth." Although Charleston is the largest city in West Virginia, it was called upon to represent rural Appalachian poverty in part because some areas of the city wind through hollows and ravines.[83] Wright's report told a moving story about what is lost when bureaucrats attempt to render lives into paperwork.[84] Rather than lamenting the failures of "Buddy" and his family, Wright set out to give a practical answer to a concern that many middle-class people in Appalachia and elsewhere had: that mountaineers lacked the "motivation" necessary to take advantage of assistance programs, let alone lead community action programs.[85] She asserted that Appalachian "passivity" was due not to an intrinsic lack of motivation but to the extrinsic dynamics of the welfare bureaucracy. Her case study provided examples, beginning with Banks, of men who tried to sign up for government assistance programs and faced barriers along the way. Some of the barriers were logistical; some were internal. Wright was attentive to the ways that poverty and anxiety fed one another, and why someone in grave need of assistance might wait in a welfare office for hours without saying a word.

Yet Wright's case study began very much like anti-idyllic eugenic family studies, typifying her main subject through the use of a landscape-based pseudonym: "Buddy Banks." Banks, like so many subjects of eugenic studies, resided in a ravine. He had built his "one room pole-and-cardboard house" himself, on a "small piece of ground" given to him by his mother-in-law so he could build shelter before the snow came. Wright ascribed a mental state to him that readers would likely find familiar. He was forty-five years old, she wrote, a sober, kindly, passive man. Banks had worked in coal mines and farms but had been "pretty badly battered up" and was now "none too stout."[86] Like "nerves," "none too stout" was an idiom for a variety of disabling yet unnamed maladies that did not require clinical terminology in order to be understood.

Wright focused on a scenario in a welfare office. She drove Banks to the office and left to run an errand. While she was away, Banks sat in the waiting room for hours, never speaking to the clerk. He told Wright he was unsure which line to stand in, though there was only one line, and she inferred that he was afraid to look foolish by approaching the interaction incorrectly. In other words, the problem was not just that Banks lacked material resources—a birth certificate, transportation into town, a radio or newspaper to hear the word that there was a new program he might qualify for—or that he lacked the cultural capital necessary to interact with the middle-class paper shufflers, both of which Wright could assist him with. The barrier, according to Wright, was Banks's *trepidation* that he lacked the necessary cultural capital—or, perhaps, his fears about what it might be like to be on welfare, to be denied welfare, or to be uncertain about his status for an interminable amount of time.

To portray this, Wright relied on fraught language. Banks, she asserted, was frozen by a "paralysis of strangeness, of lostness, of not knowing what to do."[87] Words like "strangeness" and "lostness" rendered Banks—and, by proxy, all Appalachians, poor people, and people with mental illnesses—distant and other, out of touch with the modern world and consensus reality. As Ardis Cameron contends, "topographies of strangeness" are invoked to imagine "a zone of difference—a particular place and a peculiar people" who are alien, as well as metaphors that map onto the social alienation experienced by people with mental disabilities.[88] Yet Wright located this "strangeness" not in Banks's bodymind or the geographies he called home, but in the bureaucratic, middle-class atmosphere of the welfare office. Banks may have felt a sense of strangeness, Wright intimates, because he was being actively estranged by the very offices and programs meant to support people like him.

Wright stages this anecdote as an encounter between an anxious, vulnerable person and the "kairotic space" of the rural welfare office. Margaret Price coined the term "kairotic space" to refer to the invisible infrastructure and forms of in/accessibility that undergird social interactions.[89] For example, in the classroom, infrastructure is not just a set of tables and chairs, but the "beliefs, discourses, attitudes, and interchanges that take place there." Kairotic space combines a real-time unfolding of events, impromptu communication, in-person contact, a strong social element, and high stakes. For a college student with a mental disability, the kairotic space of office hours or classroom discussions or milling-about time at a professional conference presents a host of challenges. In a social services office, the consequences of inadequately navigating kairotic space might mean no income, no food stamps for a family of twelve, or no chance at a job retraining program. With such high stakes, it was no wonder that men like Banks, having finally been offered what they needed to physically access the welfare office, still faced difficulty in navigating the emotional and social landscapes of the office.

The problem with the complicated "legal labyrinth" of poverty and welfare programs was the middle-class social norms that came to dominate welfare offices when caseworkers were necessary to assist the poor in traversing such "tortuous" systems to receive basic items like food.[90] In 1964, psychiatrist Alvin L. Schorr clearly articulated the problem with the professional interests of middle-class service workers in the culture of poverty industry.[91] Community Action Programs like AAY emphasized hiring and training "subprofessionals" or "indigenous nonprofessionals" rather than trained social workers. All too often, however, these subprofessionals were middle-class residents of the areas in question, lacking an understanding of what it was like to be hungry and scared and without clean water.[92] Betty Messer Smith, a poor women's activist from Goose Creek, Kentucky, described a woman who worked for the local poverty program and carelessly tossed off comments about how inexpensive her $8 dresses were—in an area where many women wore clothing that had been donated to them for free or cost no more than 20 cents. The poor women resented the poverty worker, Smith explained, though they would not tell her so to her face.[93]

Along with the overdetermined type of the "passive," "nervous" Appalachian man was the equally overdetermined type of his weary wife. Forced to shoulder the burden of providing for the family in light of her husband's "deficiencies," the story went, she had to navigate the alienating kairotic spaces of the welfare bureaucracy herself, lest her family starve. A 1964 *Newsweek* article on Appalachian poverty encapsulated these two figures by declaring that the "lean, inscrutable mountain patriarchs" of old had been replaced by "tired, numbly polite men presiding over clans of birth-worn women."[94] Mental health researchers turned this figure into a formal clinical pathology, asserting that many Appalachian women exemplified "a classical type of depression, brought on by a kind of social deprivation."[95] Women were expected to shoulder the family burden when men could not or would not, but they too experienced the physical and emotional symptoms of "nerves." The term "nerves" could "give voice to women's anguish" and had "at least a limited medical respectability" but did not require women to confront the "social arrangements underlying their distress."[96]

These two-dimensional renderings of Appalachian women had a kernel of truth that was partly regional and partly due to heteropatriarchal expectations writ large. Women married to coal miners, it is true, had learned to wait and wait during "long hours when a coal miner is down under the earth," taking on the roles of doctor, teacher, and parent in the meantime.[97] Yet women also bore pressure—not necessarily regional—from how men internalized economic norms. A West Virginia woman named Katherine Tiller recalled the dread and anxiety that her husband felt from being out of work—he "got to the point where he'd rather die than go down to the unemployment office"—even though she knew his unemployment was a "failure of the systems."[98] Poor Appalachian women also bore the heteropatriarchal double burden that so many Americans did, expected to manage the home (including, often, welfare paperwork) while working for pay outside the home.

The material difficulty of making it to the welfare office and keeping up with various welfare requirements was onerous, and government officials knew it was. They received many letters to that effect. Joan Linger explained to a Johnson aide that it was "unrealistic" to expect women "both to seek or maintain employment and to escort children to clinics, visit schools, and maintain appointments with housing, food stamp, and welfare offices when the latter activities are irregularly scheduled during normal working hours."[99] One man described a Kentucky woman who had been forced to make three arduous trips to pick up her food stamps, "45 miles each way, hitchhiking." On the first day, she arrived three minutes after the office's closing time; on the second, the office had closed three hours early, unannounced.[100] Notorious rabble-rouser Granny Hager colorfully explained her situation to the "good-sized women" on the Social Security board, telling them that if they had walked all the miles that the Social Security agency had forced *her* to walk in order to receive death benefits for her deceased miner husband, they too would get their "schoolgirl figures" back.[101] And Johnson heard directly from Mrs. Bowen in 1966, two years after they met in Inez. Rather than demanding that "somebody owes us something," as Marlow did, Bowen requested help signing up for food stamps and chronicled the labyrinthine welfare and disability bureaucracy that she had found herself lost in.[102]

Beyond the experience of the welfare office, we might understand bureaucratic paperwork itself—not just encounters with human gatekeepers—as a type of kairotic space. As Lisa Gitelman explains, paperwork has "worked to structure knowledge and instantiate culture" in the United States. "Blanks" on paperwork, she contends, "divid[e] mental labor," "directing and delimiting fill-in entries that form the incremental expressions of the modern, bureaucratic self."[103] Declaring oneself "disabled" (or not) could have immense consequences, even though the definition varied from form to form. If a man was physically impaired and unable to work a coal mine or farm, he might ask for disability assistance, only to then be turned down for job retraining that would have prepared him to work in a less physically taxing environment.

As Wright waited for Banks in the welfare office, she saw another middle-aged man get turned down for the job retraining program. She recounted that the official told him that since he was too disabled for work, "there's no use asking about training." Wright reached out to him, but as he began to talk, he became "embarrassed to be talking to a stranger," turned away, paused, and left. In his wake, Wright meditated on how the complexity of human experience exceeded the limitations of paperwork: "Disabled or not disabled. Employed or not employed. In need or not need. Yes or no. Black or white. Answer the question. Stand in line."[104]

Numerous firsthand accounts and activist histories from Appalachia confirm the difficulties that poor people faced in accessing welfare programs and the ways men and women supported one another.[105] In 1969, the *Louisville Courier-Journal* discussed the vexed circumstances of Charles Jones, a man judged to be "too sick to work and too well to draw welfare." Jones, much like the man Wright described, was stuck in a gray zone: ineligible for work programs because he had been classified as disabled, yet ineligible for disability support because he had worked before.[106] In

Kentucky, the Clay County Poor People's Association protested the Social Security Administration's "impossible and confusing regulations and standards" for black lung compensation claims, insisting that "total disability" was too constrained a category.[107] Both the Black Lung Association and Miners for Democracy held trainings and directly assisted disabled miners and their widows in filing claims, due to the significant barrier that the paperwork posed in accessing promised aid.[108] Disabled people who were not able to leave their homes due to inaccessibility faced barriers even when they knew they qualified for particular programs, like the disabled miner who had to write to a newspaper to get updates on the program that directly affected his well-being.[109]

The proliferation of poverty tourists meant that kairotic spaces did not end with the welfare office and the welfare paperwork. Through poverty visits, poor mountaineers' own homes were made into fraught, unsettling, and deeply consequential social spaces requiring public performances for unknown audiences. As politicians and journalists made poverty tours in the mountains, so did countless social workers, psychologists, students, and writers like Wright. The problem was not just the visitors, but the uncertainty and potentially high stakes of such encounters, leading to anxiety and suspicion of interlopers.

This sense of being hypervisible because of one's misfortunes, unsure how to behave or who is looking in on you, was evident in Wright's account of the welfare office. Interwoven throughout the narrative were insults Wright thought people might hurl at Banks: "you would say, 'White trash.' You would say, 'Welfare bums,'" she projected after describing Banks's home, or "'Country boy, come to get his check.'"[110] But, as the study went on, Wright distanced herself from invectives, switching from the second to the third person. She recognized the paradoxical position Banks was in: he'd be called a "lazy cheat" if he did request assistance and an "unmotivated ignorant fool" if he did not.[111] Sitting in the welfare office, uncertain whether he would be declared too disabled to work or too employable to be disabled, Banks was all too aware of the stark consequences that could result from those judgments.

WHITEWASHING POVERTY: THE POLITICAL USES OF APPALACHIAN POVERTY TOURS

By the spring of 1965, West Virginians were tired of hosting poverty tourists. It had been a year since Johnson famously toured Appalachian poverty to drum up support for the War on Poverty, and five years since Kennedy's primary campaign in the Mountain State. "The people of the mountains," Jack Weller wrote, "often to their grave dislike, have found themselves the objects of surveys and studies, the subjects of pictures and articles in newspapers and national magazines, the grist for the TV cameraman's mill as he grinds out pictures of poverty, malnutrition, ignorance, and loss of hope."[112] The *New York Times* and other media outlets hired reporters specifically for the white, Appalachian "poverty beat."[113] Joining politicians and journalists were thousands of other "tourists," from college students to scions like John D. Rockefeller IV. Even Sargent Shriver, head of the OEO, made jokes in public speeches about that "new breed of tourists—the poverty tourist—who is busy visiting the new scenic wonders of poverty—the shacks and shanties, the slums and rural hollows . . ."[114] Poverty tours disrupted people's lives and transformed poor people's homes into performance spaces freighted with worry and laden with economic significance.

Yet they were crafted to humanize the face of white suffering, engendering sympathy—however invasive and paternalistic—rather than the fear and resentment directed at poor communities of color. The problem of white poverty, to many, was that it prevented white people from fully realizing the privileges of being white. Over and over, poor white people were compared only to white US standards of living—evidence not of poverty but of the sense of indignity that it was suffered by whites. The *Saturday Evening Post* explained to the nation that West Virginia had "a higher ratio of illegitimate white babies than any other state."[115] Robert Kennedy asked what the "oddsmakers would say" about the reduced life chances of a "white child born somewhere in a shack in the vast hills and valleys of despair we call Appalachia."[116] Martin County, Kentucky, home of Inez, was described as the "poorest 'white political subdivision' in the country."[117]

In the end, the results were predictable: the War on Poverty provided assistance to "more white, male-headed families . . . than other demographics."[118] Within Appalachia, the focus on the mountains as home to poor whites had several consequences. Most immediately, the explicit federal focus on white poverty meant that very few resources remained for Black mountaineers.[119] It also perpetuated the myth of white Appalachian "racial innocence," allowing white residents to understand their region's predominantly white demographics as a "benign fact" instead of a "product of active practices characterized in part by persistent white supremacy."[120]

From presidents and journalists to volunteers and social workers, "tours" of white rural Appalachian poverty in the 1960s brought renewed attention to the region. Trained by eugenic family studies to be on the "lookout" for nonconforming families and by the FSA's visual iconography of rural white poverty in the 1930s, white Americans knew how to identify the peculiar rural landscape through an anti-idyllic gaze. In the 1960s, this anti-idyllic gaze was informed by the rural white aspects of culture-of-poverty theory. As with FSA photography, poverty tours aimed to highlight the "deserving" poor, and in doing so, evoke the idyllic potential of white rural life.

The social conditions indexed by these poverty tours were more complex than rehabilitation narratives allowed. Some of the people visited by poverty tours experienced addiction or had mental disabilities that made navigating the welfare office nearly impossible. Poverty tours made their lives more difficult, inviting gossip and further unwanted media scrutiny, and turning one's very home into a space with new social rules and very high stakes. Not all poverty tourists sought to tell a sympathetic, if overly simplistic, story; some wended their way into the mountains with distinctly anti-idyllic aims, seeking out and telling tales about the most grotesque situations possible. In the 1970s, the rural white anti-idyll peaked in the form of horror films that did just that, combining the feeling of a regional poverty tour with the incomprehensible violence and gender ambiguity of the Gein legend.

5: BANJOS, CHAINSAWS, AND SODOMY

Making 1970s Rural Horror Films and the Apex of the Anti-Idyll

In 1972, an adventure flick set and filmed in the north Georgia mountains became a summer smash at the box office, propelling Burt Reynolds to superstardom and inaugurating what has become a half century of hillbilly sodomy jokes set to the easy rhythm of a country banjo. *Deliverance* was supposed to be much more than that: an allegory for social and environmental injustice, a critique of white suburban masculinity, a story of moral ambiguity and uneasy resolution. Following the box-office success of *Deliverance*, low-budget exploitation films like *The Texas Chain Saw Massacre* and *The Hills Have Eyes* became cult favorites and met unexpected success on midnight movie circuits, constituting a subgenre of horror films that Carol Clover terms "urbanoia."[1] Decades later, what remains seared in American cultural consciousness is not the allegories or ambiguity of *Deliverance*, but the foolish horror of banjo savants and sodomitical hillbillies.

The anti-idyll reached its apex in 1970s urbanoia films. Urbanoia films echoed the logic of eugenics ("Talk about genetic deficiencies," a suburban *Deliverance* character intones) and the visual symbolism of FSA photography, but they sited anti-idyllic stories in mountain hollows like those where white poverty had recently been "rediscovered." The films' characters and set dressings were indebted to the story of Ed Gein, which had been briefly revived by his second trial in 1968. This manifested most obviously in depictions of violence by "psychotic," crossdressing characters and through the elaborate use of human relics that were associated, as in the Gein case, with purportedly "primitive" imperial provenances.[2] Horror films distilled the elements of the anti-idyll, then stretched and distorted them anew.

5.1 An elderly white woman, Mrs. Andy Webb, and a white disabled teenage girl sit in a small room in their home. Their walls are papered, and clothes and purses are hung neatly in the background. The woman sews, looking toward the girl, whose small frame is supported by a large pillow. Still image from *Deliverance*.

Despite the sensationalism of urbanoia films, there are moments that lend themselves to alternative interpretations. After all, as J. W. Williamson contends, urbanoia films don't reflect a pre-existing white fear of the mountains so much as they teach it to their white viewers.[3] Early in *Deliverance*, right after the dueling-banjo scene provokes viewers to leer at the folks who live in the mountains, the film takes one step further, beckoning viewers to furtively intrude into their homes. If we freeze the frame at the right moment, however, rather than peering into a poor white family's home through a darkened window, burdened with the film's ableism and heteronormativity, we might imagine the scene as part of a different story. When the film is paused, viewers see an elderly woman and teenager sitting together in a cozy living room, a colorful space filled with quilts and papered walls (fig. 5.1). The girl sits in a blanket-draped chair, her small frame supported by pillows and her legs arranged—crossed—in the other direction. The older woman, played by an extra named Mrs. Andy Webb, is sewing. They are angled toward each other and appear to be conversing. This small family, constituted by a woman and a girl several generations apart, is not a heteronormative nuclear family, but neither is it the perverse "patriarchy run amok" that is characteristic of urbanoia.[4] Webb and her young companion might fail to meet the norms of compulsory able-bodiedness, but their embodied existence appears neither perverse nor horrific.[5] If we avert our eyes from the darkened window through which *Deliverance* frames our gaze and instead consider them with queercrip values of flexible kinship and interdependence, we might imagine Webb and the girl she is raising as a daughter to be rather ordinary. Not without troubles, but hardly the shameful, hidden embodiment of "social devolution" that other scholars understand them to be.[6]

Horror films are a locus of dense entanglements between disability, gender transgression, and perverse sexual object choices; as such, they are in desperate need of queercrip analysis. Queer studies has historically embraced the monstrous, queer-coded villains of horror films, theorizing a rich array of desires and identifications through which queer viewers can relate to horror monsters.[7] Disability studies, in contrast, has been wary of the genre, and with good reason.[8] Horror films, which have material and metaphorical roots in eugenics,[9] frequently deploy disability to render characters vacant of desire and identity, thereby denying disabled viewers the slippery pleasures that queer viewers have relished. As Michael Gill contends, ableism and anti-queer sentiment often work together, as "sexual ableism," to "deny the disabled subject the ability to express sexual agency and desire" and "actively redirect queer sexual desire."[10] A queercrip analysis that considers the materiality of disability and class in horror films has the potential to generate new desires that exceed the constraints of sexual ableism.

In the landscapes of 1970s urbanoia films, all types of mental and physical disabilities were interchangeable with one another, and they were commonly associated with gender and sexual nonconformity. Through the apparent veracity of the stories and characters they depicted, horror films made implicit claims about the uneasy landscapes and social worlds available to rural white communities. In the words of Gunnar Hansen, the actor who played Leatherface in *Chain Saw*, "You watch this movie and you think, there are people like this in the world."[11] As in chapter three, we must disentangle the horrifying violence of a story from the mere existence of people with visibly nonnormative bodies, gender expressions, and sexual practices. I begin with a materialist analysis of *Chain Saw*, examining the racialized job losses of deindustrialization together with the gender transgression and apparent intellectual disability of Leatherface. Changing *how* we look in on a family does not change *that* we looked, of course, and I turn to the material conditions of anti-idyllic filmmaking in the second section. There, I analyze how disability, gender, and sexuality functioned in the quotidian experiences of filming *Deliverance*. I conclude the chapter by examining the racialized circulation and reception of urbanoia films during the 1970s, contesting claims that the rural white landscapes of urbanoia films are blank spaces of allegory.

PLANT CLOSURES AND CROSSDRESSING CANNIBALS

Urbanoia films revised anti-idyllic tropes for a postindustrial rural economy and a mental healthcare system undergoing massive shifts, while incorporating gendered inspiration from the mythology of Ed Gein. *The Texas Chain Saw Massacre*, an exemplar of the genre, bound narratives of rural white economic dispossession (slaughterhouse employees put out of work) to "monstrous" gender transgression in the form of a chainsaw-wielding nonverbal madman with masks of human skin (Leatherface). *Chain Saw* suggested that when rural white men were confronted with sweeping economic and social changes, they would cling to heteropatriarchal family structures in perverse ways.

As in many urbanoia films, the poverty of the rural landscape in *Chain Saw* is figured as the cause of the community's recent decline. Unlike *Deliverance*, which relies on the trope of the eternally poor hillbilly, *Chain Saw* attributes white rural poverty to deindustrialization. The cannibals of the Texas countryside, the film conveys, had once been respectable members of the white male working class, legitimately employed at a local slaughterhouse until technological innovations eliminated their jobs. While many urbanoia films feature antagonists who have never been employed in the formal economy—the moonshiners of *Redneck Zombies*, for example, or the poachers of *Hunter's Blood*—more socially conscious films referenced plant and mine closures, naming specific jobs lost to the economic shifts of the 1970s. In doing so, they constructed a powerful but false narrative that rural white men were particularly harmed by deindustrialization.

Chain Saw's violent conflict pits five privileged white youths from Dallas against a white male family of former slaughterhouse workers. The protagonists include two cheerful heterosexual couples—Pam and Jerry, Sally and Kirk—who are charming, trim, and physically capable of running up any creaky staircases they might encounter. The fifth wheel of the group, Franklin, presents a sharp contrast. Franklin is physically conspicuous because of his wheelchair, stout frame, and dark curly hair. His appearance so resembled that of his filmic double, Leatherface, that many viewers believed they were played by the same actor.[12] Franklin's liminality is deepened by his knowledge of his grandfather's former business in the rural Texas town they now visit as vacationers.

The protagonists first encounter their adversaries when they pick up a bloodied hitchhiker on the side of the road. The "psychotic" Hitchhiker, viewers will learn later, is supported by two brothers—the morally ambiguous Old Man and the chainsaw-wielding Leatherface—as well as their decrepit grandfather, the family patriarch. After ejecting the Hitchhiker from the van when he starts a fire and attacks Franklin, Sally and her friends eventually arrive at their destination, an abandoned home once occupied by Sally and Franklin's grandfather. When Leatherface finds them, he conducts his business quickly, knocking out Kirk with a blow to the head and stringing up Pam on a meat hook. Franklin and Jerry are hunted down next, and as nightfall approaches, only Sally lives. Sally will survive, but as the film's promotional materials forewarn, she will wish that she had not. After escaping Leatherface once, she runs through the woods to get back to the gas station for help, where the Old Man captures her and drives her back to his family's home. The climax of the film is an absurd dinner scene— Sally is to be the dinner—that fails due to the slaughterhouse family's utter incompetence. After leaping through their dining-room window into the early morning light, Sally is aided by a cattle-freight-truck driver. She ultimately survives by jumping in the back of a passing pickup truck, bloodied and screaming, as the film fades to black.

From the initial encounter through the family dinner scene near the end, *Chain Saw* strenuously emphasizes the antagonists' former employment at the local slaughterhouse. In the early scenes, this adds ominous foreshadowing of the human slaughter to come. Yet it also emphasizes class difference—not just between the Dallas interlopers and the local family, but between the local white family and local Black and Latino men. By depicting rural white gender transgression as an effect of deindustrialization, *Chain Saw* suggests that gender perversion might result from white men's desperate attempts at a middle-class heteronormativity that is denied to them and wrongly intimates that deindustrialization predominantly affects rural white men.

As the bourgeois protagonists drive through the countryside on vacation, they immediately notice the stench of the slaughterhouse. Only Franklin can name it, informing the others that "that's where grandpa used to sell his cattle," thereby positioning Franklin and Sally's family as part of the local ranching elite. A few moments later, after picking up the Hitchhiker and noticing his bloodstained face, Franklin asks Hitch if he works at the slaughterhouse. Answering no, the Hitchhiker explains, "My brother *worked* there," emphasizing the past tense and adding ominously, "My grandfather too! My family's always been in meat." When Franklin asks what he thinks about the new method of killing cattle—an air gun to the skull, rather than a sledgehammer—the Hitchhiker insists that the old way is better. "With the new way, people put out of jobs," he responds twitchily, pulling out a Polaroid of himself standing next to a dead cow and announcing, "I was the killer!" The Hitchhiker becomes demonstrably more agitated as he narrates the loss of his family's livelihood, embodying the psychological consequences of plant closings as he describes them. This theme recurs throughout the film, from the Old Man's concerned mumbling that the "cost of electricity's enough to run a man out of business!" to the brothers' insistence on literally propping up the patriarch too weak to stand—"Old Grandpa, the best killer there ever was!"—as he feebly fails to even grasp the sledgehammer.

Leatherface's gender nonnormativity is decidedly different than the "emasculation" that sociologists attributed to white former factory workers facing unemployment.[13] Rather than having his masculinity called into question by his wife's new role as breadwinner, Leatherface assumes the role of wife in a family consisting of four men. He plays multiple roles, from daughter to grandmother, and has a different mask and persona to correspond to each kinship figure, in addition to his "killing mask."[14] The family is so deeply and perversely patriarchal that it disturbed the film's prop man and inspired him to create a "petrified grandmother" to suggest that "at *one time* there were women."[15]

A scene in which Leatherface is depicted as taking pleasure in his gendered appearance was cut from the film but included in the DVD extras. In the cut scene, Leatherface chooses from an assortment of feminine masks and wigs hanging from the ceiling, interspersed with bones, like a gruesome mobile. The scenario, obviously lifted from the Gein mythos, takes Leatherface's commitment to feminine grooming a step further than Gein or Norman Bates: he powders his face, applies new lipstick, and examines his appearance in a compact mirror (fig. 5.2). Hansen later claimed that the "tittering and babbling" noises he made during the scene were supposed to approximate "You're so pretty!"[16]

The family dinner scene commences when the Old Man returns home with Sally. Furious that Leatherface has damaged their front door with his chainsaw, the Old Man yells, "Look what your brother's done to the damn door!" in the Hitchhiker's direction, then mutters, "He's got no pride in his home!" The Old Man's concern about the integrity of his home is the film's "one true comic line"—and one of its most-quoted—because it so starkly illustrates the absurdity of "family values" in a home decorated with human relics.[17] Within the social world of the film, however, the Old Man's domestic concerns and Leatherface's crossdressing are perfectly consistent: they have lost their livelihoods because of advances in slaughterhouse technology, but they are not about to give up their investments, however farcical, in respectable heterodomesticity.

The film's narrative about deindustrialization fabricates a popular sociology of the rural white South that did not fit the racial and regional realities of economic change in the 1970s. Although white men faced job losses, it was Black and Latino men who bore the brunt of manufacturing-sector cutbacks at the time.[18] Despite this reality, white men embraced a "newfound victimhood, a widespread and plaintive 'me-too-ism'" that falsely placed blame for white male unemployment on affirmative action programs that began at the same time as "massive transformations" in the US economy.[19] Indeed, white men in the rural South were the most likely to *benefit* from deindustrialization. Before blue-collar jobs moved overseas

5.2 Leatherface from *The Texas Chain Saw Massacre* looks into a compact mirror as he reapplies his makeup. He wears a disheveled wig and a messy mask of what is supposed to be human skin. Bones dangle from strings in the foreground. Still image from *The Texas Chain Saw Massacre*, deleted scenes.

in search of cheaper, less organized labor and higher profits, they moved to less industrialized areas within the United States itself.[20] In the 1970s, manufacturing in the United States shifted from the North to the South, from metropolitan regions to nonmetropolitan regions.[21] Urbanoia films indexed an emerging affirmative-action backlash among white men by putting a rural white face on manufacturing job losses that in fact benefited white men in nonmetropolitan areas and had a detrimental effect on Black and Latino workers in both urban and rural areas alike.

They did so not only by representing white men as the newly jobless, but by representing the only men of color as the only people with jobs. Considering how few characters of color there were in 1970s horror films, any appearance by or reference to nonwhite characters was remarkable. A rural character with a discernible job was also notable. It is quite meaningful, then, that *Chain Saw* not only features two scenes with employed men of color but frames the film with those scenes. The film opens with the sounds of digging and grunting, as noisy, ominous music begins to play and a scarcely audible radio newscast is heard in the background. As images of slimy, decaying, light-skinned body parts come into visual focus between flashes to black, radio narration about a recent rash of grave robberies comes into aural focus. "Sheriff Jesus Maldonado," the radio man's voice tells us, "refused to give details in the ghoulish case" but assures residents that they have out-of-state leads. The only other person in the film, including the privileged protagonists, who has an explicitly marked job is the chubby Black truck driver who ineptly attempts to help Sally escape during the final scene. Denied even the opportunity to escort Sally to safety, the Black character's blundering conjures white male concerns that "their" jobs were being given to insufficiently qualified people of color.

Rural white Southerners were the least likely to be detrimentally affected by US deindustrialization, but urbanoia films prefigured white male reactions to deindustrialization. They intimated that rural white men were losing jobs at the same time that men of color were gainfully employed, laying groundwork for the affirmative-action backlash to come. Relatedly, they suggested that when rural white men were confronted with sweeping economic and social changes, they would respond by clinging to heteropatriarchal family structures in perversely gender nonnormative ways.

PEERING INTO WINDOWS AND PLAY-ACTING AT PIG FARMS: MAKING DISABILITY IN *DELIVERANCE* AND *CHAIN SAW*

Physically disabled characters and characters with nonnormative bodily forms have long been standard fare for horror films.[22] Through the 1980s, screenwriters were explicitly taught to use disabilities as a way to visually represent a character's moral defect: a limp, for example, could suggest that a character was an "emotional cripple."[23] Yet 1970s urbanoia films were distinct in the connections they drew between mental disability and rural white sexual and gender nonconformity. The presence of amorphously disabled characters was implicitly understood to be a consequence of consanguineous intercourse. As a consequence of sexual ableism, people with intellectual disabilities are typically depicted as childlike and nonsexual or as vicious sexual predators—or both, as with Lennie from *Of Mice and Men*.[24] Urbanoia films augmented those associations, depicting characters with mental disabilities to be constitutionally unable to distinguish between sex with a man or woman, human or animal, consensual or rape. The making of *Deliverance*, which used disabled extras, and *The Texas Chain Saw Massacre*, which sent an actor to tour an institution for disabled children, reveals the disjuncture between the sensationalism of rural white disability in film and the imperfect but quotidian conditions of life for non-filmic disabled people.

Disabled characters served vital functions in many urbanoia films. Actor Michael Berryman, the literal face of *The Hills Have Eyes*—nearly all of the film's promotional materials feature his face against desert cliffs—was hired after telling director Wes Craven, "I have 26 birth defects. I think you can use me." Horror directors routinely used Berryman's anomalous physical appearance to convey intellectual disability, making him the apparent embodiment of anti-idyllic rural horror (fig. 5.3). Although Craven was quick to note that Berryman was "a sweet intelligent guy," his "defense" of Berryman—a denial of intellectual disability—came at the expense of those who do have intellectual disabilities.[25]

Deliverance forged strong relationships between the geographical isolation of a mountain community, the mental isolation that the film imagines to be characteristic of people with intellectual disabilities, and the "depraved" sexuality of the film's notorious same-sex rape scene. *New York Times* film reviewer Stephen Farber contended that the strength of the film was its hauntingly memorable images, beginning with the "face of a mute retarded mountain boy on a bridge over the river."[26] Even more than the face of that boy, Lonnie—perhaps an allusion to Steinbeck's Lennie—is that iconic banjo music. In "popular memory," Anna Creadick contends, "*Deliverance* is about two things: that rape and that song, and the metonym ensues so that the banjo is the violence, and the violence has a banjo soundtrack."[27] Decades later, with just a few strums of a banjo, a film or television show can quickly conjure the rural backwardness, sodomy, and intellectual disability that are so provocatively conjoined in *Deliverance*.[28]

Deliverance quickly establishes a close relationship between topographical insularity and disability. In the early minutes, as the protagonists wind their way through the twisting mountain roads leading to the Cahulawassee River, group leader Lewis (Reynolds) tells the others that "there's some people up there that ain't never seen a town before," explaining that the "woods up there are real deep, the river's inaccessible, except at a couple points." Moments later, Lewis and pals reach their mountain destination. They immediately encounter Lonnie, banjo in hand, and catch a glimpse of Webb tending to her disabled granddaughter. After a musical exchange between Lonnie and the guitar-playing suburbanite Drew, Lonnie looks away and steadfastly refuses to shake Drew's hand. Actor Jon Voight described Billy Redden, the teenager who played Lonnie, as "quite amazing, a very talkative fellow," a stark contrast to his sullen character.[29]

Lonnie's banjo also evokes the specter of rural sexual "depravity"—a male-male rape that many straight male viewers took as evidence that any act of anal intercourse must be horrific, regardless of consent. Lonnie is

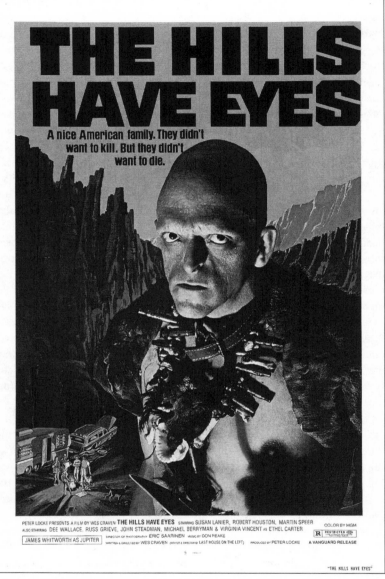

5.3 A poster for the 1977 film *The Hills Have Eyes* made Michael Berryman the literal face of rural white horror film monsters. Berryman has an usual appearance caused by a hereditary medical condition; he is bald and has a prominent fore-head. His character makes a menacing expression and holds a knife. He is draped in fur and bones, including what is obviously a set of human teeth. Cliffs rise up behind him, and he looms over a small cartoon illustration of an "all-American family" with a vacation camper. Promotional poster.

not involved in the rape scene, but his banjo-strumming specter haunts the ordeal; the horrors of the rape scene are conjured with the strum of a banjo just as they are through the infamous lines "squeal like a pig," and "he sure has a pretty mouth." The rape scene, unlike urbanoia representations of women being raped, was not eroticized. The film offered an allegorical interpretation of the assault—disenfranchised white rural male characters asserting what little power they have over the privileged white suburbanites—but viewers made intertextual associations between the same-sex sex act on screen and off-screen homosexuals.[30] In the wake of gay liberation, the cultural appearance of banjos, squealing pigs, or pretty male mouths uneasily began to evoke at least the possibility of homosexual desire, which *Deliverance* conflated with sexual assault.[31]

Lonnie, and the sense of perversion he evoked, functioned metonymically for the mountain community that he called home. These were linked through implicit filmic suggestions of consanguineous sexuality and its purported relationship to "genetic deficiencies." In a DVD commentary track, John Boorman, the English director of *Deliverance*, describes the Georgia extras, "these people up there," as being representative of the "kind of inbreeding that is so notorious in these communities."[32] The comments, made on Lonnie's first appearance, specifically associate intellectual disability with apparent "inbreeding." Further, as Boorman contends that "this strange, hostile, inward-looking . . . community grew up around that history," he hesitates before the word "community," while an image of the banjo player lingers on screen. Boorman's indecision about whether to describe the boy or the entire rural community as "strange, hostile, inward-looking" illustrates how the disabled boy was imagined to stand in for his larger community.

The trope of intermarriage and consanguineous relationships is consistently offered as one potential explanation for the existence of intellectual disabilities in geographically isolated rural communities. By the 1970s, the popular but faulty assumption that isolated rural communities fostered "inbreeding" augmented perceptions that rural life produced more congenital disabilities, both physical and intellectual, than life in more diversely populated locales. Yet the relationship between consanguinity and disability is far more complex than popular understandings would suggest. Just a few decades earlier, eugenicists encouraged intermarriage among the elite, as exemplified by Charles Darwin's marriage to a first cousin.[33] As geneticist Hanan Hamamy contends, while it is true that "close kin marriage facilitates the expression of rare recessive disease genes," it is also true that "consanguinity does not cause genetic disease."[34] Even the expression of "rare recessive disease genes" does not correlate to the visible physical anomalies—a single "cyclops" eye, for example, or a body with no limbs—preferred by horror films or the media they have influenced.

There were numerous, much more probable causes of disability in rural communities, as even James Dickey, author of the novel and the screenplay of *Deliverance*, acknowledged. In the film, one of the suburban adventurers makes a loud remark about the pitiful "genetic deficiencies" that characterize the area. In an earlier version of the screenplay, closer to the book, the line is quite different: "How is it these people here are always missing something . . . a finger, an eye, an arm, or 'in the head,'" the character wonders. "I never saw a farmer yet who didn't have something wrong with him. You'd think it would be a healthy life."[35] Rather than attributing disability to consanguineous sex, the novel and the early draft of the screenplay crystallized the tension between idyllic notions of rural life—it would be a "healthy life"—and the mundane reality that people who farmed or performed other physical labor might have injuries to show for it.

Simultaneously, researchers in the 1970s argued that the perception of disproportionately high rates of intellectual disability in Appalachia was based on a cultural misunderstanding. There was not a greater preponderance of such disabilities in the mountains, just different cultural approaches to disability and care. Rural Appalachians preferred "home care in the community,"[36] in contrast to elite wealthy families like the Kennedys, who sent their disabled children to institutions out of sight. A *Deliverance* extra, the unnamed disabled girl sharing a home with Webb, was evidence of this: by caring for disabled kin at home, rather than sending them to institutions, Appalachians made disability more visible and normalized. But to outsiders, it rendered the entire region aberrant.

Consanguineous sex and the disabilities mistakenly presumed to be the result of it were figured as the cause of other kinds of sexual deviance in urbanoia films—particularly bestiality, homosexuality, and transgressive gender expression. Austin, Texas, native and *Chain Saw* director Tobe Hooper attributed to the landscapes of rural Texas the kind of generic rural sexual deviance that elided distinctions between inbreeding, bestiality, intellectual disability, and cross-gender identities. Decades after *Chain Saw*'s release, Hooper recounted that the film was about the "city boy/country thing, where we're all afraid that out there in those kind of dark kernels of rural America . . . there are these inbred types that are doing terrible and dastardly things."[37] This assertion revised a Hooper quotation that had been widely used to promote the film after its release in the 1970s, a statement that characterized the film as being about "crazy retarded people going beyond the line between animal and human."[38] For Hooper, being "crazy," "retarded," "inbred," murderous, or unable to understand the difference between human and animal were interchangeable forms of deviance, related to one another by their location in the "dark kernels of rural America" where a self-described city boy like Hooper would never venture.

These implicit equivalences between intellectual disability, bestiality, and gender difference are even more shockingly underscored by the direction that Hooper gave Hansen as he prepared for the role of Leatherface. Leatherface, presumably assigned male at birth, paired suits with female masks and wigs, and assumed feminine household roles; Hooper described Leatherface's gender transgression as a consequence of his implied intellectual disability. Like sexual ableism, the idea that a person with a mental or communication disability cannot have a sense of their own gender has profound consequences for people with those disabilities.[39]

It was not just a sense of his own gender that Leatherface purportedly lacked, but any sense of interiority at all. He was what philosopher James Berger describes as "disarticulate," when a character who does not use spoken language is "forcibly severed from the social fabric, stigmatized, silenced," and sometimes even "physically dismembered" as a result of being "blocked from language."[40] For Hooper, Leatherface's entire identity was limited to the selection of one of three masks, which purportedly corresponded to different female personas.[41] With no intelligible lines of dialogue, all Hansen could bring to the character was his physical embodiment and the nonsense gibberish that he was directed to speak. Told by Hooper that his character should "be able to squeal like a pig," Hansen recounted that he "went out to a friend's place out in the country, and he had some pigs, and I'd stand there for hours," trying in vain to imitate their squeals.[42] The specter of bestiality is one of the most enduring themes of urbanoia films, despite the fact that sex between humans and nonhuman animals is never depicted directly. Through the line "squeal like a pig," *Deliverance* intimated that for physically and intellectually disabled hill folk, humans and pigs might be interchangeable sex objects.[43] As an influence on all urbanoia films to come, *Deliverance*'s evocation of bestiality reappeared in films like *Chain Saw*, where Hansen's squealing gibberish does, indeed, seem to be inspired by one man's interpretation of a pig farm. Leatherface does not direct his phallic chainsaw toward any farm animals, because it is Leatherface himself who is supposed to evoke the specter of the nonhuman animal. He was conceived and depicted in line with a common trope, that of intellectually disabled people depicted as "animalized human others," as Licia Carlson puts it.[44]

The lore of Hansen's preparation for the role cemented the association between a nonhuman animal and a person with intellectual, developmental, or mental disabilities. Hansen wondered, he wrote later, how someone like Leatherface, who was "crazed and mentally limited," might present himself.[45] So, after the pig farm failed to provide Hansen with all he needed, he purportedly spent several days at the Austin State School, "a residential campus for retarded persons," trying to establish a distinctive physicality that would "reflect Leatherface's mentality."[46] Granted access by his mother, who worked there, Hansen reported that he "started wandering the grounds, watching people." Hansen even recounted, with little self-awareness, that at one point he feared the school's staff might notice him—that is, might notice the strange man staring at children. When Hansen feared detection, he knew it was time to "act," to practice his role. Attempting to imitate the posture of the disabled people he had been scrutinizing, he deployed a "shambling walk" and slouched shoulders, tipping his pelvis forward.[47] As he told the story, he felt he had succeeded: "you couldn't distinguish me from someone who was a patient."[48]

This physicality was especially important because Leatherface's mental "limitations," together with their physical manifestations, bore the burden of accounting for Leatherface's gender transgression. According to Hansen, Leatherface had "no sexual identity" and his gender was "irrelevant," a function of his disability. Hooper and Hansen falsely understood a person with an intellectual or developmental disability to lack interiority and have the mind of an animal. Intellectual disability, as Sunaura Taylor argues, "has been so easily animalized" in part because "animals themselves have long been understood as intellectually inferior."[49] By attributing Leatherface's gender transgression to this "animalized" sense of disability, Hooper and Hansen extended the objectification and inferiority associated with nonhuman animals and intellectually disabled people to people who are trans or nonbinary or otherwise exceed normative gender conventions. Suggesting, as *Chain Saw* does, that a "lack" of gender and a "lack" of sexuality are innate to intellectual disability denies gender and sexual agency—including the agency to affirmatively identify as agender or asexual—to people with disabilities. This is how anti-idyllic cultural texts can locate visibly disabled, gender nonconforming characters in rural white communities without contradicting the notion that those communities have inherently conservative values: rural white folks would only crossdress or have same-sex intercourse if they were intellectually incapable of exerting any agency over it.

Yet accounts from the Rabun County, Georgia, residents who worked on *Deliverance* offer a profound contrast to the tales from big-city actors and directors. Published in *Foxfire,* a magazine started in 1966 at the Rabun Gap-Nacoochee School in northern Georgia, the interviews were conducted with people students knew who had worked on *Deliverance*: actors and extras, location scouts and caterers. The interviews suggest a different way of understanding both rural sexuality and rural disability—including the queer notion that "mountain people being that way" was, in fact, conceivable for people from that area in the 1970s.[50]

More than any of the Georgians involved with *Deliverance*, Frank Rickman, a legendary Appalachian set-builder and location scout, sought to make his mark on popular culture. When it became evident that an out-of-town actor sounded "about like Zsa Zsa Gabor," in Rickman's estimation, Rickman was asked to provide the voice for one of the rapists.[51] He indicated that he was initially unsure about the "rough scenes and things" being in the script, since he didn't "think of the mountain people being that way." Yet, by using the phrase "that way"—a common way of denoting homosexuality in the rural South—Rickman paradoxically demonstrated that perhaps some mountain people were, in fact, "that way."[52] Further, Rickman was very proud that filmmakers let him "change part of that rough script in there" and allowed him to ad-lib the infamous "squeal like a pig" line.[53] Despite his concerns about the "rough scenes," he boasted that he was personally responsible for adding "all that ugly stuff to it."[54]

The interview subjects who disapproved of the rape scene the most forcefully located the problem in its violence, not in the gender of the victim. Louise Coldren, a local hotel manager who worked as a caterer for the film crew, said she would have preferred if the film had left out the rape scene, understating the matter by noting that the rape "left the impression the local people were very unfriendly."[55] In later interviews, Rickman called the rape scene what it was—a "rape in the woods"—without conflating the assault with consensual same-sex sexuality.[56]

By focusing on the violence and cruelty of the act, Rabun County residents like Coldren shared a perspective with many gay viewers, who understood that what made the rape scene "one nightmare buttfuck" was not the act of anal intercourse but the coercive violence.[57] As Ed Madden contends, *Deliverance* fostered a kind of "homoerotic homophobia."[58] The novel was laden with homoeroticism, and the film explicitly appealed to gay male tastes of the era: Reynolds was clad, "fetishistically," in an inexplicably sleeveless turtleneck wetsuit paired with tight jeans—a combination that, in Madden's words, "looks more like a leather-daddy S-M costume than canoeing gear."[59] *The Advocate*'s 1972 review of *Deliverance*, which described the "nightmare" of the film as the scene where two men are "homosexually assaulted by a pair of mountain men," raises the question: why must a sexual assault scene be declared "homosexual" or "heterosexual," particularly if sexual assault is about power and violence rather than desire?[60]

Of greater concern to those interviewed in *Foxfire* was the perception that the disabled young people used in the film were exploited. Randall Dall, a Rabun County man who appeared in *Deliverance* as a "mountain man" extra, enjoyed the film and the filmmaking process but did not like the fact that the crew filmed the disabled teenager who appears briefly as an extra with her grandmother. This concern about the girl's quality of life and possible exploitation differed dramatically from local elites' worries about reputation. For example, a woman whose husband played a doctor—one of the only non-"hillbilly" extra roles—worried that people in the area were "portrayed as very limited," which "didn't make us [nondisabled Appalachians] feel good."[61] In contrast, Webb, the girl's caretaker, maintained that the film was ultimately good for them, as the small amount of money she earned allowed her to take better care of her granddaughter.[62]

The scene featuring the Webb family was not a transparent account of their life, of course, regardless of Boorman's voyeuristic claims that the scene was "absolutely how it was . . . peering through the window with a camera."[63] Most obviously, "peering through the window with a camera" was not how their neighbors knew them. Although Boorman's horrified gape would determine how generations came to know the Webbs—and disabled Appalachians more broadly—they had previously been known in far less spectacular ways. Even their yard, as it appeared in the film, was not "absolutely how it was" before the film crew arrived. The location scout had "created a gas station island, filled the Webb yard with junk, and called it a set."[64] The Webb family's home was mediated not just by Boorman's gaze, but by aesthetic and production decisions.

Boorman's gaze through the Webb family's window is so commanding that it even distorts the perspective of those who might seek to view the film differently. This causes Williamson, for example, to misread a scene in the film against the screenplay. Williamson assumes that a barbed line from the screenplay—describing "the acute discomfort" that the suburban men feel "when confronted with the unseemly"—corresponds to glimpses of Webb and her "retarded fourteen-year-old granddaughter."[65] Yet the line he quotes from the screenplay is from an earlier scene, when many locals are gathered around to watch the dueling banjos.[66] It is Williamson, then, not the screenwriters, who associates Webb and her granddaughter with the "acute discomfort" of the "unseemly." *Deliverance* fashions such a narrow, ableist way of looking, relying on the body of Webb's granddaughter to evoke horror, that it is nearly impossible for viewers to imagine otherwise.

Webb herself was more preoccupied with material circumstances than representational details, but not because the cultural aspects of the film were irrelevant to her. Indeed, she had "enjoyed that movie picture very much" but had concerns about the material circumstances of her family. Like the Marlow family in chapter four, whose collard patch was disturbed when President Johnson visited, Webb disliked that her visitors tore up her "awful pretty" patch of potatoes and did not adequately compensate her for it. How Webb would continue to care for the disabled thirteen-year-old sitting beside her was another pressing concern. Feeding and bathing

5.4 A disabled teenage girl with a very small frame sits in a chair, propped up by a pillow. She appears to be smiling. Still image from *Deliverance*.

the girl was "getting hard on me," she acknowledged, but it was the only option, since the girl's recent three-month hospital stay "never did do any good." As Webb remarked on her struggles, she defused them with humor. After mentioning that her age made caring for the girl difficult—Webb was "a'rubbing a hundred pretty close"—she added, tongue-in-cheek, "I ain't going to tell people my age for I might want to get married again."[67]

If the teenager in the living room was concerned about how she was represented, she was not given an opportunity to share her perspective with the media—but Redden, at least, has been interviewed about his experience. Redden was concerned about his poor compensation, plus Reynolds's rudeness. For his iconic role, Redden was paid just $500 and the banjo, which his mom later sold to pay bills.[68] He received small residual checks until changing his address in 2005; six years later, he had not pursued the matter, because the money was "not worth fighting my ex-wife for." In contrast to Reynolds's claims that the cast "cherished" Redden—supplemented with a patronizing story depicting Redden as childlike and ignorant—Redden reported that Reynolds "wasn't that nice" and was "kind of a smart-ass."[69] Further, Redden had to bear the film's associations for decades, expressing annoyance about all the publicity. In school, he had been harassed because of the film's representation of male-male sexual assault.[70] Nevertheless, Redden was less bothered by the film than his more privileged neighbors.

Privileged community members were perturbed because elite ways of looking—like Rickman's—were being shared with the wider world. Rickman's success in the Georgia film industry was predicated on his famously deep knowledge of the area. When Boorman told him to "find all the people in Rabun County who were challenged in any way—physically and mentally," Rickman knew which way to look.[71] He knew how to discern the landscape and the people who resided there; he knew exactly where Billy lived and that he "looked the part." After all, "Billy's mama was raised on the old Rickman farm up in the valley," Rickman told writer John Lane, incidentally naming a property that bore his own family moniker, suggesting he might come from a landowning family with knowledge of their tenants.[72] Other Rabun County residents were upset that Rickman shared this knowledge, because they lost control of that anti-idyllic gaze as it left their local community and spread nationally. Outside of Rabun County, viewers were not discerning enough to tell the difference between a local elite and a local outcast. The local elite who might be accustomed to gazing into the window of someone like Webb did not take kindly to being confused with her.

Urbanoia films suggested that rural white sexual deviance in the form of consanguineous relationships caused intellectual disabilities, which in turn caused sexual deviance that could take the form of homosexuality, bestiality, sexual violence, or some combination thereof. According to films like *Deliverance*, a rural same-sex sexual act could only make sense through the logic of sexual ableism, attributed to characters who were implicitly represented as intellectually disabled and therefore, like the "feebleminded" decades earlier, not capable of making or being responsible for sexual choices.

Yet, as the *Foxfire* project shows, same-sex sexuality was perfectly legible in the Georgia mountains when framed through vernacular categories like being "that way." *Foxfire* interview subjects did not express heteronormative prudishness so much as an understandable discomfort about being associated with violent rapists. In recent years, Appalachian studies scholarship has moved away from this perspective and, ironically, assumed the anti-idyllic perspective that it has purported to contest. Anthony Harkins, for example, describes *Deliverance* as representing "retarded and crippled misfits and savage sodomizers of the North Georgia wilderness," capitulating to urbanoia's insistence that visible disabilities, particularly when paired with nonnormative sexuality or gender expression, must be grotesque.[73] That perspective was not yet the norm in the Rabun County of the *Foxfire* interviews. In 1974, sexual difference and disabilities were understood as elements of the mundane social landscape of the Rabun County mountains. They were markers of a heterogeneous community like any other, associated with both difficulty and joy, not reducible to a generic rural horror.

In fact, the kayaking incident that spawned *Deliverance* transpired quite differently in reality than it did in the novel and film. Two of Dickey's friends, Lewis and Al, hit a rough stretch of rapids and busted their canoe. As Al was about to drown, "like from nowhere, this redneck boy out hunting with his dog" appeared.[74] The boy took Al home, warmed him up, and sent him off with moonshine to share with Lewis. After the novel was released, Al reminded Dickey of the difference between the real interaction and the fictionalized version: "those people were always nice to us, and none of us was ever sodomized."[75]

RACE, PLACE, AND THE LIMITS OF ALLEGORY

In 1977, NBC News aired a three-hour special called *Violence in America* that addressed an apparent tide of violence that had swept the United States in the past decade. The television special placed the violence of horror films alongside what it described as the "subculture of violence—poverty in the cities, racial segregation." In doing so, it conflated as "social problems" a largely white fictional medium with real instances of violence represented as Black.[76] Yet three years later, a *Los Angeles Times* article contradicted the prevailing wisdom that horror films inspired violence and were bad for the nation's collective mental health. The psychiatrists and psychotherapists interviewed described the generic horror film as a "cathartic nightmare" that allowed viewers to feel ownership over their "destinies" in light of the news. Film industry executives concurred, contending that the "real horrors" were "in the newspaper headlines."[77]

Psychoanalytic interpretation of horror films as a psychic release that enacts allegories for larger world problems has been the primary lens through which filmmakers and film scholars interpret horror films of the 1970s.[78] Urbanoia films have been analyzed as allegories for class and racial struggles of the 1960s,[79] for the Vietnam War,[80] and for the racialized frontier violence that had been the province of Westerns.[81] Many prominent directors, including Craven and Hooper, identified as leftists and intended for viewers to identify with the "downtrodden" rural antagonists and against the "normal" bourgeois family from the city or suburbs.[82] And, as the NBC special suggested, the white rural violence in urbanoia films could be wrapped with images of urban riots into a broader moral panic about violence. By 1980, white horror violence was reimagined as cathartic and healthy while "downtrodden" urban Black communities—whom the white antagonists of urbanoia films were meant to allegorically represent— remained stigmatized.

The fictional social worlds of horror films shaped cultural understandings of rural white sexuality beyond the theater. Or, to quote visual theorist W. J. T. Mitchell, landscapes and bodies of horror films are a force that "*makes* history in both the real and represented environment."[83] Horror films were intended to have allegorical meanings, and audiences surely made connections between on-screen filmic violence and on-screen newsreel violence from the United States, Vietnam, and elsewhere. But if horror films from all eras and all subgenres stage a basic battle between good and evil, they differ in the specific visual and narrative techniques that they use to convey the "normality" and "deviance" that mark good and evil. The "monsters" of 1970s urbanoia films were distinctly human, distinctly rural, and distinctly white. Even when urbanoia antagonists were outfitted to resemble "movie Indians," as in *Hills*, they were located in a white frontier mythology—described as the degraded descendants of "homesteading ancestors"—underneath their racial drag.[84]

By looking to the racial geographies through which urbanoia films circulated in the 1970s, we are reminded that whiteness is not a blank slate and that rural on-screen locales are not abstracted from modern social life. The rural white antagonists of urbanoia films did not ultimately function as a generic and un-racialized "other," and they could not, even symbolically, represent disenfranchised people of color in the United States and abroad. The "history" that horror films forged was rooted in the anti-idyllic visual imagery of poor, sexually deviant, and disabled rural white folks depicted on screen, rather than in the greater social struggles that horror films allegorized.

Concerns about violence in horror films and notions of an urban Black "subculture of violence" intersected in the promotion and distribution of horror films. Urbanoia films initially played on the midnight movie circuit, which was limited to theaters in working-class and often predominantly Black areas of major cities, as well as predominantly white-attended drive-ins in the rural South. While Craven assumed audiences shared his white, middle-class, repressed backgrounds, promoters and distributors typically described their audiences as working class, Black, and urban.[85] Stephen Brenner, a sales manager for the company that marketed *Chain Saw*, gave a lengthy anecdote describing the working-class Black urban audiences that he assumed to be the main demographic for the films he sold. Prefacing his comments with a qualifier intended to demonstrate that he wasn't racist, Brenner conflated race and class as he insisted, "I'm not trying to make any derogatory comments about races, but it isn't white-collar workers" who watch horror films.[86]

Even white actors in urbanoia films expressed fears that their films might prompt Black urban audiences to respond violently against white people. William Vail, the white actor who played one of the rich city kids in *Chain Saw*, recounted fearing for his own safety while watching the film in a predominantly Black theater in Times Square. "Every time one of the kids went in the door, they'd scream 'Kill him! Kill the white guy! Murder him! Smash his head!' And it was like, huh? 'Kill the honky!'" Laughing, Vail described it as a "different experience," explaining that he was afraid the audience would recognize him and respond violently—though they did not, and his fears were completely unfounded.[87]

Racist fears that urbanoia films might inspire Black violence extended to theater owners, particularly when the film featured a Black family. Concerned that a film depicting white "redneck" violence against a Black bourgeois family would provoke a riot, many theater owners refused to show the 1977 hicksploitation/blaxploitation hybrid *Fight for Your Life*. *Fight for Your Life* differed from the standard urbanoia film as the bourgeois protagonists were Black, and the violence was set in a pastoral New York suburb rather than a more remote area. Like most urbanoia films, the violence was perpetrated by a man—Jessie Lee Kane, a prison escapee obviously marked as a Southerner—though together with Asian and Latino sidekicks named "Ling" and "Ching." Theater owners who refused to show the film had unfounded worries that *Fight for Your Life* was an entirely too-faithful reproduction of white Southern violence against Black Americans. In other words, when the victims were Black, the antagonist's whiteness became too visible. White theater owners' fears were needless: Black audiences, like all horror audiences, responded to the films as the fiction and fantasy that they were.[88]

In 1980, a *Saturday Night Live* sketch called "Deliverance II" featured Reynolds, the show's host, reprising his role as Lewis. Enlisted by Anita Bryant and a local sheriff to investigate reports of "homosexual hicks" in the Georgia woods, *SNL*'s Lewis traveled all the way to New York City to find gay "bait" for his Georgia mission. Much of the skit's humor derived from embodied stereotypes of lisping, prancing, effete urban homosexuals, but its obvious premise was the apparent contradiction between a rural sexual act between men and the cosmopolitan culture of gay-identified men. In a plot twist, both Lewis's New York homosexuals and the Georgia men he hoped to entrap were also on undercover missions. Yet the sketch concludes with all six men discoing into a cozy tent together, suggesting that perhaps the Georgia mountains are as good a place as any for men to share intimacy.

From the 1910s through the 1970s, cultural forms like popular science, documentary photography, and metropolitan media stories gazed at rural white landscapes with an anti-idyllic lens. Horror films were the culmination of this genealogy, but they were not the end of it. As "Deliverance II" suggests, by the 1980s, the popular acknowledgment of the gay liberation movement and the rise of the religious right seemed to join forces to assure us that gay-identified people existed—but only in cities far away from the Bible Belt. Although horror film viewers may still think "there are people like this in the world" when they watch 1970s urbanoia films, "those people" are not "homosexual hicks" but violent monsters.

6: ESTRANGED BUT NOT STRANGERS

Nonconformity Encounters Identity in 1990s Hate-Crime Documentaries

In an upstate New York farmhouse that four brothers had shared for decades, an elderly man died in the bed he shared with his closest brother. Three and a half years later, in a southeast Nebraska farmhouse, three young people died in the home that they had shared for just a few hours. Both cases, alleged to be murders, grew into dramatic news stories and subjects of award-winning independent documentaries by New York City–based filmmakers: *Brother's Keeper: A Heartwarming Tale of Murder* (1993), directed by Bruce Sinofsky and Joe Berlinger, and *The Brandon Teena Story* (1998), directed by Susan Muska and Gréta Ólafsdottir, respectively. The films—one about an intellectually disabled farmer accused of killing his own brother, the other about a young transgender man killed in a small town he was new to—presented opposing visions of community and belonging in predominantly white rural communities struggling in the wake of the 1980s farm crisis. As *Brother's Keeper* chronicled a sensational, anti-idyllic story of fratricide and fraternal intimacy among four aging and economically marginal farmers, *The Brandon Teena Story* indexed the emergence of a nascent identity movement for transgender rights. In other words, while the former slowly revealed to viewers the tangled ball of disability, sexuality, race, and class that constituted the anti-idyll, the latter teased apart a single identitarian thread, demarcating lesbian and transgender issues as separate from race, class, and disability. Yet the underlying social circumstances of each film were remarkably similar. They shared accusations of murder and sexual assault, police with ulterior motives, the ubiquity of disability in poor communities, interracial intimacies, and unorthodox social interdependencies in depressed rural communities with a dissolving social web.

Shifts in Christian politics, farm economics, and welfare politics molded the contours of the idyll and anti-idyll. In the 1970s and 1980s, the rise of the Christian right combined and crystallized white resentment politics, homophobic sexual panics, and free-market capitalism into the idea of "Christian values."[1] These religious values were often spatialized and called "small town values," locating a prescriptive conservative sexual politics—more explicit and punitive than the implicit ideal of the farm family from past generations—in rural white landscapes.[2] The farm crisis of the 1980s, which devastated middle-class white farming communities, caused an abrupt downward mobility that was unfamiliar to many rural white people; many rural white men became drawn to white supremacist and militia movements.[3]

Simultaneously, as urban communities of color experienced economic crisis and downward mobility, the United States witnessed the rise of virulent anti-welfare politics scapegoating Black and Mexican immigrant communities. Moral panics over the "culture of poverty" and "welfare queens" castigated values such as interdependence, flexible kinship structures, and mutual aid that existed in all kinds of poor and disabled communities but were publicly associated with Black urban communities.[4] Politically, anti-welfare movements reached their height in the 1990s, with the passage of President Bill Clinton's bill to "end welfare as we know it"—the Personal Responsibility and Work Opportunity Reconciliation Act (PRWORA)—and California voters' approval of Proposition 187, which blamed the state's economic contraction and restricted welfare state on the purportedly "pathological and parasitic Mexican family."[5] Earlier in the century, moral panics about so-called "dependent classes" had included rural white components, even when they focused primarily on communities of color; for a brief moment in the early 1960s, as discussed in chapter four, poor rural white Americans were even among those associated with the culture of poverty. But by the 1990s, this history of a rural white culture of poverty had all but been erased, and the problems of so-called "fragile" family structures headed by single mothers on welfare were typically attributed to Black urban "disorder."[6] The intertwined idyll and anti-idyll of the 1990s were shaped by these interrelated political movements—the rise of the Christian right, and racialized fears of families who used welfare—but articulated primarily through the latter.

The murders at the heart of *The Brandon Teena Story* and *Brother's Keeper* took place in farmhouses, but they did not evoke the independent nuclear family–occupied farmhouses of white American mythology. The family unit that called each farmhouse home was nonheteronormative and interdependent, reliant on both welfare and neighbors. In Munnsville, New York, the farmhouse was owned by four adult brothers, with cousins and other kin living in abandoned buses and other structures on the property. In Humboldt, Nebraska, the farmhouse was a rental, occupied by single mother Lisa Lambert, who allowed friends and acquaintances, like Brandon and DeVine, to stay with her. The Ward brothers were normalized—albeit temporarily and only after the media came to town—by townsfolk who defined "capacity" not in terms of their ability to "take care of themselves," but as having "never been on welfare." By the measure of Munnsville residents, Delbert Ward was not disabled, but almost all of the white people involved with the Brandon Teena story were.

While the rural sociality of the Ward brothers was perverse through its insularity, the rural sociality of Humboldt/Falls City was perverse through its transience—or what we might think of as rural interzones. In 1995, a magazine reported that Cynthia McGown, a woman who "once lived as a 'lesbian separatist'" in the city of Lincoln, was "writing biographies of these families whose lives crossed so tragically."[7] The events were no doubt tragic, but in most rural areas—at least outside of separatist communities—lives cross in all sorts of ways. Hate crimes, rural or otherwise, do not typically abide by the stereotype of "stranger danger." Though they may be emotionally estranged, victims and perpetrators of hate crimes are typically familiar with one another and share a "sense of physical proximity."[8]

Independent film of the 1990s began to grapple with the impact of identity-based movements on the anti-idyll—not just emerging LGBT and disability movements, but also emerging claims to "white trash" identities.[9] Realist rural scripted films often grappled with this sense that disability, queerness, and poverty were related, but struggled to understand how. Billy Bob Thornton's 1996 breakout film *Sling Blade*, for example, portrayed a closeted gay person, an intellectually disabled person, and a poor single mom as discrete formations and characters, replete with belabored dinner-table conversations about the parallel—never intersecting—relationships between each person's form of "difference." In contrast to realist feature films, documentary films had much denser, knottier material to work with. Documentaries portrayed the anti-idyll with complexity, even as narrative films sought to disentangle knotted vernacular social formations into discrete identity threads. *Brother's Keeper* initially struggled to find distribution, despite being voted best documentary at the 1992 Sundance Film Festival, because it did not appeal to any particular "target groups"—that is, it did not lend itself to identity-based marketing beyond "the elderly," "organizations devoted to rural issues," and, possibly, departments of American Studies.[10] In contrast, when *The Brandon Teena Story* was released in 1998, its kindred exploration of a murder in a poor rural community found a very clear target audience in the LGBT community and cosmopolitans enthralled with the film's "anthropological" representations of Nebraska.[11]

As *Brother's Keeper* indexed a residual formation of white rural nonconformity, "Brandon" became a site of identitarian struggle between trans and lesbian activists, to the exclusion of race and disability from the story about the three young people killed in Humboldt. Queer, predominantly white activists, academics, and journalists fought over whether Brandon should, in his death, be portrayed as transgender or lesbian. But sexual and gender categories are never shaped by gender identity and sexual orientation alone; they are deeply interwoven with class, race, and region. Like Dorothy Allison, who attests that "much of the hatred directed at [her] sexual preferences is class hatred,"[12] Brandon's gender and sexual variance was firmly shaped by class. His gay high school classmates had heard Brandon called the "little dyke in the school"—a classed gender-sexual term—but primarily considered him to be of the "trailer-trash caste," a group understood to be separate and apart from gay and lesbian students.[13] As Qwo-Li Driskill contends, Brandon—whose family asserted that he was of mixed "Sioux" and white ancestry—should also be considered in relation to Two Spirit gender and sexual identities.[14] Further, Brandon's death cannot be separated from white supremacist hatred toward interracial sexuality, as his killers—who also murdered his friend Phillip DeVine, a young Black man dating a white woman—had neo-Nazi and white supremacist ties.[15] The murders of Brandon, DeVine, and Lisa Lambert raise questions about all kinds of interrelated forms of gender and sexual nonconformity, questions that are much thornier than a debate about whether Brandon was "really" transgender.

This chapter examines how, by bringing legibility to some white rural sexual/gender dissidents, queer documentary filmmaking buried capacious rural social formations like "peculiar" and "odd" that—as evidenced by *Brother's Keeper*—were still present and part of a long anti-idyllic history of rural white America. I consider unconventional access intimacies among the Wards and mundane sociality—the interracial, disabled, and transgender intersections and divergences of small-town life—in Humboldt.

THE ACCESS INTIMACIES OF QUEERLY FRATERNAL FARMERS IN *BROTHER'S KEEPER*

In June 1990, when New York state police visited the rural home of deceased sixty-four-year-old farmer William (Bill) Ward, they immediately suspected wrongdoing, even though Bill had seemingly died in his sleep. There were no obvious signs of violence on his body; there was neither a gruesome crime scene nor a murder weapon in plain sight. But police were suspicious of Bill and his brothers because of their peculiar domestic arrangements: their home was small and rundown, but more perversely, the four disabled, bachelor, middle-aged and elderly brothers shared the small space. "We're talking two grown men that sleep in a bed together because that's the only place to sleep," investigator Michael Donegan explained to CBS journalist Connie Chung months later. "They were hermits. They lived up there, they lived a very different lifestyle, and many people, I don't think, approved.... You know, anything that's not normal, or that we don't consider to be ordinary, creates doubt in our mind." The Ward brothers' "different lifestyle" was so out of the "ordinary" that police examined Bill's body for signs of strangulation, as well as sexual activity—presumably with accused murderer, and fraternal bedmate, Adelbert (Delbert).

The "different lifestyle" that made police suspect murder and fraternal sexual intimacy also enticed reporters, television producers, and filmmakers to pay a visit to the Ward brothers' home in Munnsville, New York. Among them were Sinofsky and Berlinger, who filmed *Brother's Keeper* over the course of a year. The documentary examines contradictions between Munnsville's newfound claims of support for Delbert and their decades of ostracizing the Ward brothers. Prior to Delbert's arrest, most Munnsville residents looked down on brothers Roscoe, Bill, Lyman, and Delbert, who shared a home and limited means. Yet, after Delbert was accused of Bill's murder, the town came together in support of Delbert. They accused the cops of picking on a man they considered vulnerable—a man who could not read and write, was understood to be intellectually disabled, and had naively believed the police when they said that if he confessed, he could go home and his legal troubles would be over. Munnsville residents had different theories about whether Delbert had killed Bill, and if so, why; but whether the suspected motive was "sex gone bad" or "a mercy killing," they backed Delbert over the police.

Brother's Keeper was sympathetic to Delbert Ward but also prying and intrusive, typical of anti-idyllic approaches. Berlinger and Sinofsky explained that in making films, they liked to "turn over the rock and see what's underneath, or stop at places you would normally drive by or drive through."[16] What viewers found under the metaphorical rock was the disjuncture between the idealized, pastoral vision of rural white America as virtuous, healthy, and vigorous and the reality of poverty, disability, and non-normative domestic structures in Munnsville. "Words like 'pastoral' and 'rustic' don't go nearly far enough to describe the lives of the Ward brothers," wrote *USA Today*.[17] *Vogue* magazine concurred, writing that to see the Ward brothers was "to be confirmed in your understanding of the perversity of the simple life."[18]

In the details of the Ward brothers' "very different lifestyle," however, are numerous modes of unexpected intimacy and interdependence that allowed for crip survival under difficult circumstances. Even so, the Ward

brothers are not "good subjects" of disability studies. They were not politicized disabled subjects. Delbert was accused of both incest and fratricide,
and although he was found not guilty in court, his friends and acquaintances believed that he did kill his brother.[19] After six to seven decades of
life together, the Wards shared forms of intimacy with one another—and
with their built surroundings—that were not socially expected of adult
brothers. Their lives were quite difficult, even before Delbert was accused
of murder. As Avery Gordon contends, "even those who live in the most
dire circumstances possess a complex and oftentimes contradictory humanity and subjectivity."[20] Understanding Delbert to possess complex
personhood means we must not allow, for example, pity and outrage over
ableist policing practices to exclude the possibility that though he was disabled, he may have killed his brother because of Bill's disabilities.

To many people locally and nationally, the brothers' rural fraternal intimacy was understood as "perverse" or "queer," in the sense of odd, peculiar, or strange, possibly with the implication of nonnormative sexuality.
The Ward brothers' friend and protector, Harry, explained that the police
had conducted a rape test on Bill's body, looking for evidence of anal sex
with Delbert, because Bill and Delbert "always slept together." Harry justified their sleeping habits by explaining that "they just slept together when
they was kids and why the hell change it. It was a comfortable arrangement
all the way around. Just a habit." Regardless of whether Bill and Delbert
had intercourse with one another, their living situation offered no possibili-
ties to imagine a normative adult sex life. If the semen found on Bill's body
came from a bull, it revealed the perverse proximity they shared with nonhuman animals; if it was his own, it evoked just how little privacy the men had.
But Harry did not deny or condemn the possibility that the brothers had
intercourse with one another. "Whether they'd found it [semen] or not,
what the hell matter does that make. . . . We have lesbians and gay people
all over so why the hell was they bothering with Bill and Delbert, I don't
understand that part."

Whether sexual or not, their intimacy was seen as odd because they
seemed to actively choose it—it was not solely dictated by their material
circumstances. Community members and news media suggested that it
was odd that the brothers were each other's "constant companions," that
Delbert called Bill his "best brother," and that once, when Delbert, Lyman,
and Roscoe were given separate hotel rooms at a film screening, they left
their rooms to share a single bed.[21] It was not simply that the brothers did
not marry, or that they lived in such close proximity, but that they were so
reliant on one another.

The Ward brothers' intimacies were deeply shaped by disability and
interdependency—what we might understand as forms of "access inti-

macy." Writer and community organizer Mia Mingus describes access intimacy as a kind of "closeness" that she feels with certain people with whom her "disabled body just felt a little bit safer and at ease," people who accept and habituate themselves to how her body functions, people who are able to anticipate her needs just as an abled person's needs are invisibly but structurally anticipated and accommodated.[22] The Ward brothers likewise seemed to feel a comfort and ease with one another at least partially related to disability. For example, the brothers were invariably described by news media as difficult to communicate with, presented as suffering from a variety of linguistic and social "deficiencies": Delbert as "socially estranged" and "inarticulate," Lyman as a "twitchy hermit," and Roscoe as hard of hearing.[23] Yet they did not have difficulty communicating with each other, nor with their extended family. This was not because they shared a secret familial language, nor solely because they were familiar with one another's speaking styles. Rather, it was because they knew each other's communications needs and did not treat them as impediments. Instead of treating Roscoe's hearing as a burden, Delbert and Lyman spoke loudly enough for Roscoe to understand, and they combined their vocalizations with gestures that conveyed meaning. Likewise, when Lyman became overwhelmed and needed to remove himself from a social situation, Roscoe and Delbert allowed him the space he needed.

Beyond basic sociality, access intimacy between the unmarried Ward brothers, all disabled in different ways, allowed them to live together and depend on one another without an abled caretaker (whether sibling, nurse, or neighbor). It offered social safety and protection when they were refused access to desired medical or social services. In other words, the access intimacy that the brothers shared—among other forms of intimacy—was what allowed them to live interdependently. They cared for one another, but not in the ways typically expected of family carers. For decades, the Ward brothers modeled a form of horizontal care that is underdiscussed: care by people who shared roughly the same age, social status, gender, race, and approximate levels of disability. The Ward brothers had different types of impairments, described in characteristically vernacular terms, but the differences in their impairments allowed them to complement each other's contributions to their shared household. As the brothers' disabilities changed with age, their relationships with one another changed as well. What became particularly difficult was that they had few resources to turn to for palliative medicine, let alone in-home care.[24]

Bill's death starkly revealed the limits of such family care. Those who believed Delbert killed him had different theories as to why: a sense of "mercy," irritation with his bedmate's loud cries of pain, or simply being tired of living in Bill's shadow. Yet the small body of existing disability

6.1 Lyman Ward walks away from the filmmakers, down a country road. Still image from *Brother's Keeper*.

studies scholarship about the Ward case fails to address Bill as a subject of carer violence, focusing instead on Delbert and guidelines for police interrogations of people with mental disabilities.[25] In the decades since Bill died, disability advocates have organized a powerful movement against carer violence. Yet the frameworks that work well for most of the cases that receive public attention—a nondisabled parent harming or killing a disabled child—do not apply neatly to Bill and Delbert Ward, brothers who were both disabled.

The Ward brothers experienced a form of intimacy with built structures—their home, barn, cows, and land—that was perceived as strange. Perhaps access intimacy is not found only in other people, but in nonhuman animals or even inanimate objects and structures. The idea that a nonhuman animal might provide comfort or facilitate access, whether emotional, mental, or physical, is not new to many disabled people, particularly those who work with service or support animals. Jacks Ashley McNamara, writing for the Icarus Project, elaborates Mingus's theory of access intimacy through the example of Rosebud, an imaginary psychiatric service goat who was made available for "all our (self-identified) crazy crip friends."[26] And Mel Chen questions the ontological distinctions between human, animal, and object by describing a "toxic period," an ill period, in Chen's life, when, "anyone or anything that I manage to feel any kind of connection with, whether it is my cat or a chair ... or my partner, I think they are, and remember them as, the same ontological thing."[27] This experience—epitomized by a moment when Chen conflates Chen's couch and Chen's partner—causes Chen to reconsider the concept of intimacy, having now "encountered an intimacy that does not differentiate, is not dependent on a heartbeat." Even if one does make an ontological distinction between objects, animals, humans, and built structures, the idea that one might feel safer, more comfortable, or, perhaps, more intimate, with certain objects or spaces—a beloved childhood blankie, a bed that has been chosen carefully to minimize painful positions, the inviting home of your best friend, and so on—is not unheard of. As Tanya Titchkosky contends, "Access is a way to orient to, and even come to wonder about, who, what, where, and when we find ourselves to be in social space."[28]

It may be little wonder, then, that in the disorienting social world that the Ward brothers inhabited after Bill's death—a social space of intrusive media, tailing filmmakers, and neighbors who abruptly claimed to be the brothers' best friends after decades of ostracizing them—they embraced the access intimacy that they shared with one another and with their cow barn. *Brother's Keeper* begins with a shaky handheld camera journey into the Ward brothers' home, lingering on broken appliances, dirty hands, and one of the infamous shared beds, bare of linens. These establishing shots appeal to viewers' sense of disgust and pity and draw on long-standing anti-idyllic tropes about rural poverty. They also show off the filmmakers' intimate access to the brothers' lives: "being inside the house . . . was always very special," Sinofsky and Berlinger explained later, because outside of the brothers themselves, "only two or three people had ever been in that house."[29] Beyond the house, the filmmakers spend time with the brothers outdoors, and in the courthouse during Delbert's trial. One place the filmmakers spend very little time, however, is inside the barn.

The cow barn facilitated the brothers' queer "reclusiveness" in a particular way, providing them comfort or intimacy that Munnsville residents did not. Time after time, when Delbert or Lyman felt sad or anxious or lonely, he turned to the barn. Delbert slept in the barn after Bill's death, for example, eschewing the bed that the two had once shared, until family friend Harry convinced him to go back to the house.[30] In a front-page *New York Times* article shortly after Delbert was arrested, reporter Elizabeth Kolbert described Delbert as "at ease only when talking about the family's cows," and Kolbert's insight held true for the barrage of media interviews Delbert conducted over the next two years.[31] Lyman's attachment to the barn and the animals inside is represented in two viscerally upsetting scenes in the documentary. In each scene, Lyman, made visibly anxious by

6.2 Lyman Ward slips through the door to his family's barn in order to remove himself from conversation with the filmmakers. Still image from *Brother's Keeper*.

the filmmakers' questioning, seeks refuge: he rambles away from the cameras, shaking and wheezing, desperately trying to climb through a broken door into the barn.

Viewers' very first glimpse of Lyman in *Brother's Keeper* sees him taut and nervous, hunched over, turning his body away from the filmmakers almost as though he might retch at any moment. Sinofsky, recalling the moment, asserted that although the scene made him "feel bad as a human being," he ultimately loved it—in part, he claimed, because Lyman's conversations with the filmmakers later show how much more he trusted them.[32] Still, the scene is upsetting and intrusive, described by reviewers as feeling "invasive."[33] Wearing an unbuttoned plaid work shirt, unzipped work pants, and a green Burton hat perched askew on his head, Lyman leans on a car for support as he loses his breath. Sinofsky and Berlinger ask him about his police interrogation following Delbert's arrest, and Lyman narrates the nervousness that he felt at the police station, as he clearly becomes more nervous before them. Lyman explains that at the police station he was "all shook up" and "bad down there." When the filmmakers ask him why, he explains simply, still on edge, "Cuz I'm nervous." When the filmmakers ask if their presence is making Lyman more nervous, he responds, "Everything makes me nervous. Always was, ever since—" and gestures to a child's height. As the filmmakers probe, starting to ask whether he remembers a beginning to his nerves—a root cause—Lyman interrupts them: "No . . . I was probably born to be nervous," adding, upon questioning, "I ain't the only one that's nervous. There's a lot of guys down here that's nervous," and insisting that "all these farmers" are nervous. He walks away in the middle of speaking, hiding behind tractors so the filmmakers, following closely behind, can't reach him. He moves toward his solace, the barn, still hunched over and wheezing. Lyman strains to squeeze into the barn through a broken door, his hat nearly falling off his head in the process. Film critics described this scene in which Lyman "can no longer cope, and rips his coat while escaping quickly through a half-opened door," as "one of the most poignant moments in the film."[34]

Before viscerally displaying his anxiety, Lyman explains his apparent mental disability as being "nervous," elaborating that being nervous is part of his nature and that being nervous is part of the nature of farming. Local newspapers concurred with Lyman's assessment of himself, reporting that "All his life, the reclusive Lyman hid from strangers," often riding with his brothers into town but staying outside while his brothers ate or shopped.[35] Lyman contradicts stereotypes of the laconic farmer, while reaffirming anti-idyllic associations between "nervousness" and reclusiveness that were forged through Appalachian poverty tours in the 1960s.

In a second scene that mirrors the first, several months have passed, and Lyman, standing with Roscoe, seems more at ease with the filmmakers. Yet, as the conversation turns toward marriage and girlfriends, Lyman again becomes noticeably distressed. The filmmakers ask whether the brothers "used to, you know, have, like, girlfriends?" Lyman responds, "Naw, I wouldn't have 'em around," and Roscoe interrupts to add, "Lyman never wanted a girlfriend." The brothers and filmmakers laugh together at a reference to Sinofsky's ongoing divorce, and Lyman seems relatively at ease—at least, as at ease as he ever appears on screen. Then the filmmakers casually ask whether Lyman or Roscoe had ever considered marriage. Lyman quickly and vehemently responds, "Noooo," and Roscoe laughs, and Lyman begins to walk, nervously, away from the cameras again and toward the barn. The cameras follow Lyman toward the barn as Roscoe explains in the background that their deceased brother Bill "didn't want no women, neither," nor did their cousin Ike, who lived on their property. Then, as before, Lyman slips through the broken barn door, bucket in hand, extricating himself from the difficult topic of marriage.

To outsiders, the cow barn was a contradictory space. It was a peculiar emotional refuge for Lyman but also the site of the brothers' primary economic activity and an important social space. The pastoral puffery introducing the *A Current Affair* story about the Ward brothers began by

6.3 Walter and Theodora Geisler sit beside each other in folksy rocking chairs. As they present themselves to filmmakers as saintly supporters of the Ward brothers, they also divulge the contingency of their support, and the underlying aversion they had had for the Ward brothers. Still image from *Brother's Keeper*.

describing Munnsville as a "sleepy farming town in New York State, where barns and silos dot the lush green countryside," leaving no doubt as to the idyllic nature of a barn that decorates a landscape, whether or not it functions for farming.[36] But the Wards' working cow barn—a structure that is rarely shown in the film—offered the greatest testimony for the brothers' "humanity" and "capacity" as measured by normative standards like cleanliness and economic productivity. It was much cleaner and in much better repair than their home, since their milking operation was subject to frequent inspections—which they passed with honors.[37]

Delbert's ability to farm, albeit interdependently with his brothers, and with a very low profit margin, even hurt him in court. Prosecutors used his "competence" in farming to suggest that he was not intellectually disabled, as Delbert's defense attorney asserted and as his school records suggested. Whether the brothers were ashamed of their house or simply more comfortable in the barn, most of their friends visited them in the barn and never saw inside their house. And locally, their identities as farmers were used to rehabilitate their reputations and put them on the same social plane as their neighbors: "We're farmers. We stick together."[38] A Syracuse journalist summarized this tendency in 1993 when he wrote that despite "their reclusiveness, lack of education and abject poverty," they evoked a sentiment from their neighbors that "they were gentle men whose character and behavior were those of the farmer."[39] In other words, the abstract vocational virtues associated with farming helped humanize men whose poverty, disabilities, and unconventional family formation estranged them. Yet, as the cow barn was the primary site of agrarian virtue and economic competence, it was also a site of injury and pain as well as a site of unconventional intimate attachments.

Brother's Keeper and much of the national media focused on the seemingly idyllic public support that Munnsville voiced for Delbert after his arrest. A field producer for *A Current Affair* explained, "The essence of the story is the community support."[40] Yet the downside of the "territorial pride" that the *New York Times* lauded—a newly found pride that followed years of indifference and outright rejection—was condescension and possessiveness. The *Times* illustrated this territorial pride with a sentiment purportedly circulating in the area: "the Ward boys might be oddballs, but they were Munnsville oddballs."[41] In fact, the line "making the rounds" in upstate New York went differently: "They may be the Ward Boys but they're our Ward Boys."[42] The distinction speaks to the gulf between rural vernacular language and urban approximations of it. The formation that the Ward brothers exemplified wasn't a generic category of folksy otherness like "oddball," but the iconoclastic Ward brothers themselves, and "our Ward boys" was considerably more patronizing than "our oddballs," infantilizing men in their sixties and seventies.

Long before Delbert's arrest and subsequent local fundraisers at the Sugar Shack, a few residents of the Munnsville area provided substantial yet quotidian material support to the brothers. Harry looked out for them, of course, and their extended family—their cousins, as well as several of their late sister's adult children—also cared about them. Nephew Moses Frank, who appears briefly in the film, quit his paid job as a farmworker to help his uncles after Bill's death, and niece Sandra Dodson talked to them regularly about how the media attention was affecting them.[43] During the last three years of Delbert's life, when he lived in a nursing home, Dodson visited him every day.[44] Police officer Eugene Rifenburg claimed that he had been known to pitch in as well, driving Roscoe home after he got drunk and passed out on the side of the road—and generously, in his estimation, refraining from charging him with a crime.[45] As they got older, the Ward brothers received Meals on Wheels.[46] Their community support was not just about bare survival, though. After Berlinger and Sinofsky paid the brothers a percentage of the film's proceeds, Delbert and Lyman purchased a car, a gray Chrysler Fifth Avenue. They enjoyed the car, painting it silver and playing with the sunroof, but neither brother had a driver's license. When they wanted to go for a ride, neighbor Kenny Elmer volunteered to be their chauffeur.[47]

When Munnsville-area residents came to the Ward brothers' defense, however, they emphasized that what made the brothers worth defending, in spite of their peccadilloes, was the racialized sense that they were "self-sufficient"—or, more precisely, that they "never took welfare."[48] The brothers' community belonging, however fleeting, was thus implicitly conditioned on their whiteness. Sociologist Robert Bogdan, who visited Munnsville and interviewed residents during the trial, registered the frequency with which Munnsville residents invoked welfare in their defense of the brothers. Although they worked inefficiently, they were described as "hard workers" because they were "not on welfare."[49] Delbert was defended on the basis of his "self-pride," defended by "his refusal to accept charity or welfare, his strong work ethic, his gentleness and his honesty."[50] The brothers were defended for doing without, for eating "bread sandwiches" (day-old bread and margarine) rather than using food stamps. On *A Current Affair*, a Munnsville resident described them as "simple people." "They're honest, they're polite," the person stated, "they mind their own business, they don't ... draw welfare."

The Ward brothers' belonging may have been conditional on their own whiteness and local roots, but it was also conditional on their large, mixed-race extended family who lived nearby. The Ward brothers had seven nieces and nephews, the children of their sister Emma, who had died of cancer in 1988, and her husband Charles, who passed away a year later.[51] Frank, one of those nephews, appears in the documentary's most notorious scene, in which he slaughters a hog for the brothers. Later, nieces Dodson and Jane Hatch frequently spoke with the media on their uncles' behalf, and when they became co-administrators of the brothers' estate— after Lyman passed away in 2008—they expressed a strong bond with their uncles and insisted they would keep their farm in the family.[52] Although no one in the film or media ever commented on the brothers' interracial family, their deceased brother-in-law, Charles Frank, was Black, and their nieces and nephews were mixed-race Black locals.[53] Perhaps the Wards' neighbors felt a paternalistic "tolerance" or a misguided sense of "color-blindness" because Frank's family had deep roots in the community, or perhaps the film and media avoided topics that challenged their white, anti-idyllic frame.

If the Ward brothers had lived in a larger community where keeping a herd of twenty-three dairy cows was not sufficient to maintain a home, or where their childhood neighbors did not continue to help them out at the bank or diner when they came by as adults, they might not have been able to live independently. That is to say, if the Ward brothers—who were tolerated in part because they were seen as an anachronistic throwback to older times—had even been born into the very same community, just ten or twenty years later, they may have been institutionalized. Even in 1991, their friends feared that the police were trying to incarcerate Delbert in order to force Lyman and Roscoe into "a home." The Ward brothers farmed more slowly and less efficiently than their neighbors, but they were competent and skilled, using the language of farming, which they knew, to explain themselves to outsiders. In other words, they asserted the less valorized queercrip knowledge, skills, and intimacies that they possessed in spite of their eccentricities.

THE HUMBOLDT MURDERS: THE RUPTURE OF MINIMART SOCIALITY

In 1998, the documentary *The Brandon Teena Story*, together with the more famous, Oscar-winning narrative film *Boys Don't Cry*, inaugurated what Jack Halberstam terms the "Brandon archive": the array of cultural productions created after a triple homicide in Humboldt, Nebraska, on New Year's Eve 1993, when John Lotter and Marvin "Tom" Nissen took the lives of Phillip DeVine, Brandon Teena, and Lisa Lambert (ostensibly seeking to kill Brandon a week after brutally assaulting him).[54] Five years after *Brother's Keeper* revived anti-idyllic optics and trained them on the Ward brothers, *The Brandon Teena Story* transformed the murders of three young Nebraskans into a single story of the tragic fate of a rural, white transgender person. As C. Riley Snorton contends, transforming the Humboldt murders into a trans liberation narrative requires rendering the death of DeVine— a Black, physically disabled Iowan who was dating the sister of Brandon's girlfriend—as "ungeographic and untimely," evacuating his "constitutive presence to and place within" the Brandon archive.[55]

Yet, as Snorton and Driskill both recognize, beyond the heart of the Brandon archive as constituted by trans activists and scholars, most contemporaneous accounts of the Humboldt murders—from articles in the *New Yorker* and *Playboy* to a true-crime pulp novel—told much knottier stories.[56] Rather than focusing narrowly on questions of trans or lesbian identity, they drew upon a long history of white poverty, family "instability," interracial sociality, violence, physical and mental maladies, and welfare. Indeed, eugenic laments about the "social residuum" of the country are hardly discernible from how *New Yorker* writer John Gregory Dunne editorialized about the "drifting and woefully underequipped stratum" of southeastern Nebraska.[57] The intersections of disability studies and transgender studies have been studied through the formation of bodies, medicalization of difference, law, access, and identity; they can also be ascertained through working-class socialities and intimacies.

The murder victims, their friends, and their murderers lived on the social margins and shared the barstools, minimarts, and workplaces through which people meet, mingle, and make out in small towns—what Dunne chauvinistically termed "lumpen hangouts."[58] Brandon and DeVine's social circles in Nebraska were centered in the town of Falls City, about twenty-five miles from Lambert's Humboldt farmhouse, where they were killed. Although Brandon and DeVine were both new in town, small-town gathering places and the social circles of their girlfriends—sisters Lana Tisdel and Leslie Tisdel, respectively—brought them into close proximity, perhaps even friendship, with Lotter and Nissen.[59] Many of the friends and acquaintances who interacted at Kwik Trip, karaoke bar the Oasis, and the Tisdels' mother's home shared common experiences of disability and psychiatric confinement, being on welfare, and the social stigma assigned to interracial relationships. Yet these shared social worlds were fraught, combining an uneasy mix of love and violence, familiarity and estrangement. The Humboldt murders ultimately reveal the limits of such intimacies: the brutal rupture when the limits of "tolerance" and working-class sociality were violently enforced against the transgender white-passing man and cisgender Black man deemed "out of place" and too proximate to white cisgender women.

While cities have been valorized by queer scholars for "random, inter-class, and interethnic social encounters," small towns have, until recently, largely been seen as homogeneous and homogenizing.[60] *The Brandon Teena Story* seems to confirm this, yet it also reveals how small-town homogeneity is manufactured. Early in the documentary, an unattributed voice-over haltingly insists that "Falls City is a . . . white community. We may've had one or two families in here that were Black, but as far as . . . having gay people come in, Falls City would, I'm sure, escort 'em out of town." This assessment of Falls City as a "white community" is not a description—it is a threat. Falls City was a white community because it wished to remain a white community, not because people of color had never lived there or visited. The voiced threat to "escort" gay people out of town, following a conflation of Blackness and gayness, supports rumors that Falls City was a sundown town—a town that uses violence and intimidation to threaten Black people who remain in town after sundown—and confirms the community's entrenched hostility toward "others."[61]

Efforts to portray Falls City and Humboldt as idealized farm towns struggled in the face of ubiquitous anti-idyllic narratives about the towns' young adults. To deny that racial and sexual difference existed in their town, both towns had to distance their communities from the social group that put them on the map. The managing editor of the *Falls City Journal* insisted that no one else in town knew any of the people involved: they were no "Future Homemakers of America," he explained, choosing a gendered example targeting the women who dated Brandon and DeVine rather than the men who were ultimately convicted of their murders.[62] The *Humboldt Standard* took "consolation" in the fact that "none of the victims, or the accused, were from Humboldt."[63] Local leaders were defensive for a reason. Dunne's condescending *New Yorker* piece, which cataloged in great detail the supposed "drifting and woefully equipped stratum" revealed by the Humboldt murders, was endorsed by urban Nebraska newspapers.[64] The *Omaha World-Herald* so strongly embraced Dunn's perspective that his judgment was cited as fact in numerous editorials, by different writers, who lamented the social conditions of Nebraska's economically depressed rural communities.[65]

The young people who met and mingled at the minimart belied the town's claims to homogeneity, even as two of them—Lotter and Nissen—committed murder in part to enforce those claims. The friends and acquaintances who orbited the Tisdels' home shared experiences of interracial intimacy, disability, institutionalization (or threats of it), and the challenges of being on state welfare aid. It is not surprising that people like Brandon and DeVine might share space and intimacy with Lambert, the Tisdels, Lotter, Nissen, and their ilk—there was a logic to their sociality, even as their shared experiences had hard limits. Brandon and DeVine, like many victims of violence, were simultaneously familiar with and estranged from their attackers.[66] Rather than focus on Brandon, DeVine, and Lambert's social circles in the way anti-idyllic accounts do—to suggest that violence within a group of "unpopular dropouts and derelicts" was inevitable, a move that makes victims and killers equally culpable—I focus on the complicated and ambiguous relationships they shared in order to emphasize that victims who know their attackers, as most do, are no more culpable for their own murders than someone killed by a stranger.[67]

Despite the pronouncement that Falls City was an all-white town, that was never the entire truth. Leslie, who was known to date only Black men, had a mixed-race Black child from a previous relationship (as did Brandon's sister Tammy); DeVine was not even the only Black man staying at her home at the time.[68] The men who murdered DeVine were not strangers to him, nor were they unacquainted with Black men generally; indeed, "routine fraternization" between Black men and poor white men has long driven white resentment and anti-Black violence.[69] Sometimes this violence was more mundane (though by no means benign): a Black man being denied service at Hardee's, or the regular opprobrium that both Leslie and Lana faced for "associate[ing] with Black people."[70] That Lotter and

Nissen could go out drinking with Black acquaintances did not undermine their associations with or support from white supremacist groups.[71] After DeVine's death, his mother expressed regret that "With no friends there, he befriended someone—if that's the correct word—and it happened to be the wrong people."[72] Her sentiment could easily refer to the white men, friends of DeVine's girlfriend, who knew he was at the Humboldt farmhouse that night. Yet in context, it's clear she's referring to Brandon, as though—as so many suggested—Brandon was blameworthy for his own murder while DeVine and Lambert were "innocent." That Brandon and Lambert were the very friends who picked DeVine up at the bus station when he arrived in Nebraska, weeks earlier, was irrelevant.[73] In death, the victims were estranged even from each other.

In lesbian and trans narratives, perceptions that Brandon was both innocent and white further estranged him from DeVine and Lambert. Despite many accounts describing Brandon as white, Brandon's family said that his paternal grandfather was "full-blooded Sioux."[74] It is difficult to determine whether Brandon's family did belong to Očhéthi Šakówiŋ peoples or whether they told that story as many families tell tall ancestral tales, claiming indigeneity without any real belonging to Native communities. Regardless, it is undeniable that his perceived whiteness fostered identification from white trans people and lesbians across the United States—and that such identification required, as Driskill contends, white queer and trans people to erase his Nativeness.[75] Brandon would not have received the same kind of cultural attention were he perceived as Indigenous. A young man quoted in Beth Loffreda's account of another hate crime— the 1998 murder of Matthew Shepard, a white gay man, in Laramie, Wyoming— starkly names the consequences of being perceived as Native rather than white. Jay, described as a "Shoshone-Northern-Arapahoe-Navajo American Indian born on the Wind River Reservation," told Loffreda, "If that was me hung on the fence, they'd just say, oh, another drunk Indian. No one would have paid much attention."[76] Perceived as white, Brandon was treated differently.

Disability and shared histories of institutionalization were another reason why Brandon, DeVine, and their rural Nebraska cohorts contradicted the area's self-image of wholesome, healthy, normative life. DeVine was born with multiple physical disabilities; as an infant, doctors pressured his mother to put him in an institution, fearing "he would never be able to function."[77] DeVine's companions had mental disabilities. Brandon's family and friends had him committed to a psychiatric institution for a week in January 1992, after which he was reportedly discharged to outpatient care with two diagnoses: transsexualism and a personality disorder.[78] According to Jones, Brandon also struggled with eating disorders, compulsive showering, and attempted suicide.[79] Leslie, Nissen, and Lotter had all attempted suicide, and Lotter had been institutionalized off and on since his early childhood; Lana and her mother were often represented as experiencing addiction, though they challenged those representations.[80] In other words, disability was everywhere in the story of the Humboldt murders, not just in the prosthetic limb used by DeVine.

Brandon and Lana bonded over being "crazy" and the threat of institutionalization that it carried. In an outtake from *The Brandon Teena Story*, Lana reads a letter written by Brandon, which he had signed, "We both understand, we're both crazy." Lana explained to Muska and Olafsdottir that Brandon's reference to being "crazy" was an inside joke. Her parents, friends, and neighbors thought she and Brandon were crazy and had threatened to send her to a place "in Lincoln or Omaha, somewhere up there," a place whose name she could not remember except as a "Crazy Home" in one of those indistinguishable, faraway cities. The threat to institutionalize Lana recalls the criminalization of interracial relationships, wherein Black men dating white women were often incarcerated, while their white girlfriends were institutionalized for the "insanity" of desiring to date a Black man.[81]

Brandon's gender and sexuality were understood through disabled and racialized experiences of class and the reputations they engendered: as the "type of person" who socialized at so-called "lumpen hangouts" when he got out of jail or the psych ward, who grew up on welfare, or who came from a non-Black family that associated with Black people. Lesbian activists in Lincoln and Omaha—unlike those in New York, who were less familiar with the class dynamics of rural Nebraska—never even wondered if Brandon might belong to their community.[82] Brandon strenuously distinguished himself from lesbians, but when he lived in Lincoln, he had gay roommates and patronized gay bars with straight girlfriends. In Falls City, Brandon fit into a more elastic category: "He was a pervert, just a regular guy," according to a girl he met at a party who used "pervert" as paradoxical slang to refer to a man who expressed a commonplace sexual interest in women.[83] When forced to explain the apparent incongruity between his gender and his sexed body, Brandon deployed language from tabloid talk shows or partial recollections from his psychiatric stay, asserting that he was a "hermaphrodite," had a "sexual identity crisis," or was seeking a "sex change."[84] These were almost universally unfamiliar to his friends in Falls City and Lincoln. In an outtake from *The Brandon Teena Story*, John Lotter recounts seeing a trans woman once in Lincoln—a big city, and therefore, he assumes, a place where "most people are well off." Lotter uses the story about the woman in Lincoln to brag that "I've seen this stuff [before]," claiming the sophistication that he associates with the city, even as he acknowledges that he'd "had no idea" that the woman was trans. In 1993, the knowledge it took to make Brandon's gender legible required cultural capital that his friends in Falls City did not have. Then again, Brandon's gender had not been legible in Lincoln, either, and in Falls City—at least for a while—legibility hardly seemed to matter. As Tisdel explained in amorphous language characteristic of rural white Midwestern communities in the 1990s, her relationship with Brandon felt odd "in a way, but in a way not."[85]

In the view of critics, what united the minimart crew most was "irresponsibility." When Dunne insisted that Nebraska's best-known sexual nonconformist, Willa Cather, would have seen Brandon's "obsession with gender and its discontents as self-indulgent," as an "excuse to abdicate personal responsibility," he drew on multiple historical narratives: the psychiatric view of homosexuality as narcissism, the false notion that trans people are inherently "deceptive," and the discourse of welfare reform.[86] "Irresponsibility" was (and is) the kind of capacious term that could tie together racialized welfare recipients, people with mental illness, and people who disobey sexual norms (whether interracial, same-sex, out of wedlock, with a trans person, or any combination thereof). Irresponsibility was a component of the "psychopathologies of damaged masculinity and low self-esteem" that, as Christina Hanhardt contends, since the 1970s were imagined to be the root of homophobia and attributed to a racialized culture of poverty.[87] The white supremacist and trans-antagonistic violence perpetrated by Lotter and Nissen was attributed to their own belonging to homophobic cultures of poverty that were associated with the racialized communities they sought to distance themselves from.[88] Perhaps because of this, Lotter and Nissen held on to their whiteness possessively; when the innate superiority they felt over a Black man like DeVine was not evident in their respective class statuses or the women they dated, Lotter and Nissen enacted their supremacy with violence.

In fighting for disability rights, for trans rights, and even for welfare rights, activists are often too quick to parse identities that are rarely so neatly parsed in real life—for example, to name rural white poverty as the provenance of Brandon's killers but not of Brandon himself, despite their shared experiences of growing up "on disability," of psychiatric institutionalization, and of interracial sociality; or to say that disability isn't relevant because Brandon was "really" trans and therefore wrongly considered to have a mental disability, or because his and Lana's moms' disabilities were not apparent and triggered accusations of malingering; or to say that DeVine was killed because he was "in the wrong place at the wrong time," without wondering why DeVine was in that place at that time or what social forces put an aspirational young Black man in the same social circles as white folks with so much less ambition.

In *Exile and Pride*, Eli Clare writes that "Gender reaches into disability; disability wraps around class; class strains against abuse; abuse snarls into sexuality; sexuality folds on top of race . . . everything finally piling into a single human body."[89] Gender, disability, class, abuse, sexuality, race, violence, welfare—these intersect not only in our human bodies and minds, but in our social stratifications, in the very idea of "those people" who hang out at the minimart.

CONCLUSION: SEIZING THE LENS

Decades after both *Brother's Keeper* and *The Brandon Teena Story* were released, another acclaimed documentary dove into anti-idyllic rural imaginaries of violence, disability, gender nonconformity, and working-class white masculinities: *Marwencol*. *Marwencol* follows Mark Hogancamp, a man rebuilding his life in the wake of a vicious physical attack outside a bar that left him with a nine-day coma, a traumatic brain injury (TBI), and post-traumatic stress disorder (PTSD). Hogancamp builds extraordinarily intricate dioramas using G.I. Joes, Barbies, and all sorts of other materials. He photographs the scenes and stories he creates, sometimes walking down winding forest roads with his figures to find and set up the right shot. The center of this creative world is a fictional town that he calls Marwencol, which is named for three of its main characters: Mark (himself), Wendy (a woman he has a crush on), and Colleen (another woman he has a crush on). Marwencol exists during World War II, and Hogancamp's staged battle scenes function as a form of therapy, a thrifty crip method of working through trauma after his insurance has cut him off. Marwencol is also art, though, and Hogancamp is discovered by an art magazine one day while staging a photograph on the side of the road. That discovery in turn leads the documentary filmmakers to Hogancamp, and the film follows him from a relatively ordinary life in rural Kingston, New York, to an art-show debut in New York City.

The attack left Hogancamp with amnesia, and without a desire for many of the things he enjoyed prior to his injury, including large quantities of vodka. But one desire, once he is reminded of it, is immediately reactivated. Hogancamp was attacked, he learns, because he told the men at the bar that he was a crossdresser. He begins ordering heels and stockings like he orders miniatures: online and in the dozens. At his art show, he decides that New York City is the perfect place to try on a new, yet old, identity as a crossdresser. Hogancamp has survived violence based on his gender expression (or desired gender expression) but also become disabled by it. Yet his disability—or rather, his self-made ways of reckoning with disability in lieu of adequate medical and social services—has helped him accept the gender nonconformity that precipitated the violence.

This is one of many circumstances that might seem to be contradictory to outsiders but seem to co-exist without angst for Hogancamp. He reconnects with a feminine gender expression by creating a world in which he is a masculine war hero. (Even more perversely, one of Hogancamp's realistic battle photos regularly circulates on social media, falsely presented as a photograph of human men at war and invoked as an example of masculine heroism used to shame and harass transgender and gender nonconforming people for being "frivolous.")[90] Hogancamp struggles to remember how a ruler works, yet he constructs a village and intricate battle scenes. He expresses excitement about crossdressing in New York City but also has no trepidation about crossdressing in the small town where he was bashed. A middle-aged man who was once dismissed as a "hermit" just "playing with dolls in a doll village," Hogancamp is now considered an artist and has created a way to connect with "other brain-injured people."[91] Rather than connecting Hogancamp with people who understand him, however, it has given people with TBIs permission to "create their own world" that they, too, can occupy in isolation.[92]

These apparent contradictions might invite Hogancamp into another world, should he desire it: the neuroqueer community. Autistic rhetoric scholar Melanie Yergeau theorizes *neuroqueer* as a kind of "asocially perverse" motioning.[93] Corbett O'Toole elaborates that neuroqueerness often results from experiences of neurodivergence in which a person's "inside worlds" do not "match their outside presentations."[94] The term is primarily associated with autistic people, but Hogancamp's experiences of neurodivergence (TBI and PTSD) are likewise filled with "lurching" incommensurabilities of gender, sociality, craft, and place. Then again, neuroqueer communities might not wish to have Hogancamp join them. It's not clear that he understands himself as "queer," let alone as "neuroqueer"; moreover, his unreciprocated romantic interest in women might make him unwanted company.

We might think of Hogancamp as seizing the lens of the anti-idyll, albeit in a contradictory, neuroqueer way. *Marwencol* and the visual art world figure Hogancamp as an "outsider artist," an eccentric rural figure who seems queer in a quaint, throwback sort of way. As *Marwencol* director Jeff Malmberg trained his cameras on this odd figure in upstate New York, he told a story with many of the same social circumstances that are hallmarks of anti-idyllic filmmaking. Yet Hogancamp also had a lens. More urbane artists might condescend to Hogancamp and the artistic skills that he seems to have stumbled on to through patience and obsession, but Hogancamp's work as a photographer is skilled and focused, with a precise eye for world-making.[95] The film is split between the world of Marwencol and the world of its creator, but Hogancamp's persistent vision prevents *the film* from fully embracing an anti-idyllic approach to its subject matter. *Marwencol* does not quite tell the story of a city dweller entering a strange rural world, nor does it closely adhere to the story of a neurotypical person entering the internal world of a person with a mental disability—two pathologizing narratives that share a common structure. *Marwencol* does both—but also neither.

My first encounter with the anti-idyll was through the gaze of a New Yorker in a white, working-class Hudson River Valley community—not *Marwencol*, but Richard Dugdale's 1877 proto-eugenic family study, *The Jukes*, which I read for my college thesis. Raised in the rolling hills of the Missouri Ozarks and the woods of northern Wisconsin, New York State was worlds away. I had never sought out the anti-idyll; in the eugenic tales of hovel families, I encountered distorted glimpses of rural social formations that obliquely resembled those with which I was familiar—formations that were much more complicated than metronormative queer narratives allowed. Yet through the lens of the anti-idyll, these social formations were made alien; they were used to justify involuntary institutionalization and forced sterilization, to justify settler colonialism and to make false claim to the innate superiority of the "white race."

By countering the anti-idyll with the mundane and the material, and by holding space for the complexity of the people, places, and social dynamics rendered through it, I have sought to analyze anti-idyllic optics without assenting to their ways of looking. *Peculiar Places* has traced the anti-idyllic lens from its nationalization in the 1910s to its apex in the 1970s and its lingering remnants in the 1990s. The anti-idyll's cultural manifestations range from popular science to horror films, and from documentary film and photography to government poverty programs, and far beyond. It can be deployed in quite singular scenarios—to make sense of revelations that a nearby farmer has a gruesome collection of human relics made of one's neighbors, for example—or in much more common ones. As this analysis unsettles normative appeals to the inherent virtue and health of white rural life, these stories affirm how deeply interdependent gender, sexuality, disability, class, and race are—and how fraught those interdependencies can be, particularly on the spatial and social margins.

ACKNOWLEDGMENTS

This book, like all books, is only possible because of intellectually, socially, and materially interdependent networks of support. I offer here a humble gesture to some of those who nourished me.

First, I thank my dissertation advisors, Roderick Ferguson, Regina Kunzel, and Kevin Murphy, and my committee members, Jennifer Gunn and Omise'eke Natasha Tinsley. I could not ask for more intellectually generous and caring mentors, and I feel extraordinarily fortunate to have worked with them. I appreciate the support of Colin Johnson, as well as the mentorship of Pete Daniels and Katherine Ott at the National Museum of American History. I'm also deeply grateful to Douglas Baynton, Adria Imada, Alison Kafer, Molly McGarry, and Susan Schweik for workshopping an early draft of my manuscript in 2016. I find myself returning to my workshop notes regularly, and this book is considerably improved thanks to their astute guidance and nourishing conversation.

Many friends and colleagues have read drafts of chapters along the way. I thank Charlotte Karem Albrecht, Elizabeth Ault (who also answered countless questions about publishing and functioned as my "shadow editor" at times), Emily Smith Beitiks, Pamela Butler, Karisa Butler-Wall, Krystal Cleary, Ari Eisenberg, Megan Faragher, Michael David Franklin, Perla Guerrero, Charles Hughes, Karissa Isaacs, Doug Jensen, Rushaan Kumar, Cathryn Josefina Merla-Watson, Ryan Murphy, Karla M. Padrón, Juliana Hu Pegues, Jesús Estrada Perez, Rebecah Pulsifer, Thomas X. Sarmiento, Maia Surdam, Jasmine Tang, and Jess Waggoner. Thank you especially to Karla and Rushaan for their support over the difficult last months.

At the University of Chicago Press, I thank my editors, Timothy Mennel and the late Douglas Mitchell, as well as Susannah Marie Engstrom. I'm indebted to wise comments from John Howard and an anonymous reader.

I am fortunate to have had excellent research support by Amanda Eke, Elizabeth Seeley, and, in particular, June Wayee Chau. I thank Robert Bogdan and Scott Hassett for sharing their time and research materials with me, Cathy Hannabach for indexing, and Erika Clowes for weekly writing support. I am indebted to many librarians and archivists as well as university staff members and countless others.

This project has benefited from generous institutional support. It was made possible through the Jacob K. Javits Doctoral Fellowship, American Philosophical Society Library Research Grant, Lyndon B. Johnson Presidential Library Grant, Smithsonian Institution Predoctoral Fellowship, ACLS New Faculty Fellowship, University of California Humanities Research Institute Junior Faculty Manuscript Workshop Grant, and Hellman Family Fellowship, in addition to support from the University of California, Davis. I'm very grateful to my colleagues at the NEH Summer Institute on "Global Histories of Disability," led by the incomparable Sara Scalenghe, for a month of stimulating conversation.

I am so fortunate to be surrounded by genuinely supportive colleagues at UC Davis. I'm grateful for the mentorship of Caren Kaplan and Julie Sze, and support from Javier Arbona, Charlotte Biltekoff, Jemma DeCristo, Anjali Nath, Eric Smoodin, Carolyn Thomas, and Grace Wang, as well as Angie Chabram, Ofelia Cuevas, Elizabeth Freeman, Kathleen Frederickson, Sara Giordano, Hsuan Hsu, Rana Jaleel, Lisa Pruitt, Julie Wyman, and Susy Zepeda. I am appreciative to Cathy Kudlick for laying the disability studies groundwork that allows my work and presence at Davis.

I thank my parents, Roy and Joyce, my sister, Sara, and Chayse, Kaylee, and Sawyer. My abiding friendship with Karla M. Padrón has been a source of sustenance even across thousands of miles. And most of all, I am grateful to Tristan Poehlmann.

NOTES

INTRODUCTION

1. *Brother's Keeper.*

2. *Making the San Fernando Valley*, 11.

3. Jeremy Egner, "'X-Files' Writers Recall the Show's Most Disturbing Episode," *New York Times*, October 30, 2015, https://www.nytimes.com/2015/10/30/arts/television/the-x-files-home-scary-tv.html.

4. *Face to Face with Connie Chung.*

5. Gonzalez, "Delbert Takes Manhattan—Big City Holds Little Charm for the Wards of Munnsville," *SHA*, September 27, 1992; McKenna, "Truth Behind 'Brother's Keeper,'" F4.

6. Stack, "'Brother's Keeper's' True Confessions," C4.

7. Dick Case, "On the Farm, Ward Boys Shrug off the 'Fuss,'" *SHA*, February 16, 1992, G1; Bogdan, "Simple Farmer," 315; chapter six.

8. Jina B. Kim, "Toward a Crip-of-Color Critique: Thinking with Minich's 'Enabling Whom?,'" *Lateral* 6, no. 1 (Spring 2017).

9. Bell and Gill Valentine, quoted in Bell, "Anti-Idyll," 94; Mitchell, *Biopolitics of Disability*, 29.

10. Bell, "Anti-Idyll."

11. Gordon, *Ghostly Matters*, 3.

12. "Body Shame, Body Pride," 264.

13. "Body Shame, Body Pride," 263.

14. Cacho, *Social Death*, 26.

15. Kolbert, "Dairy Town Doubts," A1.

16. Commentary, *Brother's Keeper*; Howe, "True Crime, Artful Drama," 42; Sarah Stegall, "Family Plot," Munchkyn.com, January 25, 2016 [1996], http://munchkyn.com/tv-reviews/the-x-files-home/.

17. Schneider, "Blood Secrets."

18. McKenna, "Truth Behind 'Brother's Keeper,'" F4; Schneider, "Blood Secrets."

19. Weiss, "Brothers Grim."

20. Gordon, *Ghostly Matters,* 4.

21. Rogers and Merrill, *Vale of Siddem*, 38.

22. In contrast to the very precise sexual and subcultural meanings "queer" held in prewar New York, as described by George Chauncey, in regions across the rural United

States, "queer" was used in a much more capacious way through the 1960s and sometimes beyond. *Gay New York*, 14–15; 19; Howard, *Men Like That*, xvi. By the early twenty-first century, "queer" functioned both as an umbrella term for anyone in the LGBTQIA+ community and as a name for an antinormative politics.

23. Queer functioned as a "nebulous eccentricity" until the early 1960s. *Men Like That*, xvi.

24. Somerville, *Queering the Color Line*; Rogers and Merrill, *Vale of Siddem*, 35–36.

25. Rogers and Merrill, *Vale of Siddem*, 36.

26. "Out of Sorts," *feminist killjoys*, October 15, 2014, http://feministkilljoys .com/2014/10/15/out-of-sorts/.

27. *Queer Limit of Black Memory*, 13–16.

28. Herring, *Another Country*, 8.

29. On how rural is defined through its urban opposite: Herring, *Another Country*, 13; Johnson, Gilley, and Gray, *Queering the Countryside*, 12. On "metronormativity": Halberstam, *Queer Time and Place*, 36–37; Herring, *Another Country*, 14–17. On queerness and the suburbs: Tongson, *Relocations*. Regarding the significance of "the region" for scholarship on queer diaspora: Gopinath, *Unruly Visions*, 5. On rural queer studies: Howard, *Men Like That*; Ferguson, "Sissies at the Picnic," 188–196; Johnson, *Just Queer Folks*; Weston, "Get Thee to a Big City"; Johnson, *Sweet Tea*.

30. Manalansan et al., "Queering the Middle," 4.

31. Ferguson, *Aberrations in Black*, 10. On the state and social regulation of urban people of color: Carby, "Policing the Black Woman's Body"; Mumford, *Interzones*; Shah, *Contagious Divides*; Yu, *Thinking Orientals*, 49–50.

32. Roosevelt, "Special Message," 10.

33. Lovett, *Conceiving the Future*, 8, 89–91; Casey, *A New Heartland*, 4.

34. Casey, *New Heartland*.

35. Wald, *Nature of California*, 5, 4.

36. Harris, "Whiteness as Property," 1734.

37. Harris, "Whiteness as Property," 1721; Lipsitz, "Possessive Investment in Whiteness," 371.

38. DuBois, *Black Reconstruction*, 700–701.

39. Shah, *Stranger Intimacy* 267.

40. Shah, *Stranger Intimacy*, 6; Cohen, "Deviance as Resistance," 29.

41. Miranda, "Extermination of the *Joyas*"; Driskill, *Asegi Stories*.

42. Piatote, *Domestic Subjects*, 2; Rifkin, *When Did Indians Become Straight?*, 152–153.

43. Ferguson, *Aberrations in Black*, 13.

44. Mitchell, *Lie of the Land*; Williams, *Country and the City*.

45. Ferguson, *Aberrations in Black*, 13.

46. Shah, *Stranger Intimacy*, 90, 124.

47. Shah, *Stranger Intimacy*, 8.

48. Albrecht, "An Archive of Difference," 136.

49. Lydia X. Z. Brown, "Legal Ableism, Interrupted: Developing Tort Law and Policy Alternatives to Wrongful Birth and Wrongful Life Claims," *Disability Studies Quarterly* 38, no. 2 (2018), http://dsq-sds.org/article/view/6207/4903.

50. For example: Jarman, "Dismembering the Lynch Mob," 89–107; Akemi Nishida in "Developing and Reflecting on a Black Disability Studies Pedagogy: Work from the

National Black Disability Coalition," *Disability Studies Quarterly* 35, no. 2 (2015), http://dsq-sds.org/article/view/4637/3933; Downs, *Sick from Freedom.*

51. Bailey and Mobley, "Work in the Intersections"; Talila A. Lewis, "Longmore Lecture: Context, Clarity, & Grounding," *Talila A. Lewis Blog,* March 5, 2019, talilalewis.com/blog/longmore-lecture-context-clarity-grounding; Baynton, "Disability and the Justification of Inequality in American History," in *New Disability History,* 33–57.

52. McRuer, *Crip Theory,* 8.

53. Brown, "Legal Ableism, Interrupted."

54. Harris, "Whiteness as Property," 1749.

55. As Tiffany Willoughby-Herard contends, writing about the settler-colonial nation of South Africa, *The Poor White Study* unintentionally "revealed that the ideology of white supremacy could not guarantee white success." *Waste of a White Skin,* 32.

56. Lange and Taylor, *An American Exodus: A Record of Human Erosion in the Thirties* (New Haven, CT: Yale University Press, 1939), 135.

57. "OVERVIEW: The AAY Target Population and Its Characteristics," undated, Box 10, DKP.

58. Dunne, "Humboldt Murders," 49.

59. DuBois, *Black Reconstruction*; Lye, *America's Asia,* 142.

60. Willoughby-Herard, *Waste of a White Skin,* 8.

61. Clare, *Exile and Pride,* 70.

62. "Thinking about the Word Crip," EliClare.com, October 15, 2009, http://eliclare.com/poems/thinking-about-the-word-crip; refer also to Leroy F. Moore Jr., "Krip-Hop Nation, Is Moore than Music," *Wordgathering* 22 (2009), http://www.wordgathering.com/past_issues/issue22/essays/moore2.html.

63. On crip as a politicized term that emerged from disability communities: Clare, "Thinking about the Word Crip"; Hamraie, *Building Access,* 12; Longmore and Umansky, "Introduction," in *New Disability History,* 2. On crip theory as an academic field of analysis: Sandahl, "Queer and Crip Identities"; McRuer, *Crip Theory*; Kafer, *Feminist Queer Crip.*

64. Burch and Patterson, "Not Just Any Body," 130.

65. Longmore and Umansky, *New Disability History*; Kudlick, *Reflections*; Serlin, *Replaceable You*; Burch and Joyner, *Unspeakable*; Burch, "Disorderly Pasts"; Boster, *Slavery and Disability*; Virdi, "Prevention and Conservation"; Rose, *No Right to Be Idle*; Jennings, *Out of the Horrors of War.*

66. Berne et al., "Disability Justice—A Working Draft," 15. On crip of color critique, see Kim, "Toward a Crip-of-Color Critique."

67. Sandahl, "Queer and Crip Identities," 25–56; Schalk, *Bodyminds Reimagined*; Hamraie, *Building Access,* 12; Siebers, *Disability Theory,* 25–33; Berne et al., "Disability Justice," 15; Erevelles, *Disability and Difference,* 129.

68. Minich, "Enabling Whom?"

69. Bailey and Mobley, "Work in the Intersections," 7.

70. Johnson and McRuer, "Cripistemologies," 129.

71. Burch and Patterson, "Not Just Any Body," 130.

72. Kafer, *Feminist Queer Crip,* 15.

73. Shah, *Stranger Intimacy,* 8.

74. Shah, *Stranger Intimacy,* 8.

75. Cohen, "Punks, Bulldaggers, and Welfare Queens," 441.

76. Stryker, "(De)Subjugated Knowledges," 7.

77. My use of "pry bar" is inspired by Eli Clare's usage. In *Brilliant Imperfection*, Clare's pry bar poses questions to institutional case studies (114), his imagination (115), and his bodymind (180).

78. Sandahl, "Queer and Crip Identities," 37.

79. On cure: Clare, *Brilliant Imperfection*. On pain: Patsavas, "Recovering a Cripistemology of Pain," 203-218.

80. Brandon Teena, for example, one of the subjects of chapter six, apparently told friends and girlfriends that he was a "'morphodite," presumably a nonstandard pronunciation of "hermaphrodite." That term has since been replaced by the less offensive "intersex." There is no evidence that Brandon was intersex, but it is not uncommon for non-intersex trans people—particularly before widespread Internet access—to learn about intersex conditions and surmise that that could explain their sense of gender dissonance. Some non-intersex trans people have made false claims to being intersex as a mistaken attempt to avoid stigma. These claims are widely upsetting to intersex people, both because of the ignorance they manifest and because they elide the most harmful aspect of being intersex, which is the "shame, secrecy, [and] attempts at eugenicist elimination" (through nonconsensual operations on infants). Emi Koyama, "Is 'Gender Identity Disorder' an Intersex Condition?," Intersex Initiative, [May 14, 2006], http://intersexinitiative.org/articles/gid.html; Costello, "Intersex and Trans* Communities," 105-107.

81. On the necessity of understanding the "experience of the addicted body" through disability studies perspectives: geoff, "Destabilizing Disability," 67.

82. In *Race Rebels*, Robin D. G. Kelley contends that labor history need not only address "engaged workplace struggles" but also the cultural terrain of "identity, dignity and fun" (3). If "we regard most work as alienating," Kelley argues, particularly under conditions of racist and sexist oppression, then acts that were interpreted by racist Southern ideology as "ineptitude, laziness, shiftlessness, and immorality" might instead be considered acts of workplace resistance (21-22).

83. Gordon, *Ghostly Matters*, 5; Williams, *Alchemy of Race and Rights*, 10.

84. Mitchell and Snyder, *Biopolitics of Disability*, 29.

85. Kim, "Toward a Crip of Color Critique."

86. Perske, "Crimes They Did Not Commit," 63; Yar and Rafter, "Justice for the Disabled," 802. Ward was even used as a "textbook case" to teach police "how to question people with mental disabilities." Mike Dickinson, "Ward Trial Becomes Textbook Case," *SPS*, April 13, 1991.

87. Cameron, "When Strangers Bring Cameras," 412.

88. Bell, "Anti-Idyll," 95, italics in original. The "armchair countryside" that Bell refers to was coined by Michael Bunce in 1994 in the context of the English countryside. Bell contends that the more commonly idealized rural formations in the United States are the small town, the farm, and the colonial "frontier life" of the US West.

89. Williams, *Country and the City*, 165.

90. Wolfe, "Settler Colonialism," 392.

91. DuBois, *Black Reconstruction*, 130.

92. I thank Roderick Ferguson for this insight. Also: Creadick, "Banjo Boy," 64.

93. Cameron, "When Strangers Bring Cameras," 412.

94. Klotter, "Black South and White Appalachia."

95. Quoted in Wray, *Not Quite White*, 33.

96. Reynolds, "White Trash in Your Face," 360.

97. Sedgwick, *Epistemology of the Closet*, 24; Holmes, "What's the Tea," 55-56.

98. Ruby, review of "Appalachia Portraits," 339.

99. Jacoby, *Crimes Against Nature*, xvi, 3-4.

100. *Shocking Truth*.

101. Bliss, "Tell Gein's Crime Motive," 1.

102. Harrington, *Other America*, 16.

103. Clover, *Chain Saws*, 124-137.

CHAPTER 1

1. J. R. Ross, *Bartlett-Flint Pedigree*, September 1912, Microfilm Roll 1769581, Box 52, ERO.

2. Maude R. Williams, *Lottie Kickland*, c. 1914, Microfilm Roll 1822182, Box 56, ERO.

3. H. B. Webster, *Grindle-Bowden Family*, 1915, Box 5, Series VIII, ERO.

4. Harry W. Crane, "Family History: Burns Carmon Neely," December 1, 1915, Microfilm Roll 1822198, Box 57, ERO.

5. Sadie Myers, *Report of Survey of Salt Lake, Cache, and Sanpete Counties*, July 1912, Box 4, Series VIII, ERO.

6. On the influence of the Kallikaks in popular culture: Smith, *Minds Made Feeble*; Leila Zenderland, "Parable of The Kallikak Family," in *Mental Retardation in America*; Christina R. Belcher, "Turning Backward: The Kallikaks and Rural Programming in the 1970s" (presentation, American Studies Association, Los Angeles, CA, November 8, 2014).

7. Roberts, *Killing the Black Body*, 61.

8. Roberts, *Killing the Black Body*, 9.

9. Although the original face of eugenic sterilization laws was the feebleminded white woman in the 1900s-1910s, coercive sterilization—often at the hands of agencies like the Department of Health, Education, and Welfare or the Bureau of Indian Affairs—dramatically increased in the 1920s-1930s and targeted women of color. On periodization: Reilly, *Surgical Solution*; Roberts, *Fatal Invention*, 47-49. On racial dynamics and state programs of sterilization: Lawrence, "Indian Health Service"; Stern, *Eugenic Nation*, 189-210; Davis, *Women, Race and Class*; Novak et al., "Disproportionate Sterilization of Latinos"; Nelson, *Women of Color*.

10. Charles B. Davenport, "Importance of Eugenical Field Work for the State of Rhode Island," c. 1913, Box 26, Series I, CBD.

11. Rafter, *White Trash*, 2.

12. Many of these studies were collected and published in Rafter, *White Trash*.

13. Reed, *Trix Family: A Study of a Defective Family in a Rural Community*, 1916, Series VIII, ERO.

14. Park and Burgess, *The City: Suggestions for Investigation of Human Behavior in the Urban Environment* (Chicago and London: University of Chicago Press, 1925), 385.

15. Lovett, *Conceiving the Future*.

16. Roosevelt, *Strenuous Life*.

17. Fiske, *Challenge of the Country*, 45.

18. Isaac, *American Tropics*, 77.

19. Fiske, *Challenge of the Country*, 47.

20. Bederman, *Manliness and Civilization*, 200–206. Roosevelt was concerned that falling white birthrates represented, in Bederman's words, the "ultimate racial nightmare—impotent, decadent manhood" (200).

21. On the "fracturing of whiteness" and its reconsolidation in the 1920s: Jacobson, *Whiteness of a Different Color*, 7–8.

22. Burch and Patterson, "Not Just Any Body," 124.

23. Snyder and Mitchell, *Cultural Locations of Disability*, x.

24. Gill, *Already Doing It*, 147.

25. Somerville, *Queering the Color Line*, 31.

26. Researchers were careful to make classed and racialized distinctions between "perversion," which they saw as a disease that might afflict the upper classes, and "perversity," which they interpreted as either willful or mindless acts of vice committed by people who were racially or economically marginalized. Prince, "Sexual Perversion or Vice?"; Terry, *American Obsession*, 47–49.

27. By reading against the grain of colonial archives, literature, and film, postcolonial scholars from the Subaltern Studies Group to queer diasporic scholars like Gayatri Gopinath present models for how to study "non-metropolitan" spaces in the sense of spaces outside the metropole. Gopinath, *Impossible Desires*; Arondekar, "Without a Trace"; Guha, *Peasant Insurgency*.

28. Siebers, *Disability Aesthetics*, 27.

29. Kim, "Toward a Crip-of-Color Critique."

30. The phrase "ingenuity of living" comes from Mitchell and Snyder, *Biopolitics of Disability*, 29.

31. Harris, "Whiteness as Property."

32. Carlson, *The Unfit*, 162–172.

33. "Medical Notes," 112–113.

34. Round, "Introduction," viii.

35. Abramowitz, "Family Ethic," 15–26.

36. Stanley, *From Bondage to Contract*.

37. Dugdale, *Jukes*, 60.

38. Dugdale, *Jukes*, 60.

39. Hartman, *Scenes of Subjection*; Stanley, *Bondage to Contract*; Katz, *Shadow of the Poorhouse*.

40. "Current Literature," *Galaxy: An Illustrated Magazine of Entertaining Reading* 24, no. 4 (October 1877): 575.

41. Gelb, "Not Simply Bad," 361.

42. Rafter, *White Trash*.

43. Harrigan, "Rural New England," 583.

44. Hyde, "Impending Paganism"; Harrigan, "A Remote Village," 577–587; Sanborn, "A Farming Community."

45. Harrigan, "A Remote Village," 583. On how modernist poetry engaged with this "anti-rural strain" of thought: Farland, "Modernist Versions of Pastoral."

46. Hartt, "Its Revival"; Hartt, "Its Condition."

47. On the "hovel type," Laughlin, "Proposed Program of Sterilization," 140.

48. Davenport, "Nams."

49. Harry H. Laughlin, *Eugenics Record Office*, Report (Cold Spring Harbor, NY: Eugenics Record Office, June 1913): 485–486.

50. Laughlin, "Report," 18; Davenport, "Official Records in the History of the E. R. O.," Series I, CBD.

51. Davenport, "Importance of Eugenical Field Work for the State of Rhode Island," c. 1913, Series I, CBD.

52. "Directions for the Guidance of Field Workers," n.d., Box 116, Series II, CBD.

53. Goddard to Davenport, March 15, 1909, Series I, CBD.

54. White, "Conclusion," 61.

55. Davenport, "Eugenics in America," n.d., cited in Bix, "Experiences and Voices," 662n52; Goddard to Davenport, March 15, 1909.

56. Davenport, "Eugenics in America."

57. Saidee Devitt to A. C. Rogers, September 6, 1913, Box 109.H.13.8 (F), Faribault State School and Hospital, State Archives, Minnesota Historical Society (MHS).

58. English, *Unnatural Selections,* 143.

59. Fieldworkers were described as a "sort of sociological detectives" in "The Book of the Month: The Kallikak Family," *Hearst's Magazine* 23, no. 2 (February 1913): 329–331.

60. U.S. Public Health Service and Bureau of Education, *Sex Education*; "Kallikaks Moved to Harrisburg."

61. Smith, *Minds Made Feeble,* 62–64; H. W. H., "Restricted Ambition," 858; Belcher, "Turning Backward."

62. K. M. G., "Dwellers in the Vale of Siddem," *Social Hygiene* 6, no. 4 (October 1920): 583–584.

63. Harry W. Crane, Notes, April 8, 1916, Microfilm Roll 1822198, ERO.

64. Davenport, "Eugenical Field Work."

65. Goddard, *Kallikak Family*; Randolph, "Canton Kallikaks," 279–281; Kansas Commission, *Kallikaks of Kansas.*

66. Estabrook, "Country Slums."

67. Estabrook, "Country Slums," 9.

68. Myers, *Survey of Salt Lake.*

69. Gesell, "Thousand Souls," 11.

70. Schweik, *The Ugly Laws,* 73.

71. Gesell, "Thousand Souls," 12–13.

72. Gesell, "Thousand Souls," 11–12.

73. Gesell, "Thousand Souls," 11.

74. Harris, "Arnold Gesell's Progressive Vision," 324, 326.

75. Roosevelt, *Strenuous Life,* 8.

76. Trent, *Inventing the Feeble Mind,* 141; Popenoe, "Heredity and Behavior," 4.

77. Kite, "The 'Pineys,'" 7.

78. Groves, "Feeble-Minded."

79. Zenderland, *Measuring Minds.*

80. Carey, *Margins of Citizenship,* 63; Gould, *Mismeasure of Man*; Ladd-Taylor, "'Sociological Advantages,'" in *Mental Retardation in America,* 286–287; Roberts, *Fatal Invention,* 39–40.

81. Hodson, "What Minnesota Has Done."

82. The definition of feeblemindedness comes from the Association of Medical Officers of American Institutions for Idiotic and Feeble-Minded Persons and American Association for the Study of the Feeble-Minded, "Report of Committee on Classification of Feeble-minded," *Journal of Psycho-asthenics* 15, no. 1 (1910): 61. The quoted concerns are by Robinson, "State Supervision."

83. R. M. Phelps to John Kuhlmann, "Comments on Feeblemindedness," December 6, 1923, Box 1: 107.G.18.1 (B), Psychological Services Bureau, Public Welfare Department, MHS.

84. Phelps to Kuhlmann, "Comments on Feeblemindedness."

85. Kline, *Building a Better Race*, 29.

86. Olson, "Psychopathic Laboratory."

87. Sadler, *Race Decadence*, 266–267.

88. Reed, *Trix Family*.

89. *Minnie D'Agosta*, 1913, Box 1, Series VII, ERO.

90. Davenport to Mrs. E. H. Harriman, February 5, 1916, Box 45, Series I, CBD.

91. Kempton and Kahn, 1991; Wilkerson, "Sex Radicalism."

92. Goddard to Davenport, July 4, 1910, Box 41, Series I, CBD.

93. Gavisk et al., *Mental Defectives in Indiana*. Emphasis in the original.

94. Contributors' Club, "Heritages of the Lord," 142–143.

95. Mulder, *Bram*, 95.

96. Quillen, "Where the Fence."

97. Ernest Bicknell, "Care of the Adult Feeble Minded," in *Proceedings of the Fourth Minnesota State Conference of Charities and Corrections* (St. Paul, MN: Pioneer Press Company, 1895), 45.

98. Anna Peterson, *Bertha Yorski*, November 14, 1913, Box 4, Series VIII, ERO.

99. John Cramer, "Va. Indians Still Hunt Federal Recognition," *Roanoke Times*, January 6, https://roanoke.com/archive/va-indians-still-hunt-federal-recognition/article_5b8c9ee2-0bd3-5013-9f81-0b5f8898e513.html. Also: Gonzales et al., "Eugenics as Indian Removal."

100. Estabrook and McDougle, *Mongrel Virginians*, 199.

101. Zenderland, *Measuring Minds*, 311–320; Noll, *Feeble-Minded in Our Midst*, 90.

102. English, *Unnatural Selections*, 45–46.

103. Carpenter, "Feebleminded and Pauper Negroes"; Sadler, *Race Decadence*, 233.

104. Hodson, "What Minnesota Has Done," 211; W. D. L., "Being a Pauper Idiot: How Kentucky Has Changed Her Century-Old System of Pensioning the Feebleminded," *The Survey* 40, no. 1 (April 6, 1918): 11–12.

105. Gesell, "Thousand Souls," 11.

106. On "temperamental peculiarity": Knox, "Tests for Mental Defects," 123. On loafing: Merrill, "Minnesota's Heritage," 564.

107. Jordan, *Heredity of Richard Roe*, 102, 104.

CHAPTER 2

1. According to the Agricultural Adjustment Administration (AAA), the poorest areas were the Great Lakes cutover and the "Appalachian-Ozarks" region. Saloutos, *American Farmer*, 153.

2. "Round Table Transcript" (1952), 43–44, Box 10, JVP.

3. What I call the "FSA" went by three different names: Resettlement Administration (RA; 1935–1937), Farm Security Administration (1937–1942), and Office of War Information (1942–1943).

4. Levine, "Historian and the Icon," 28; Smith, *Making the Modern*, 328; Retman, *Real Folks*.

5. "Still Photography," c. 1937, Box 6, Series II, RES.

6. "Still Photography." On the forces that shaped FSA photography: Stange, "Record Itself"; and Finnegan, *Picturing Poverty*.

7. Shah, *Stranger Intimacy*, 6.

8. Kozol, "Madonnas of the Fields," 10–13; Hall et al., *Like a Family.*

9. Gordon, "Dorothea Lange," 699; Daniel, "Transformation," 237.

10. Melosh, *Engendering Culture*, 53–81; Wyman, "Affirming Whiteness."

11. On rehabilitation as both medical science and cultural process: Linker, *War's Waste*, 10; McRuer, *Crip Theory*, 110–116; Serlin, *Replaceable You*, 10.

12. Breeden, "Disease as a Factor," 11–12.

13. On rural rehabilitation programs as "nationalizing work": Lye, *America's Asia*, 164–165. As Lawrie contends, US rehabilitation efforts after World War I characterized disabled Black veterans as "congenital racial cripples" who were therefore unable to be rehabilitated. "'Salvaging the Negro,'" 330.

14. Stiker, *History of Disability*, 128; McRuer, *Crip Theory*, 111–112.

15. Hariman and Lucaites, *No Caption Needed*, 58; Kozol, "Madonnas of the Fields"; Murphy, "Picture/Story."

16. Watson and Martin, "The Miss America Pageant."

17. Stryker to Vachon, March 18, 1942, Correspondence with John Vachon, RES.

18. Lipsitz, *Possessive Investment in Whiteness*; Lange and Taylor, *An American Exodus*, 135.

19. Approximately one-fifth of RA/FSA photographs depicted people who were on relief or otherwise "useful for agency promotion efforts." Natanson, *Black Image*, 59–60.

20. As Currell contends in "Eugenic National Housekeeping," FSA photographers often "relied on welfare workers and a network of other local officials" to "gain access to the people they wanted to capture" (490).

21. Post to Stryker, May 15, 1940, RES.

22. Serlin, *Replaceable You.*

23. Interview by Suzanne Riess, July 3, 1968 (conducted 1960–1961), Regional Oral History Office, Bancroft Library, University of California, Berkeley, https://archive.org /details/cabeuroh_000012.

24. Stein, "Peculiar Grace," 75, 73.

25. Serlin, *Replaceable You.*

26. Spirn, *Daring to Look*, 11.

27. "Log House and White Rural Nonfarm Family," July 9, 1939, 1, Box 7, HWO.

28. "From Natchitoches, La," 1940, Correspondence with Marion Post Wolcott, RES.

29. "Journal entry from Neosho, Missouri," February 4, 1942, Box 10, JV.

30. Currell, "Eugenic National Housekeeping," 510.

31. "Spooner Hospital Purchased for Home for Aged," *Baudette Region*, October 1, 1937. Created in 1936, OAA differed significantly from Old Age Insurance (OAI), which is closer to Social Security as we know it today. OAA was not funded by the Social Security payroll tax and was not limited to people who worked in "qualifying"—deeply racialized and gendered—fields. Gordon, *Pitied but Not Entitled*, 282–284.

32. The Beltrami Island Project was launched in 1934 by the Land Policy Section of the AAA, then managed by the Minnesota Rural Rehabilitation Corporation (MRRC), and later by the RA. Wasson, "Grubstake Plan."

33. Canady, *Straight State*, 93.

34. Shah, *Stranger Intimacy*, 267, 268.

35. Child, *Holding Our World Together*, 81; Mittelholtz and Graves, *Historical Review*, 28–40.

36. Mittelholtz and Graves, *Historical Review*, 38.

37. Anton Parieda—also spelled Antoine Paradais—staked a claim in or near the town of Faunce in 1905, shortly after the state of Minnesota took that land from Red Lake Ojibwe. R. W. Murchie, E. L. Kirkpatrick, C. R. Wasson, rough draft of "Beltrami Island, Minnesota," bulletin (Agricultural Experiment Station, University of Minnesota: May 1937), Box 1, Entry 267, RG 83, Chicago NARA.

38. The FSA sought to fence off or compel Red Lake Ojibwe to sell allotments within the proposed area of the Wildlife Refuge. Collier to Rex Tugwell, December 9, 1936; and Nowell to Tugwell, January 8, 1937, Box 401, entry 71, RG 96, Archives II.

39. MRRC, "Certification of Incorporation," 1935, MRRC, MHS.

40. Fred Newhouse, "Minnesota's Last Frontier (a case study of families in a submarginal area)," c. 1937, 34, Box 1, Entry 267, RG 83, Chicago NARA.

41. Shah, *Contagious Divides*, 78.

42. McRuer, *Crip Theory*, 90–95.

43. Longmore and Goldberger, "League of the Physically Handicapped," 892; Snyder and Mitchell, *Cultural Locations of Disability*, x.

44. Shah, "Ordinary Americans"; Shah, "Policing Privacy"; Boag, *Same-Sex Affairs*, 35–36.

45. Shah theorizes the normalization of white men involved with men of color in *Stranger Intimacy*, 146. On claims that same-sex intercourse in bunkhouses was merely "situational," refer to Parker, *Casual Laborer*, 73–74.

46. Theodore J. Karamanski, *Deep Woods Frontier: A History of Logging in Northern Michigan* (Detroit: Wayne State University Press, 1989), 107–112; Tomczik, "Lumberjack Work Culture."

47. Whittles, *Lumberjack Sky Pilot*, 100.

48. Malloch, "Love of a Man," 12–13.

49. Kunzel, *Criminal Intimacy*, 2–4; Boag, *Same-Sex Affairs*, 21–35.

50. Pérez, *Taste for Brown Bodies*, 3, 10.

51. The figure of the lumberjack, like the sailor, soldier, and cowboy, fuses mythologized national masculinity with idealized homoerotic masculinity.

52. Serlin, *Replaceable You*, 40.

53. Kozol, "Madonnas of the Fields," 2.

54. Nowell, "Resettlement Administration Program," 216.

55. The published report that seems to be referring directly to the Pioneers' Home is Farm Security Administration, *Beltrami Island Farms*, 5; E. L. Kirkpatrick and Carl F. Kraenzel, *"Rural Relief in Relation to Rehabilitation: Cut-Over Problem Area Survey,"* Final Report (c. 1935), 74, Box 1, Entry 153, RG 83, Archives II; E. L. Kirkpatrick and C. F. Kraenzel, "The Lakes States Cut-Over Area: Beltrami County, *Minnesota"* (Federal Emergency Relief Administration, December 5, 1934) 3, Box 1, Entry 155, RG 83, Archives II.

56. Kirkpatrick and Kraenzel, *"Beltrami County,"* 3.

57. On New Deal housekeeping programs: Klein and Boris, "Making of Home Care," 298–300.

58. Newhouse, "Minnesota's Last Frontier"; Noyes, "Delano Red Cross Nurses," 1120.

59. Nowell, "Experience of Resettlement Administration," 216.

60. Murchie and Wasson, *Beltrami Island*, 15. Social Security policies in the 1930s—which allowed people to receive old-age assistance grants only if they did *not* live in public homes—resulted in the closure of numerous almshouses and county poor farms, and Lake of the Woods County had struggled to maintain county poor relief before that. McClure, *More Than a Roof*, 165, 157.

61. A. C. Hanson to Ernest Lundeen, March 3, 1937, Box 401, Entry 71, RG 96, Archives II; Board of Directors of the Minnesota Rural Rehabilitation Corporation, "Board Meeting Notes," July 20, 1935, MRRC.

62. Kirkpatrick and Kraenzel, *"Problem Area Survey,"* 77; Murchie and Wasson, *Beltrami Island*, 34.

63. Underwood, *Log of a Logger*, 30.

64. Lequier, "Lumber Jacks"; Mitchell, "Timber Strikes of 1937," 274.

65. Arthur Cooley household, 1920 US Federal Census, Morris, Beltrami County, MN, accessed via Ancestry.com, Library Edition.

66. Haynes, "Timber Beasts."

67. Wyman, *Lumberjack Frontier*, 33.

68. Kirkpatrick and Kraenzel, *"Beltrami County,"* 2.

69. N. S. Boardman to M. W. Torkelson, "Location of RA offices," June 26, 1937, Box 706, RG 96, Chicago NARA.

70. "Spooner Hospital Purchased."

71. The homes remained the property of the state, but if the families became self-supporting—either because a disabling illness abated, or because young children grew old enough to be productive farmworkers—the family could purchase the home outright. Murchie and Wasson, *Beltrami Island*, 41.

72. "Spooner Hospital Purchased."

73. Ethel McClure, "Re: Pioneer Nursing Home, Baudette," November 1968, Box 3, Ethel McClure Papers, MHS.

74. Mittelholtz and Graves, *Historical Review*, 103.

75. Child, *My Grandfather's Knocking Sticks*, 55.

76. Child, *My Grandfather's Knocking Sticks*, 61–66.

77. "Method of Handling Old Age Assistance in County," *Baudette Region*, February 28, 1936.

78. Northern Minnesota was home to a large Finnish immigrant community, which was known for their radical socialist politics. In 1908, a Minnesota court determined that Finnish immigrants were white because they "looked" like "common sense" notions of a white person, though Finns were a purportedly "Mongolian" race. Cameron, "Sleuthing Towards America," 18–20.

79. Beck, "Radicals in the Northwoods," 56; Mitchell, "Timber Strikes," 265. Logging in northern Minnesota was majority white, but it was not entirely white. Mixed-heritage Ojibwe lumberjacks held prominent roles in the strikes.

80. Mitchell, "Timber Strikes," 275–276.

81. Kirkpatrick and Kraenzel, *"Beltrami County,"* 16; Kirkpatrick and Kraenzel, *"Problem Area Survey,"* 31.

82. Kirkpatrick and Kraenzel, *"Beltrami County,"* 7–8.

83. Kirkpatrick and Kraenzel, *"Beltrami County,"* 16.

84. Anderson, "Beltrami Island Resettlement Project," 74.

85. Rifkin, *When Did*, 147.

86. Child, *My Grandfather's Knocking Sticks*, 25–26.

87. Child, *My Grandfather's Knocking Sticks*, 95.

88. On the "workings of domesticity": Piatote, *Domestic Subjects*, 5. On how the WPA and CCC shifted wild-rice harvesting from women's hands to men's: Child, *My Grandfather's Knocking Sticks*, 180–181.

89. Kristine L. Bradof, "Ditching of Red Lake Peatland During the Homestead Era," in *Patterned Peatlands of Minnesota*, 263–279.

90. McDowell, *Farming on the Cut-Over*.

91. Melissa L. Meyer, "Red Lake Ojibwe," in *Patterned Peatlands*, 251–261.

92. Hanson to Lundeen; Nowell to Tugwell, "LU—Big Game Fence Project LD-MN-3," January 8, 1937, Box 401, Entry 71, RG 96, Archives II.

93. In major cities, palace hotels were quite elite, though nonetheless associated with sex work and homosexuality. Whether this was the case in a town like North Platte is unclear. Groth, *Living Downtown*, 46, 239, 120, 217.

94. John Vachon to Millicent (Penny) Vachon, October 28, 1938, Box 4, JVP.

95. Vachon Penny, October 21, 1938, Box 4, JVP.

96. Vachon to Stryker, October 30, 1938.

97. Vachon to Penny, October 28, 1938.

98. Penny's concerns are often evident through John's defensive reactions to them. Vachon to Penny, November 2, 1938, Box 4, JVP.

99. Goldman, *Prostitution and Social Life*, 2–5.

100. RA, *America's Land* (Washington: Government Printing Office, September 1935), Box 12, Series III, RES; Murphy, "Picture/Story," 101.

101. Vachon to Penny, October 27, 1938, Box 4, JVP.

102. "Brant . . . ," n.d., Box 11, JVP.

103. Vachon to Stryker, October 30.

104. Vachon to Penny, October 28.

105. Vachon to Penny, October 28.

106. Goldman, *Gold Diggers*, 116.

107. Murphy, "Private Lives," 32; Goldman, *Gold Diggers*, 116–120; Boyd, *Wide-Open Town*, 83–91.

108. Rosen, *Lost Sisterhood*, 114.

109. For example, sexology had long understood lesbianism and prostitution to be interrelated "perversions." Miller, "Sexologists Examine," 71–72; 81–82. The science of sexology also informed criminal prosecution. Goldman recounts the case of a crossdressing woman in late nineteenth-century Nevada who defended her request to wear pants in public by procuring documents affirming that she "had no desire to be a prostitute," suggesting that the courts might have assumed otherwise. Goldman, *Gold Diggers*, 120.

110. Nestle, *Restricted Country*, 155.

111. For example, the styles in Faderman, *Odd Girls*; and Kennedy and Davis, *Boots of Leather*. As Genter contends, butches in the postwar era often expressed masculinity in circumspect ways: for example, wearing tailored skirt suits rather than dresses, or mixing a masculine signifier (such as a structured jacket) with a more feminine one (like a slim skirt). "Butch-Femme Fashion," 610–611.

112. Goldman, *Gold Diggers*, 76, 116.

113. Goldman, *Gold Diggers*, 118; Murphy, "Private Lives," 32–33.

114. Greene, *North Platte Canteen*, 249, quoting Larry McWilliams, who spent his boyhood in North Platte during the 1930s and 1940s.

115. Sandoz, *Old Jules*, 174–175; Fink, *Agrarian Women*, 86; Greene, *North Platte Canteen*, 153, 102.

116. Sullenger, "Criminality in Omaha."

117. Vachon to Penny, October 28; Vachon to Stryker, October 30.

118. Goldman, *Gold Diggers*, 66.

119. Vachon to Penny, October 28; Vachon to Penny, November 7, 1938, Box 4, JVP.

120. Heap, *Slumming*, 2.

121. Vachon to Penny, November 10, 1938, Box 4, JVP.

122. "Filmmaker Commentary, *Brother's Keeper.*

CHAPTER 3

1. Clover, "Her Body, Himself," 192; Sullivan, "Ed Gein."

2. Wahl, *Media Madness*, 3; Skidmore, "Good Transsexual," 272.

3. Duggan, *Sapphic Slashers*, 34.

4. Skidmore, "Ralph Kerwineo's Queer Body," 158.

5. Gordon Culver, "2C Worth," *NLP*, November 21, 1957; Walter H. Brovald, editor of the *Cadott Sentinel*, printed in "Many Letters Received from Former Residents and Others," *PS*, December 12, 1957.

6. Schreiner, "Left Hand of God," 22; Frank, "When Bad Things Happen," 208.

7. I use "psy fields" to emphasize that in the popular press of the 1950s—the focus of this chapter—disciplinary distinctions between different psychosciences were generally immaterial.

8. Price, *Mad at School*, 19. In the popular imagination, distinctions between mental illness, developmental disabilities, intellectual disabilities, learning disabilities, autism, and other types of mental disabilities are often muddy. Notably, the figure of the "mad man" or "psycho killer" of the 1950s era has transformed into an "odd loner" or "autistic killer" stereotype, though people with autism are no more likely to commit violence than anyone else. Bronner, "'Wild Child' Narratives"; Foss, "Building a Mystery"; "Violence Is Rare in Autism: When It Does Occur, Is it Sometimes Extreme?," *Journal of Psychology* 151, no. 1 (2017): 49–68; Im, "Template to Perpetrate."

9. "Portrait of a Killer," *Time*, December 2, 1957, 40; Miller and Scherschel, "House of Horror," 29. I use the term "mental disability" to avoid reproducing the sensationalism of 1950s psycho scares.

10. Clare, "Body Shame, Body Pride," 263. Also: Gayle Rubin, "Of Catamites and Kings: Reflections on Butch, Gender, and Boundaries," in *Transgender Studies Reader*, 472; Love, *Feeling Backward*, 114.

11. Phillips, *Transgender on Screen*, 106.

12. Quotations from Clover, "Her Body, Himself," 194.

13. Frank and Glied, "Assessing the Well-Being," 136.

14. Chauncey, "Postwar Sex Crime Panic," 164.

15. Caputi, "New Founding Fathers," 8; Clover, "Her Body, Himself," 192; Wood, *Hollywood from Vietnam*, 75; Hyler et al., "Homicidal Maniacs"; Allen and Nairn, "Media Depictions," 375; Cooke, *Moral Panics*, 53–54.

16. Fox and Levin, "Multiple Homicide"; Wahl, "Stop the Presses," 58.

17. Caputi, "New Founding Fathers," 2; Fox and Levin, "Multiple Homicide," 413.

18. Mingus and Zopf, "Explaining Mass Shootings," 73.

19. Paul Bowden, "Pioneers in Forensic Psychiatry," 119.

20. Cohen, "Criminal Sexual Psychopath Statute," 456.

21. Summers, "'Suitable Care,'" 84.

22. During World War II, white psychiatrists rejected Black draftees on the basis of psychopathy more often than white men. Dwyer, "Psychiatry and Race," 125–126, 140–141.

23. Freedman, "'Uncontrolled Desires,'" 98.

24. Chauncey, "Postwar Sex Crime Panic," 170.

25. On state laws for the "indefinite civil commitment" of homosexuals, Lave, "Only Yesterday," 549. On immigration laws: Canaday, *Straight State*, 214–254; Luibhéid, *Entry Denied*, 91–93.

26. Chauncey, "Postwar Sex Crime Panic," 171.

27. Miller, *Sex-Crime Panic*.

28. Whittle, "Foreword," in *Transgender Studies Reader*, xii; Susan Stryker, "(De)Subjugated Knowledges: An Introduction to Transgender Studies," in *Transgender Studies Reader*, 1–2; Kunzel, "Queer History, Mad History."

29. For example: Hale, "Tracing a Ghostly Memory"; Stone, "*Empire* Strikes Back."

30. Clare, "Body Shame, Body Pride," 265.

31. Phillips, *Transgender on Screen*, 107.

32. Chmielewski, "Silver Screen Slashers," 33.

33. Prendergast, "Rhetorics of Mental Disability," 57.

34. Metzl, *Protest Psychosis*.

35. Brekke et al., "Risks for Individuals"; Choe, Teplin, and Abram, "Perpetration of Violence."

36. Wang, *Collected Schizophrenias*, 147, 148.

37. Nakamura, *Disability of the Soul*, 114–115.

38. "Identity, Disability, and Schizophrenia," 249–251.

39. Clare, "Body Shame, Body Pride," 264.

40. "Trans, Feminism," 826.

41. Elizabeth Lunbeck, *The Psychiatric Persuasion: Knowledge, Gender, and Power in Modern America* (Princeton, NJ: Princeton University Press, 1994), 102.

42. On the explosion of interest in psychiatry and psychology after World War II: Erb, "'Have You Ever Seen,'" 47; Meyerowitz, *How Sex Changed*, 105; Genter, "Cold War Psychopath," 135, 145–146.

43. "Portrait of a Killer." On the media enacting medicalized case studies of mass murders, Price, *Mad at School*, 146; Bronner, "'Wild Child' Narratives," 35.

44. On suggestibility, Milton Miller testimony, *State of Wisconsin v. Edward Gein* (January 6, 1958), 72.

45. Ed Marolla, "Gein's Village Is Still a Nice Place to Live," *MJ*, November 24, 1937.

46. Allan Punzalan Isaac highlights the racialized, imperial media disconnect about spree killer Andrew Cunanan in Filipino American press versus national media. *American Tropics*, xviii.

47. Vidich and Bensman, *Small Town*, 40.

48. Farrell and Cupito, *Newspapers*, 81.

49. Price, *Mad at School*, 145.

50. Murray, "Interpreting Insanity," 9; Bruce, "Mad Is a Place," 304.

51. Gambino, "Savage Heart"; Murray, "Interpreting Insanity," 9. The white "mad man" is still normalized in relationship to Black and Indigenous "mad men."

52. "3 Say Late Sheriff Used Force on Gein in Probe," *CT*, April 25, 1968, 4; "Confession of Ed Gein" (case no. 4781, Waushara Circuit Court, 1957), transcript, Disc 5A, 1–3; Confession transcript, Disc 2A, 24; Confession transcript, Disc 1A, 3; Confession transcript, Disc 1, 4; Confession transcript, Disc 6, 1.

53. Confession transcript, Disc 3, 1–6.

54. Bliss, "Tell Gein's Crime Motive," 1.

55. "'Strange Sex Complex' Led to Sadistic Killings," *ODN*, November 21, 1957, 13; "Report Sex Motive Behind Gein's Actions," *SPDJ*, November 21, 1957, 1; "Butcher-Slayer Enters Insanity Plea," *JDG*, November 21, 1957, 1; "Paper Bares Story of Strange Compulsion," *Sacramento Bee*, November 21, 1957, A14.

56. "Secrets of the Farm," 30.

57. Hays, *In Cold Blood* (review), 64.

58. Robert W. Wells, "Incredibly Dirty House Was Home of Slayer," *MJ*, November 19, 1957, 1; Confession transcript, Disc 1, 13.

59. "Complex First of Kind," 1.

60. For example, Tharp, "Transvestite as Monster"; Fox and Levin, *Extreme Killing*; Jody Roy, *Love to Hate: America's Obsession with Hatred and Violence* (New York: Columbia University Press, 2005). Fox and Jack went so far as to describe Gein as having "women's panties filled with vaginas" (3).

61. Raymond, *Transsexual Empire*, 30. On how this influences violent anti-trans discourse: Bettcher, "Evil Deceivers," 55.

62. Daly, *Gyn/Ecology*, 72.

63. Two examples, of many: joannadeadwinter, "How to, like, totally defend a psycho sex killer of women from, like, a totally feminist perspective!," *Dead of Winter* (blog), August 17, 2016, accessed October 31, 2018, https://joannadw.wordpress.com/2016/08/17/how-to-like-totally-defend-a-psycho-sex-killer-of-women-from-like-a-totally-feminist-perspective/; Lisa, "Autogynephilia: The Truth Behind 'Transgender,'" *The Mind-Body Politic* (blog), November 5, 2015, accessed October 30, 2019, https://lila rajiva.com/2015/11/05/autogynephilia-the-truth-behind-transgender/.

64. "Portrait of a Killer"; Miller and Scherschel, "House of Horror," 26.

65. Bliss, "Tell Gein's Crime Motive," 2; "Gein Admits Killing Woman, Kileen Reveals," *ODN*, November 18, 1957, 1.

66. Paul Holmes, "15 Horror Victims Found," *CDT*, November 20, 1957.

67. Leigh M. Roberts and George W. Arndt to Judge Robert Gollmar, "Re-Evaluation of Gein, 12/6/73, re: *State of Wisconsin vs. Edward Gein*," 1.

68. Harry S. Pease, "Barred Door Swings Behind Shy Ghoul, Most Likely for the Last Time," *MJ*, January 7, 1958, 1, 16.

69. Edward F. Schubert testimony, *Wisconsin v. Gein* (1958), 52; Roberts and Arndt to Gollmar, "Re-Evaluation of Gein," 4.

70. "Gein Pleads Insanity," *WSJ*, November 22, 1957, 1–2; Confession transcript, Disc 3, 1. After Gein's confession, the director of the Wisconsin Crime Lab speculated that Gein might have an oedipal complex, contextualized by a quote from the Webster's dictionary definition. Two days later, a wire service article asked laypeople to leave

questions about oedipal complexes to *psy* professionals. "Possibility of Sex Complex is Seen," *JDG*, November 21, 1957, 2; George Armour, "Science Unable to Explain Gein," *Monroe (LA) Morning World Sun*, November 24, 1957, 8A.

71. Confession transcript, Disc 3, 1.

72. Bliss, "Tell Gein's Crime Motive," 1.

73. Skidmore, "Good Transsexual," 277.

74. Stryker, *Transgender History*, 54–57.

75. Stryker, *Transgender History*, 68.

76. "Good Transsexual," 272.

77. Stryker, "Jorgensen's Transsexual Whiteness," 80; Skidmore, "Good Transsexual."

78. Mitchell, "Legend Formation," 28; "Male Scientist Becoming Woman, Says He Will Be 'Sister' to Wife," *Evening Times* (Sayre, PA), November 25, 1957, 1.

79. "Complex First of Kind," 1.

80. Clare, *Brilliant Imperfection*, 140–141.

81. T. W. McGarry, "'Psycho' Sequel Cannot Match Horrible Reality," *Los Angeles Times*, June 26, 1983, WS6; Joanna Coles, "Baby-Sitter, Killer and Cannibal," *The Times* (London), July 19, 2001, 16.

82. Confession transcript, Disc 3, 12; Confession transcript, Disc 3, 2.

83. Confession transcript, Disc 3, 3–4.

84. Psychiatrist Milton Miller testified that Gein was "the kind of individual in whom distortions are easily produced by the interrogator." *Wisconsin v. Gein* (1958), 72.

85. Confession transcript, Disc 3, 1–4, 7–8.

86. Confession transcript, Disc 4A, 19–20.

87. Miller, Eichman, and Burns, "Sanity Hearing," 100.

88. George Bliss, "Identify Head of 2d Woman on Farm," *CDT*, November 20, 1957.

89. Wells, "Youth Recalls," 1; Wells, "Dirty House," 1.

90. Bliss, "Gein Tells Motive," 1.

91. Mitchell, "Legend Formation," 8.

92. R. Marc Kantrowitz, "The Mad Butcher of Plainfield," *Massachusetts Lawyers Weekly*, October 8, 2014.

93. Schreiner, "Left Hand of God," 25, 30; Coles, "Baby-Sitter, Killer and Cannibal," 16; Fox and Levin, *Extreme Killing*, 3.

94. Roberts and Arndt to Gollmar, "Re-Evaluation of Gein," 10; Miller, Eichman, and Burns, "Sanity Hearing," 100.

95. Miller testimony, *Wisconsin v. Gein* (1968), 259.

96. Confession transcript, Disc 2A, 8.

97. Bliss, "Tell Gein's Crime Motive," 1; Arndt, "Community Reactions," 106.

98. "Gein Admits Killing Woman," 1; "Feeling High in Plainfield," *ODN*, November 18, 1957, 1.

99. Frank Worden testimony, *Wisconsin v. Gein* (1958), 53. Frank was Bernice's son, and Gein was his first suspect.

100. Confession transcript, Disc 4A, 14–15.

101. Miller, Eichman, and Burns, "Sanity Hearing," 100.

102. Confession transcript, Disc 4A, 1.

103. Confession transcript, Disc 1A, 10–11.

104. Roberts and Arndt to Gollmar, "Re-Evaluation of Gein," 4.

105. "Portrait of a Killer," 40.

106. Victor Cohn, "'Jack the Ripper' Slayers Linked to Peeping Toms, Schizophrenics," *MT*, November 19, 1957.

107. Metzl, *Protest Psychosis*, xviii.

108. Cohn, "Peeping Toms, Schizophrenics."

109. Stenographic record of a statement made by Gein when questioned by Waushara County district attorney Earl Kileen, "Gein's Statement Tells of Butchering Widow," *MJ*, November 19, 1957.

110. Miller and Scherschel, "House of Horror," 27.

111. Roberts and Arndt to Gollmar, "Re-Evaluation of Gein," 11.

112. *Wisconsin v. Gein* (1968), 193.

113. *Wisconsin v. Gein* (1968), 556.

114. "Is Farmer Cannibal or Mass Slayer? Evidence Indicates He's Both," *CD*, November 20, 1957, 9, quoting Kileen; Miller, Eichman, and Burns, "Sanity Hearing," 99.

115. Roberts and Arndt to Gollmar, "Re-Evaluation of Gein," 9.

116. Confession transcript, Disc 1A, 2.

117. "Science Unable to Explain," 8A.

118. Milton, Eichman, and Burns, "Sanity Hearing," 102.

119. Jim Foree, "Foree Compares The 2 'Butchers,'" *CD*, December 7, 1957, 5.

120. Schubert testimony, *Wisconsin v. Gein* (1968), 528.

121. "Public Outraged by Crime at Plainfield," editorial, *SPDJ*, November 20, 1957, 4.

122. Robert W. Wells, "Tiny Village Stunned by Macabre Slaying," *MJ*, November 18, 1957, 1.

123. Gorman, "Quagmires of Affect," 312.

124. Richard C. Kienitz, "Villagers Call Gein Lonely, Odd Man," *MJ*, November 18, 1957, 12.

125. On Ho-Chunk camping traditions: Gabriel, "Ne-rucha-ja," 40. On Ho-Chunk removal and return, Loew and Mella, "Native American Newspapers," 108–109; Amy Lonetree, "Visualizing Native Survivance: Encounters with My Ho-Chunk Ancestors in the Family Photographs of Charles Van Schaick," in *People of the Big Voice: Photographs of Ho-Chunk Families by Charles Van Schaick, 1879–1942*, ed. Tom Jones et al. (Madison: Wisconsin Historical Society Press, 2011), 13–22.

126. "Farmers Ask for Help Getting in the Food," *New York Times*, July 7, 1943, 8; Hill, *Migratory Agricultural Workers*; Surdam, "Families on Farms."

127. Jim Foree, "Gein's Region Liberal on Racial Issue," *CD*, November 25, 1957, 3.

128. "Waupun Migrant Project; Report of the Fourth Season," unpublished manuscript of the Community Council on Human Relations, Waupun, Wisconsin, 1953, 1, quoted in Mary Nona, "Apostolate in a Sugar-Beet Camp, *Religious Education* 51, no. 3 (January 1, 1956): 108.

129. Robert W. Wells, "Youth Recalls That He Saw Two of Heads [*sic*]," *MJ*, November 20, 1957, 3.

130. Wells, "Youth Recalls," 3.

131. "Shocking Contents of Gein Home Described," *WRDT*, November 19, 1957.

132. "2C Worth," *NLP*, November 21, 1957.

133. Bederman, *Manliness and Civilization*, 181, 205.

134. "Youth Tells of Seeing Gein's Heads," *SPDJ*, November 20, 1957, 1; "Gein Called Quiet, Solitary Bachelor," *MT*, November 19, 1957; Scott Hassett, "Our Psycho," *Isthmus* (Madison), November 30, 2007, https://isthmus.com/news/cover-story/our-psycho/.

135. Gonzalez, "Headhunter Itineraries," 145; Walker, "Displaying American Indians," 63.

136. For example: "20 Years Later, Gein's Name Still Evokes Painful Memories," *CT*, September 26, 1977, 16; Wells, "Dirty House," 1; Holmes, "15 Horror Victims Found"; John Patrick Hunter, "Gein Case: Psychiatric Field Day," *CT*, January 16, 1968; "Shy Gein Feared Women, Pal Says," *MS*, November 21, 1957.

137. "Ed Gein Sweet to Woman He Asked to Wed," *CDT*, November 21, 1957.

138. Roberts and Arndt to Gollmar, "Re-Evaluation of Gein," 6; Confession transcript, Disc 3A, 3–4.

139. Douglas, "Shrunken Head of Buchenwald," 42.

140. Smith, *Hard Boiled*, 27; Eby, "All Man!," 151–152.

141. On display at the University of Michigan are human skulls that anthropologist Carl Guthe personally exhumed from burial grounds in the Philippines between 1922 and 1925. See, *Filipino Primitive*, 28–39.

142. See, *Filipino Primitive*, 39.

143. "Village Stunned by Brutal Murder," *PS*, November 21, 1957, 1; "5 Slain on Murder Farm," *CDT*, November 18, 1957; "Neighbors Say Gein's Smile Was a Sneer," *MT*, November 18, 1957.

144. On gastrointestinal complaints: Arndt, "Community Reactions," 108; Scott Hassett, "Like Lizzie Borden, Gein's Story Now Part of Our Folklore, As Well," *CT*, September 26, 1977, 16.

145. Gollmar, *America's Most Bizarre Murderer*, 39.

146. Robert Enstad, "Judge Digs Up the Ed Gein Case," *CDT*, January 27, 1982.

147. "The Depths of Depravity," editorial, reprinted in *SPDJ*, November 27, 1957.

148. "Gein Also Admits He Killed Mary Hogan," *SPDJ*, November 20, 1957, 1; Confession transcript, Disc 6, 13.

149. Miller and Scherschel, "House of Horror," 30.

150. Confession transcript, Disc 6, 16–17; Confession transcript, Disc 3A, 2–3.

151. Mitchell, "Legend Formation," 25.

152. Quoted in Gollmar, *America's Most Bizarre Murderer*, 18.

153. Confession transcript, Disc 3A, 4.

154. Roberts and Arndt to Gollmar, "Re-Evaluation of Gein," 5.

155. Confession transcript, Disc 2A, 15, and Disc 3A, 10.

156. Confession transcript, Disc 2A, 7–8.

157. Robert W. Wells, "Local Folks Still Stunned," *MJ*, November 24, 1957, 28.

158. "Solitary Bachelor."

159. "Police Find 10 Heads in Gein's Home," *Hartford Courant*, November 19, 1957.

160. "Killer Enters Insanity Plea in 'Butchery,'" *MS*, November 21, 1957, 2; "Is Farmer Cannibal"; "Rundown Farmhouse Was Murder Factory," *MJ*, November 18, 1957, 12; "Smile Was a Sneer"; "Solitary Bachelor."

161. Wells, "Youth Recalls."

162. Freedman, "Uncontrolled Desires," 89.

163. "Remember Gein Joking on Murder," *CT*, November 21, 1957, 4.

164. Hogan was divorced and had a daughter in Illinois whom she had left to foster care at age ten, but her neighbors had assumed she was a spinster until after her death. "Mary Hogan's Life Story Has Big Gaps," *SPDJ*, December 22, 1954; "Discover

$3,000 in Tavern of Missing Woman," *SPDJ*, December 20, 1954; "Mary Hogan, Barkeeper, Recalled as One Able to Take Care of Self," *CDT*, November 21, 1957, 3.

165. "Barkeeper, Recalled," 3.

166. "Hogan Riddle May Be Answered," *SPDJ*, November 18, 1957, 1.

167. "Truck Found, Owner Not Involved, Says Sheriff," *SPDJ*, December 10, 1954.

168. Robert and Arndt to Gollmar, "Re-Evaluation of Gein," 2.

169. "War Food Head Says Labor Is Very Essential," *Atlanta Daily World*, September 17, 1943, 2; Doris P. Slesinger, "The Role and Future of Migrant Farmworkers in Wisconsin Agriculture," *Wisconsin Academy Review* 33, no. 1 (December 1986): 32–35.

170. "Jamaicans Refuse to Pick Cotton; Quit Farm Jobs," *CD*, October 21, 1944, 5; "Jamaica Farmers, Angry at U.S. Race Curbs, Seek Passage Back to Islands," *CD*, July 10, 1943, 2.

171. *Migratory Agricultural Workers in Wisconsin: A Problem in Human Rights* (Madison: Governor's Commission on Human Rights, June 1950).

172. The *Defender* advisedly used the word "overseer" to describe the white Wisconsin man who managed Black farmhands from the US South: "Indians, local and imported whites, Mexicans and Jamaicans." "Cherry-Picking Time Brings Flocks of Migrant Workers to Wisconsin," *CD*, August 18, 1962, 7.

173. "Gein Polite, Mild-Mannered His Plainfield Neighbors Say," *Wisconsin Rapids Tribune*, November 18, 1957.

174. "Sheriff Believes Mary Hogan Also Victim," *SPDJ*, November 19, 1957, 1.

175. Pease, "Barred Door Swings," 1, 16.

176. "Village Psychoanalyzed."

177. Arndt, "Community Reactions," 109.

178. Wells, "Village Stunned"; "Town Reacts with Disbelief and Anger," *WRDT*, November 18, 1957, 9; Mike King, "A Most Bizarre Murder Case," *Oshkosh Advance-Titan*, November 9, 1978, 28.

179. "Curious View Ashes of Gein Farm Home; Auction Next Sunday," *PS*, March 27, 1958, 1; "It's a Good Thing That House of Evil Is Gone," editorial, *SPDJ*, March 22, 1958, 4; "Let the Sad Memories Die," opinion, *WSJ*, March 21, 1958, 10; Foote, *Shadowed Ground*, 180–181. Foote contends the Gein farm arson circumvented the "normal process of bereavement" (208).

180. *Des Moines Register* editorial, reproduced in "Views of the Press," *WRDT*, February 1, 1958, 4.

181. Gorman, "Quagmires of Affect," 312.

182. Gordon Culver, "2C Worth," *NLP*, November 28, 1.

183. Wyman, "Affirming Whiteness," 38; Knobloch, *Culture of Wilderness*, 3; Johnson, *Heartland TV*, 5; Fry, *Constructing the Heartland*, 41.

184. "Adams County Man Missing, Search Focuses in Waushara," *Waushara Argus*, December 3, 1952, 1.

185. Gordon Culver, "2C Worth," *NLP*, November 19, 1957, 1.

186. Culver, "2C Worth," November 28.

187. "Two Graves Found Empty; Att'ney General Enters Case," *PS*, November 28, 1957.

188. "Adams County Man Missing," 1.

189. Culver, "2C Worth," November 19.

190. On bank robbers and chicken thieves: Culver, editor's note, *NLP*, December 2, 1957, 2. Gollmar and Hassett, an attorney and freelance journalist, had two conversations wherein they recalled hearing about high murder rates in the Plainfield area. Interviews c. 1977A and c. 1977B, Hassett's collection.

191. Gregory, *Dead Heart of Australia*; Anderson, "Geography, Race and Nation"; Rowland, "Urbanization in Australia."

192. Tuck and Yang, "Not a Metaphor," 6.

193. Culver, "2C Worth," November 19.

194. Firkus, "Agricultural Extension," 473.

195. Brenda Child, "Review of *Native American Communities in Wisconsin*," *Journal of American History* 83, no. 4 (March 1997): 1370–1371.

196. Loew and Mella, "Black Ink," 109; Hofman, "American Indian Music," 289; Arndt, *Ho-Chunk Powwows*.

197. On Indigenous hauntings: Tuck and Yang, "Not a Metaphor," 6; Tuck and Ree, "Glossary of Haunting." An example of Indigenous Wisconsin place names used as haunting: Schreiner, "Left Hand of God," 22. Gein was referred to as the "mad butcher of Roche-a-Cri," which named both that general region of Wisconsin and a large bluff with petroglyphs created by ancestors of the Ho-Chunk. "Plainfield Businesswoman Murdered; Wisconsin's Most Horrible Crime Is Unfolding," *HCN*, November 21, 1957; Ron Seely, "Vandalism Defaces History, Culture at a Rock Art Site," *LaCrosse Tribune*, August 7, 2007, https://lacrossetribune.com/couleenews/news/local/vandalism-defaces-history-culture-at-a-rock-art-site/article_e634afa0-1363-5155-b637-4b896ef2c495.html.

198. Fletcher, "Texture of the Soil," 532; "Heart," 123.

199. Culver, "2C Worth," November 19.

200. Gollmar, interview by Hassett, c. 1977B, 4, and c. 1977A, 2.

201. Johnson, *Heartland TV*, 5.

202. "Lester Tells Story of His Discovery," *SPDJ*, December 10, 1954.

203. Culver, "2C Worth," November 19.

204. "Two Graves Found Empty"; Franklin Otto, guest editorial, *PS*, December 5, 1957.

205. Gruhlke, *Small Town Wisconsin*, 8.

206. Culver, "2C Worth," November 19.

207. Schreiner, "Left Hand of God," 27.

208. Letter to the editor, *PS*, December 5, 1957.

209. Gollmar, interview by Hassett, c. 1977B.

210. Simplican, *Capacity Contract*, 3.

211. Letter to the editor, *NLP*, December 2, 1957, 2.

212. "Plainfield a Fine Village of Many Good Citizens," *SPDJ*, November 25, 1957.

213. Culver, "2C Worth," November 19.

214. Otto, guest editorial.

215. "Disbelief and Anger."

216. Interview by Hassett, c. 1977A.

217. Interview by Hassett, c. 1977B.

218. Otto, letter to the editor, 2.

219. "Franklin Otto Leaving Plainfield," *HCN*, March 20, 1958; "Plainfield Sun Sold," *PS*, June 26, 1958, 1.

220. Holmes, "15 Horror Victims Found."

221. Schreiner, "Left Hand of God," 22.

CHAPTER 4

1. Batteau, *Invention of Appalachia,* 144, 167.

2. Claude E. Hooton Jr., recorded interview by Charles T. Morrissey and Ronald J. Grele, March 24, 1966, 12, Oral History Collection, JFKL.

3. Hooton claimed the family did not believe their ruse and "just didn't want us to come in." They entered anyway. Hooton oral history, 11.

4. Hooton, interview by Morrissey and Grele, 8.

5. Gilens, "Racialization of American Poverty," 101.

6. Gilens, "Racialization of American Poverty," 115.

7. Orleck, *Storming Caesar's Palace*; *New Grassroots History*; Hanhardt, *Safe Space,* 35–80; Meeker, "Queerly Disadvantaged."

8. OEO Administrative History, vol. 1, Box 1, LBJL.

9. Vincent, "Retarded Frontier," Frost, "Our Contemporary Ancestors."

10. Allen, "Cumberland Gap on Horseback"; Frost, "Our Contemporary Ancestors," 60.

11. Frost, "Our Contemporary Ancestors."

12. See 1960s recollections of earlier discourses: Dick Nelson to Lady Bird Johnson, "Kentucky Trip," Box 5, Liz Carpenter's Files, WHSF; Duscha, "Trail of Misery," E1.

13. Brown, *Gone Home,* 6.

14. Nielsen, *Disability History,* 157–160; Smith, *Digging Our Own Graves*; Muncy, "Coal-Fired Reforms."

15. Billings and Blee, *Road to Poverty*; *Back Talk.*

16. Lewis, *Five Families.*

17. Mumford, "Untangling Pathology."

18. Ferguson, *Aberrations in Black,* 124.

19. Ferguson, *Aberrations in Black,* 117–118; Nadasen, "Struggle for Welfare Rights," 281–282.

20. Vance, *Hillbilly Elegy,* 8. For critiques: see *Appalachian Reckoning* and Catte, *Wrong about Appalachia.*

21. Hartman, "West Virginia Mountaineers."

22. Harris, "Damage of Dew." The article circulated widely and received considerable media attention.

23. Harrington, *Other America,* 2. On how the idea of a "culture of poverty" was transformed into the psychologized notion of "cultural deprivation," which became a "near euphemism for the urban, poor black community," Raz, *What's Wrong,* 39.

24. Harrington, *Other America,* 16.

25. According to Jani Scandura, this double meaning of "depression" as both economic and psychological began after the 1929 stock-market crash. *Down in the Dumps,* 4.

26. "The Region: A New Survey," in *Southern Appalachian Region,* 8.

27. Looff, *Appalachia's Children,* 170.

28. Looff, *Appalachia's Children,* 73.

29. Looff, *Appalachia's Children,* 74.

30. Yarmolinky, Memorandum, March 2, 1959, Box 24, AYP; R. Sargent Shriver to Harrington, Jacobs, and Mankiewicz, "The Long-Term View," n.d., OEO Administrative History, vol. 2, Documentary Supplement, Box 2, LBJL; Harrington, Jacobs, Mankiewicz to Shriver, "Your Headache," February 6, 1964, Box 43, Series III, RSS; CEA, "Attack on Poverty," December 20, 1963, Confidential File, LBJL. On connections between 1910s eugenic family studies and 1960s culture of poverty theories: Briggs, *Reproducing Empire*, 163; and Patterson, *America's Struggle*, 116.

31. Caudill, *Night Comes*, 286, 287.

32. Caudill, *Night Comes*, 16.

33. Caudill, *Night Comes*, 283.

34. Jolliffe, "Deficiency Disease," 33; Arny, "My Nerves Are Busted," 24–29; Mabry, "Lay Concepts of Etiology," 382.

35. Ferguson, *Aberrations in Black*, 122.

36. Nadasen, "Struggle for Welfare Rights," 281–282.

37. Nadasen, "Struggle for Welfare Rights"; Kandaswamy, "Domestic Violence," 254.

38. Gordon, *Ghostly Matters*, 3, 4; Jacobson, *Alchemy of Race*, 10.

39. "Goddard Seeks Picket-Recruits," *Raleigh Register*, August 8, 1960, 3.

40. "Back Up Material," [1964], Box 131, BDM.

41. Handwritten comment on Mrs. Marlow to Bill Moyers, September 20, 1964, attached to Joel Fleischman to Hayes Redmon, Memorandum, "Mr. William D. Marlow," October 1, 1964, Box 16, WHCF.

42. The family was also required to participate in social welfare programs (Aid to Dependent Children and a trial food stamps program in Nash County) and meet certain logistical requirements. Farnum Gray, "Marlow Family Deeply Impressed by Visit of Johnson and Daughter," *RMET*, May 8, 1964; "LBJ, Lynda Bird Get Tumultuous," *Nashville (NC) Graphic*, May 14, 1964, 11; George M. Stephens to Josh L. Horne, June 29, 1964, Box 19, Series 1.2.1, NCDF; "Marlows Give Up Crops on Their Farm in Nash County," *RMET*, August 22, 1964, 1A; "The President's Visit," *Raleigh News and Observer*, May 6, 1964.

43. Kathy Futrell, "Political Situation—Nash-Edgecombe Area (Draft)," 1, Box 381, Series 4.10, NCF; "A Description of Counties That I Started a While Ago—Might be Helpful," 1, [1965 or later], Folder 4729, Box 380, Series 4.10, NCF.

44. "Marlows Give Up Crops," 1A.

45. "Back Up Material," [May 1964], Box 131, BDM; "Itinerary for Georgia Appalachian Trip," Box 104, Statements File, LBJL.

46. Harris, "Whiteness as Property."

47. "Marlows Give Up Crops," 1A.

48. "Viewpoint #863," Editorial, Capitol Broadcasting Company, May 21, 1964, attached to Bowler to Sanford, Note, May 28, 1964, Box 444, Sanford Papers.

49. Kafer, *Feminist Queer Crip*, 25–26.

50. Gray, "Marlow Family Deeply Impressed."

51. "Marlows Give Up Crops," 1A.

52. "Sharecropper Reflects on LBJ Visit: 'He Didn't Seem Like A Stranger,' Says Farmer," *Raleigh Times*, May 8, 1964, 5; Gray, "Marlow Family Deeply Impressed."

53. James M. Dumbell, "No Handouts, Thanks, For Appalachia," *Charlotte Observer*, November 22, 1964, B1.

54. Paul M. Popple to [Secretary of HEW], White House Office Referral, March 19, 1966, Name File, WHCF; Bowen to Johnson, March 14, 1966, Name File, WHCF.

55. Carroll Kilpatrick, "LBJ Answers Critics of Attack on Poverty," *Washington Post,* May 8, 1964, A5.

56. Tom Wickers, "President Spurs Drive on Poverty in Six State Tour," *New York Times,* May 8, 1964, 1, 14.

57. William Capron oral history, quoted in *Launching the War on Poverty,* ed. Michael L. Gillette (Cary, NC: Oxford University Press, 2010). Capron was a senior economist in the Kennedy and Johnson administrations.

58. "Report to the NCRP by the Organization for Social and Technical Innovation (Cambridge)," July 1967, Box 203, JCG.

59. "Eligibility Criteria and Guidance Mechanism," Box 53, Series III, RSS; Christopher Weeks quoted in *Launching the War on Poverty,* 221. On initially excluding girls: Quadagno and Fobes, "Making Good Girls." On the accusations that the Job Corps fostered homosexuality and lesbianism: "Youth Camps to Ban Delinquent 'Queers,'" *New Pittsburgh Courier,* December 5, 1964, 19; "Arrested at Job Camp," *New York Times,* January 12, 1965, 19; "Prostitution, Drunkenness, and Fights in Girls' Job Center Revealed: West Virginia Camp Has Problems," *Chicago Tribune,* January 10, 1966, 22.

60. "Experimental Approach to Mental Health Needed," *Science News Letter* 89, no. 135 (February 26, 1966): 135.

61. Herman M. Somers, "Poverty and Income Maintenance for the Disabled," in *Poverty in America: Proceedings of a National Conference Held at the University of California, Berkeley, February 26–28, 1965,* ed. Margaret S. Gordon (San Francisco: Chandler Publishing Company, 1965), 251–252.

62. James M. Dumbell, "Johnson Sees Appalachia's Poverty," *Greensboro Daily News,* April 25, 1964.

63. "City Prepares for Visit Here by President Lyndon Johnson," *RMET,* May 5, 1964, 1A; Esser to Chancellor John T. Caldwell, May 12, 1964, Box 18, Series 1.2.1, NCF.

64. "Presidential Trip," May 7, 1964, Box 131, BDM.

65. "Marlows Give Up Crops," 2.

66. Esser to Caldwell, May 12, 1964; Esser to C. A. McKnight, May 14, 1964, Box 18, Series 1.2.1, NCF.

67. "Virginia Newspaper Has Look at President's Visit to Area," *RMET,* June 18, 1964, 8A. It recounts the circuit of the gossip from the neighbor to the *Charlotte Observer*'s Clyde Osborne, to the politically motivated "Lights! Camera! Poverty!" editorial in the *Richmond News-Leader.*

68. "Marlows Have Had Little Privacy," *RMET,* May 25, 1964, 1.

69. "Marlows Give Up Crops." On the Klan's active presence in Rocky Mount: "Nash Funds Slated for Mental Health Program," *SHE,* May 7, 1964, 1; Futrell, "Political Situation," 2.

70. David Cooper, "Marlow Family Has Trouble Returning to Everyday Life," *Winston-Salem Journal,* May 9, 1964, 1.

71. "Remarks of the President and Miss Lynda B. Johnson in a Courtroom in City Hall, Rocky Mount North Carolina," Box 104, Statements File, LBJL.

72. Cooper, "Everyday Life," 1.

73. Ivie Lane Wilder, "The Enterprise Takes Part in LBJ's Visit to Nash County," *SHE*, May 14, 1964; Vivian Smith McMillan, "The Day the President Came," *RMET*, May 8, 1964, 6A.

74. "Johnson's Program for Poor Recalled," *Norfolk (VA) Journal and Guide*, February 3, 1973, 11.

75. "Marlow and Wife Seek VA Aid; Son Quits Home," *RMET*, July 10, 1964, 3B.

76. Tullos, *Habits of Industry*, 255-284; Rose, "'Crippled' Hands," 49; Hall et al., *Like a Family*, 81-82, 358-360; Kathy Kahn, *Hillbilly Women*, 188-189.

77. Marlow to Moyers, September 20, 1964.

78. Marlow first wrote to Johnson on August 25, 1964. On September 13, Moyers instructed her to be in touch with Sanford. When Marlow wrote Sanford a week later, she thanked him for the $200 she had received on behalf of someone who "wished to be unknown," presuming it to be the "assistance from the Governor's office you spoke of," but said it was not sufficient. On October 4, state officials sent a man to Rocky Mount to "find a job for Marlow." Fleischman to Redmond, "Mr. William D. Marlow"; Fleischman to Redmon, October 4, 1964; Marlow to Moyers, September 20, 1964; Moyers to Marlow, September 13, 1964; Eddie to Mr. Hopkins, September 8, 1964; Marlow to Johnson, August 25, 1964, all in Box 16, WHCF.

79. "Johnson's Program for Poor Recalled," *Norfolk Journal and Guide*, February 3, 1973, 11.

80. Gray, "Marlow Family Deeply Impressed," 1A.

81. Charleston Youth Community, Inc., "Summary of Appalachian Action for Youth: A Demonstration Project for Youth," February 1964, Box 9, DKP.

82. According to Virginia Burns, the former head of the Office of Juvenile Delinquency (OJD) training section, AAY received the grant for "political reasons." OJD was run by Robert F. Kennedy at the time. Recorded interview by Daniel Knapp, November 28, 1967, 5, Oral History Collection, JFKL.

83. "Kennedy in West Virginia."

84. Wright, "Aspects of Motivation in Appalachia," January 1964, Box 9, DKP.

85. Wright, "Motivation in Appalachia," 1.

86. Wright, "Motivation in Appalachia," 1.

87. Wright, "Motivation in Appalachia," 3.

88. Cameron, "When Strangers Bring Cameras," 412; Prendergast, "Rhetorics of Mental Disability," 47.

89. Price, *Mad at School*, 60-61.

90. OEO Administrative History, 3, vol. 1, Box 1, LBJL.

91. Schorr, "Nonculture of Poverty," 908.

92. Psychiatrist Frank Riessman in OEO Administrative History, Narrative History, vol. 1, pt. 2 (of 3), Box 1, LBJL.

93. Oral history, in Kahn, *Hillbilly Women*, 52.

94. Burnham, "Appalachia," 30-32.

95. National Institute of Mental Health, *Mental Health in Appalachia*.

96. Van Schaik, "Social Context of 'Nerves,'" 96, in *Appalachian Mental Health*.

97. Kahn, *Hillbilly Women*, 15.

98. Tiller, in Kahn, *Hillbilly Women*, 57.

99. Joan W. Linger to Joseph Califano, April 4, 1967, Box 33, JCG.

100. James Daniels to Johnson, February 22, 1967, attached to George Christian, memorandum, February 25, 1967, Box 36, WHCF.

101. Hager oral history, in Kahn, *Hillbilly Women*, 48.

102. Bowen to Johnson, March 14, 1966; Popple to White House Office Referral, March 19, 1966; Marlow to Johnson, August 25, 1964.

103. Gitelman, *Paper Knowledge*, 24, 30.

104. Wright, "Motivation in Appalachia," 8–9.

105. Wilkerson, *You Have to Fight*, 124.

106. Vance, "Confusion in Poverty."

107. Hopkins, "Miners for Democracy," 227–228.

108. Hopkins, "Miners for Democracy," 206–207; Worthington, Smith, and Ryan, "Miners for Democracy," 288.

109. For example: Howard C. Donald in "Ring Register," *Raleigh Register*, September 20, 1968, 1.

110. Wright, "Motivation in Appalachia," 3.

111. Wright, "Motivation in Appalachia," 9.

112. Weller, *Yesterday's People*, 134.

113. Eller, *Uneven Ground*, 64; Bowler, "Ribbon of Social Neglect."

114. "Draft/Mr. Shriver's Speech—Huntington, WV 4/21/65," Box 46, RSS.

115. Tunley, "Strange Case," 20.

116. Kennedy, *Pursuit of Justice*, 15.

117. "Federal Anti-Poverty Funds Bring Hope to Appalachia," *Cincinnati Enquirer*, June 4, 1967, 11H.

118. Hartman, *In the Shadow*, 135.

119. Thomas Kiffmeyer, "Looking Back to the City in the Hills: The Council of the Southern Mountains and a Longer View of the War on Poverty in the Appalachian South, 1913–1970," in *A New Grassroots History*, 378.

120. Smith, "De-Gradations of Whiteness," 43.

CHAPTER 5

1. Clover, *Chain Saws*, 124–137.

2. John Pym, "The Texas Chain Saw Massacre," *Monthly Film Bulletin* 43, no. 504 (1976): 258.

3. Williamson, *Hillbillyland*, 151. Black viewers, of course, have been taught to fear white Southern landscapes and soundscapes through centuries of violence, from overseers to lynchings. Creadick, "Banjo Boy," 64.

4. Clover, *Chain Saws*, 125.

5. McRuer, *Crip Theory*.

6. Harkins, *Hillbilly*, 208.

7. Halberstam, *Skin Shows*, 38–177; Benshoff, *Monsters in the Closet*.

8. Snyder and Mitchell, *Cultural Locations of Disability*, 9.

9. Smith, *Hideous Progeny*; Snyder and Mitchell, *Cultural Locations of Disability*, 156–181.

10. Gill, *Already Doing It*, 185.

11. *Shocking Truth*.

12. *Shocking Truth*.

13. Broughton, "Downsizing Masculinity," 6.

14. Hansen, *Chain Saw Confidential*, 54.

15. *Shocking Truth*.

16. Hansen, *Chain Saw Confidential*, 126.

17. Worland, "Slaughtering Genre Tradition"; Commentary, *Chain Saw*.

18. Mukherjee, *Racial Order of Things*, 16; Bluestone, "Deindustrialization and Unemployment."

19. Mukherjee, *Racial Order of Things*, 12.

20. Nelson and Lorence, "Industrialization and Income Change."

21. Fisher and Mitchelson, "Forces of Change."

22. Smith, *Hideous Progeny*; Chivers, "Becoming 'One of Us.'"

23. Norden, *Cinema of Isolation*, 5.

24. Block, "Sexuality, Fertility, and Danger"; Wilkerson, "Sex Radicalism." This stereotype has dangerous consequences for disabled men, particularly disabled Black men and other disabled men of color, who suffer severe consequences for the assumption that they are sexual predators. For example: Burch and Joyner, *Unspeakable*.

25. Taylor, "Thing from Another Swamp," 179.

26. Farber, "'Deliverance'—How It Delivers."

27. Creadick, "Banjo Boy," 72.

28. As of 2010, the Internet Movie Database (IMDB) lists over 200 "movie connections" for *Deliverance*, almost of all of which mention banjos and/or one of the iconic lines of dialogue from the rape scene. "Deliverance (1972)—Movie Connections," *Internet Movie Database*, http://www.imdb.com/title/tt0068473/movieconnections.

29. Ed Potton, "Jon Voight on Making Deliverance," *Times* (London), September 22, 2007.

30. Place, "Deliverance"; Mason, "Hillbilly Defense."

31. Madden, "Buggering Hillbilly."

32. Commentary, *Deliverance*.

33. Rafter, "Introduction," in *White Trash*; Davenport, "Laws Against Cousin Marriages."

34. Hamamy, "Consanguineous Marriages." Also: Paul and Spencer, "Cousin Marriage Controversy"; A. H. Bittles and M.L. Black, "Impact of Consanguinity."

35. Dickey and Boorman, "Deliverance" [film script], 15.

36. Keefe, "Introduction," in *Appalachian Mental Health*, 9.

37. *Shocking Truth*.

38. Pym, "Texas Chain Saw Massacre," 258.

39. Gill, *Already Doing It*, 3.

40. Berger, *Disarticulate*, 2.

41. Pym, "Texas Chain Saw Massacre," 258.

42. Commentary, *Chain Saw*.

43. Madden contends the "hillbillies" are represented "not as homosexual but as bestial." "Buggering Hillbilly," 198.

44. Carlson, *Faces of Intellectual Disability*, 132.

45. Hansen, *Chain Saw Confidential*, 24.

46. Commentary, *Chain Saw*.

47. Hansen, *Chain Saw Confidential*, 25.

48. Commentary, *Chain Saw*.

49. Taylor, *Beasts of Burden*, 74.

50. Taylor, Thomas, and Brunson, "Deliverance Will Come," 304.

51. Taylor, Thomas, and Brunson, "Deliverance Will Come," 306–307.

52. Howard, *Men Like That*.

53. Taylor, Thomas, and Brunson, "Deliverance Will Come," 303–304. "Squeal like a pig" is an allusion to a scene in *Tobacco Road*.

54. Rickman interview quoted in Lane, *Chattooga,* 59.

55. Taylor, Thomas, and Brunson, "Deliverance Will Come," 301.

56. Bethea, "Mountain Men."

57. Creadick, "Banjo Boy," 72. Creadick recalls a conversation shortly after *Deliverance*'s release in which a gay male friend made that distinction for a straight friend who described it as a "nightmare buttfuck."

58. Madden, "Buggering Hillbilly," 196.

59. Madden, "Buggering Hillbilly," 205.

60. Fairbanks, "Rollin' Down the River," 18.

61. Bethea, "Mountain Men."

62. Taylor, Thomas, and Brunson, "Deliverance Will Come," 299.

63. Commentary, *Deliverance*.

64. Lane, *Chattooga,* 61.

65. Williamson, *Hillbillyland,* 164.

66. Dickey and Boorman, "Deliverance," 17 (Webb), 13 ("unseemly").

67. Taylor et al., "Deliverance Will Come," 299–300.

68. Lane, *Chattooga,* 61.

69. Bethea, "Mountain Men."

70. Interview with Ashley York and Sally Rubin, cited in Creadick, "Banjo Boy," 68.

71. Bethea, "Mountain Men."

72. Lane, *Chattooga,* 60–61.

73. Harkins, *Hillbilly,* 206.

74. Dickey, *Summer of Deliverance,* 99.

75. Graham, "Twenty Years After 'Deliverance,'" M1.

76. "Violence in America," *NBC News Reports,* transcript, National Broadcasting Company, aired January 5, 1977; Sander Vanocur, "Exploring 'Violence in America,'" *Washington Post,* January 5, 1977.

77. Isenberg, "Horror Films."

78. Farley, "Impresario of Axploitation Movies"; Beale, "Changes the Face of Horror."

79. Muir, *Wes Craven.*

80. Wood, *Hollywood From Vietnam,* 70–94; Williams, *Hearths of Darkness.*

81. Clover, *Chain Saws,* 134–136, 162–165; Sharrett, "Neoconservative Culture."

82. Muir, *Wes Craven*; Farley, "Impresario of Axploitation."

83. Mitchell, *Landscape and Power,* 2, emphasis in original.

84. Clover, *Chain Saws,* 16; Farley, "Impresario of Axploitation."

85. Bob Ross, "Worth the Rent," *Tampa Tribune,* October 27, 1995; Glenn Lovell, "The 'Professor' Who Makes Horror Movies," *Philadelphia Inquirer,* January 21, 1985.

86. Farley, "Impresario of Axploitation."

87. *The Shocking Truth.*

88. Commentary, *Fight for Your Life.*

CHAPTER 6

1. Moreton, "Sex in Christian Conservatism"; Ferguson, "Sissies at the Picnic," 192–194.

2. Moreton, "Sex in Christian Conservatism"; Lancaster, *Sex Panic,* 40–41.

3. Ferber and Kimmel, "Right-Wing Militias," 139.

4. Reagan originated the myth of the welfare queen during his 1975 presidential run, based on the incomplete, distorted story of a single woman—a con artist who was likely white and passing herself off as Black. Levin, *The Queen*.

5. Cacho, "Ideology of White Injury," 399.

6. Lancaster, *Sex Panic*, 39.

7. Atcheson, "Culture Vultures," 100.

8. Mason, "Stranger or Familiar?," 587.

9. Hartigan, "Unpopular Culture."

10. Grimes, "Box Office Poison," C11. *Brother's Keeper* was reviewed in one gay and lesbian publication, which seems to be the exception rather than the norm: Don Kerne, "Front Row: *Brother's Keeper*—An Unforgettably Stunning Documentary," *Gay and Lesbian Times*, February 25, 1993, 30.

11. Joe Duggan, "Teena Brandon Film Packs N.Y. Theater," *LJS*, October 1, 1998, A1.

12. Allison, *Skin*, 23.

13. Minkowitz, "Love Hurts," 28.

14. Driskill, "Stolen from Our Bodies."

15. Snorton, *Black on Both Sides*; Brody, "Boyz Do Cry," 92. On Nissen and white supremacy: Dunne, "Humboldt Murders," 56.

16. Commentary, *Brother's Keeper*.

17. Garner, "Strange Tale."

18. Weiss, "Brothers Grim."

19. Commentary, *Brother's Keeper*.

20. Gordon, *Ghostly Matters*, 4.

21. "'I Didn't Do It,' Farmer Says," *Watertown Daily Times*, March 25, 1991; John Nicholson and Jackie Robinson, "Up Front," Channel 3 in Syracuse, in Bogdan collection; Sam Howe Verhovek, "To Village's Disbelief, Farmer Is Indicted in Brother's Death," *New York Times*, August 4, 1990, 27; Hart Seely, "A Death Makes Stars of Backwoods Brothers," *SPS*, June 16, 2000.

22. Mia Mingus, "Access Intimacy: The Missing Link," *Leaving Evidence*, May 5, 2011, https://leavingevidence.wordpress.com/2011/05/05/access-intimacy-the-missing-link/.

23. On Delbert: Arthur, "Famous Yokels." On Lyman: "Brother's Anxiety Attack Halts Ward Trial Temporarily," *SHA*, March 21, 1993; David. J. Krajicek, "His Brother's Keeper," *New York Daily News*, March 25, 2008; Stack, "'Brother's Keeper's' True Confessions." On Roscoe: Kolbert, "Dairy Town Doubts," A1; Commentary, *Brother's Keeper*.

24. Mike Dickinson, "Brother's Suffering Keyed Ward Killing, Papers Say," *SPS*, September 6, 1990.

25. Thomas M. Kemple, "Litigating Illiteracy: The Media, the Law, and *The People of the State of New York v. Adelbert Ward*," *Canadian Journal of Law and Society* 10, no. 2 (Fall 1995): 73–97; Perske, "Search for Persons"; Conti, "False Confessions." *SPS* reported in 1991 that police in New York State would study the case of Delbert Ward in order to "learn how to question people with mental disabilities." Mike Dickinson, "Ward Trial Becomes Textbook Case," *SPS*, April 13, 1991, B1.

26. Jacks Ashley McNamara, "On Access Intimacy and Mental Health," *Icarus Project*, August 26, 2013, http://www.theicarusproject.net/article/on-access-intimacy-and-mental-health, accessed April 22, 2015.

27. Chen, *Animacies*, 278.

28. Titchkosky, *Question of Access*, 3.

29. Commentary, *Brother's Keeper*.

30. Krajicek, "His Brother's Keeper."

31. Kolbert, "Dairy Town Doubts," A1.

32. Commentary, *Brother's Keeper*.

33. Julie Salamon, "Film: Aftermath of a Small-Town Murder," *Wall Street Journal*, September 10, 1992, A12.

34. Garner, "Tells Strange Tale."

35. Hart Seely, "A Death's Tale Goes National," *SPS*, June 14, 2000, A1; Seely, "Death in the Family," *SHA*, June 11, 2000, A1.

36. *Current Affair*, in Bogdan collection.

37. Seely, "Death in the Family," A1.

38. Dick Case, "Wards Linger in Memory," *SHA*, October 25, 1998, B1.

39. Richard Grossman, "Ward Film Shows Truth Isn't Neat," *SPS*, January 4, 1993, A6.

40. Mike Dickinson, "William and Delbert Ward Case to be 'A Current Affair,'" *SPS*, June 23, 1990, B1.

41. Vincent Canby, "State Says Delbert Killed Bill; Delbert Says Bill Just Plain Died," *New York Times*, September 9, 1992, C15.

42. Canby, "State Says," C15; Peter Stack, "'Brother's Keeper's' True Confessions," *San Francisco Chronicle*, October 16, 1992, C4; Hart Seely, "Brother's Death Becomes Murder," *SPS*, June 12, 2000, A1.

43. Mike Dickinson, "Murder Probe Pulls Community Together," *Syracuse Herald-Journal*, June 12, 1990; Rocca LaDuca, "Last Surviving Ward Brother Dies at 84," *Utica Observer-Dispatch*, August 17, 2007, 1A.

44. Hart Seely, "The Ward Boys Are Now Just One After Roscoe's Death," *SPS*, June 27, 2007, A1.

45. "'The Boys Were the Boys, You Know?,'" *SHA*, June 12, 2000, A5.

46. Dick Case, "Wards Linger in Memory," *SHA*, October 25, 1998, B1.

47. Hart Seely, "Ten Years Later: The Boys Are Older, Slower, and On the Farm—A Reunion, A Lifetime Later," *SPS*, June 17, 2000, A1; Seely, "Death Makes Stars," A1.

48. Dick Case, "On the Farm, Ward Boys Shrug off the 'Fuss,'" *SHA*, February 16, 1992, G1; Seely, "Death in the Family," A1; Bogdan, "'Simple' Farmer," 308.

49. Bogdan, "'Simple' Farmer," 309.

50. Bogdan, "'Simple' Farmer," 308.

51. "Emma M. Frank," obituary, *SPS*, October 4, 1988, A8; "Charles A. Frank," obituary, *SPS*, May 25, 1989, B2.

52. Glenn Coin, "Ward Farm's Fate Falls to Kin—Last of Brothers Died without Will," *SPS*, February 2, 2008, B2.

53. According to his gravestone, Frank's husband was "Negro" and the grandson of Josiah Frank of Smithfield, NY. Andrew L., "Charles A. 'Pete' Frank" (memorial ID 34784737), *Find A Grave*, March 13, 2009, https://www.findagrave.com/memorial/34784737/charles-a_-frank. A local census confirms that Josiah Frank was a Black farm laborer in Madison County. "1870 Census," *African Americans in Madison County*, compiled by Donna Burdick, Madison County, NY Archival Records, https://www.madisoncounty.ny.gov/335/Archival-Records.

54. Halberstam, *Queer Time and Place*, 23.

55. Snorton, *Black on Both Sides*, 180.

56. In 1999, Dion Manley recognized that the book was especially interesting because "it's about working-class folk like myself," even as Manley found it "frustrating" due to the "non-transperson's bias." "All *He* Wanted?," book review, *FTM Newsletter* 45 (Summer 1999): 18.

57. Blackmar, "*Smoky Pilgrims*," 485; Dunne, "Humboldt Murders," 61.

58. Dunne, "Humboldt Murders."

59. Brandon moved to the Falls City area about six weeks before his death.

60. Delany, *Times Square Red*, 280.

61. Minkowitz, "How I Broke."

62. Scott Shock quoted in Jones, *All She Wanted*, 313.

63. "Three Murdered Near Humboldt Create National Attention," *Humboldt Standard*, January 6, 1994, 1.

64. Blackmar, "*Smoky Pilgrims*," 485; Dunne, "Humboldt Murders," 61.

65. For example: John Keenan, October 21, 1998; Tony Moton, October 18, 1998; January 17, 1998; and, most notably, the October 3, 1998, editorial.

66. Brandon himself experienced this in Lincoln. According to a friend, "There were guys who were his (Brandon's) friends who wanted to tear his clothes off" one night. Joe Duggan, "Brandon Was Threatened in June," *LJS*, January 22, 1994, 1.

67. Konigsberg, "Death of a Deceiver," 196.

68. Jones, *All She Wanted*, 226. Snorton discusses DeVine's relationship with Lenny Landrum in more depth.

69. Forret, *Race Relations*, 157.

70. Minkowitz, "Love Hurts," 28.

71. "Activists Hold Brandon Teena Murder Trial Vigil," *In Your Face* 2 (Fall 1995), 2, in Periodicals Collection, GLBTHS.

72. Frank Santiago, "Slain Iowan 'Friendly, Trusting," *DMR*, January 4, 1994, 2.

73. Jones, *All She Wanted*, 16.

74. Jones, *All She Wanted*, 29.

75. Driskill, "Stolen from Our Bodies," 56.

76. Loffreda, *Losing Matt Shepard*, 27.

77. Jones, *All She Wanted*, 196.

78. Jones, *All She Wanted*, 83; Konigsberg, "Death of a Deceiver," 193.

79. Jones, *All She Wanted*, 76. The detail about compulsive showering also appears in Ed Will, "Murder in a Small Town," *Denver Post Magazine*, March 6, 1994, 10.

80. Ann W. O'Neill, "Double Life Engenders Double Lawsuits," *Los Angeles Times*, October 24, 1999; Dunne, "Humboldt Murders," 53; Jones, *All She Wanted*, 152–153; Chris Burbach, "Lotter's Life a Struggle, Mother Says Problems Started at Birth, Court Told," *OWH*, November 23, 1995, 29.

81. Bederman, *Manliness and Civilization*, 4.

82. Minkowitz, "Love Hurts," 28; Chris Burbach, "Play Recounts Murder of 3," *OWH*, May 16, 1997.

83. Jones, *All She Wanted*, 126.

84. Dunne, "Humboldt Murders," 60; Chris Burbach and Henry J. Cordes, "Romance, Deceit, and Rage Surround Three: The Victims, The Accused," *OWH*, January 9, 1994, 1A. Brandon was not intersex, but non-intersex people experiencing gen-

der dysphoria have sometimes claimed to be when that is the only explanation they can find for their feelings.

85. Larry Fruhling, "Charade Revealed Prior to Killings," *DMR*, January 9, 1994, 4B.

86. On the narrative that trans people are "deceptive": Bettcher, "Evil Deceivers"; on masculinities as "counterfeit," Halberstam, *Queer Time and Place*, 44–45.

87. Hanhardt, *Safe Space*, 21–22, 113.

88. Hanhardt, *Safe Space*, 10.

89. Clare, *Exile and Pride*, 143.

90. Ronson, "Marwencol."

91. Lisa Hix, "Hogancamp's Heroes: How Playing with Dolls Lets a Hate-Crime Survivor Fight Back," *Collector's Weekly*, March 29, 2016, https://www.collectorsweekly .com/articles/how-playing-with-dolls-lets-a-hate-crime-survivor-fight-back/.

92. Ryzik, "(Imagined) War Hero."

93. Yergeau, *Authoring Autism*, 18–19.

94. "What is Neuroqueer? And why should I care?," *NeuroQueer Blog*, February 16, 2015, http://neuroqueer.blogspot.com/2015/02/what-is-neuroqueer-and-why -should-i.html/.

95. For example, Hogancamp's camera does not have a working light meter.

BIBLIOGRAPHY

ARCHIVAL COLLECTIONS

American Philosophical Society, Philadelphia, PA
    Charles B. Davenport Papers (CBD)
    Eugenics Record Office Records (ERO)
Gay, Lesbian, Bisexual, and Transgender Historical Society, San Francisco, CA
    (GLBTHS)
    Periodicals Collection
John F. Kennedy Presidential Library, Boston, MA (JFKL)
    Walter H. Heller Papers (WHH)
    John F. Kennedy Oral History Collection
    Robert F. Kennedy Oral History Collection
    Daniel Knapp Papers (DKP)
    R. Sargent Shriver Papers (RSS)
    Adam Yarmolinsky Papers (AYP)
Library of Congress, Washington, DC
    Farm Security Administration/Office of War Information Photograph Collection
    John Vachon Papers (JVP)
Lyndon Baines Johnson Library, Austin, TX (LBJL)
    Confidential File
    Office Files of the White House Aides
        James C. Gaither (JCG)
        Bill D. Moyers (BDM)
    Oral History Collection
    Statement File
    White House Central Files Collection (WHCF)
    White House Social Files Collection (WHSF)
Minnesota Historical Society (MHS), St. Paul, MN
    Faribault State School and Hospital, Minnesota State Archives
    Ethel McClure Papers
    Minnesota Rural Rehabilitation Corporation Records (MRRC)
    Public Welfare Department Records, Minnesota State Archives
National Archives, Chicago, IL (Chicago NARA)
    Records of the Bureau of Agricultural Economics, RG 83
    Records of the Farmers Home Administration, RG 96

National Archives, College Park, MD (Archives II)
    Records of the Bureau of Agricultural Economics, RG 83
    Records of the Farmers Home Administration, RG 96
State Archives of North Carolina, Raleigh, NC
    Governor Terry Sanford Papers
University of Louisville, Special Collections, Louisville, KY
    Roy Emerson Stryker Papers (RES)
University of North Carolina, Southern Historical Collection, Chapel Hill, NC
    North Carolina Fund Records (NCF)
    Howard Washington Odum Papers (HWO)
University of Wisconsin–Stevens Point, Special Collections, Stevens Point, WI
    Ed Gein Clippings File
Waushara County Courthouse, Wautoma, WI
    Confession and Court Records of Ed Gein

PRIMARY SOURCES

Dissertations and Theses

Anderson, Alton Anders Robert. "A Study of the Beltrami Island Resettlement Project." Master's thesis. University of Minnesota, 1937.
Hopkins, George Williams. "The Miners for Democracy: Insurgency in the United Mine Workers of America, 1970–1972." PhD dissertation. University of North Carolina–Chapel Hill, 1976.

Government Documents

Farm Security Administration. *Beltrami Island Farms.* Washington, DC: Department of Agriculture, 1940.
Hill, George Williams. *Texas-Mexican Migratory Agricultural Workers in Wisconsin.* Madison: Agricultural Experiment Station of the University of Wisconsin, 1948.
Kansas Commission on Provision for the Feeble-Minded. *The Kallikaks of Kansas.* Topeka: Kansas State Printing Plant, 1919.
Kirkpatrick, E. L. *Analysis of 70,000 Rural Rehabilitation Families.* Social Research Report No. IX. Washington, DC: Department of Agriculture, August 1938.
McDowell, J. C. *Farming on the Cut-Over Lands of Michigan, Wisconsin, and Minnesota.* Washington, DC: Department of Agriculture, 1916.
Migratory Agricultural Workers in Wisconsin: A Problem in Human Rights. Madison: Governor's Commission on Human Rights, June 1950.
Moynihan, Daniel Patrick. *The Negro Family: The Case for National Action.* Washington, DC: Department of Labor, 1965.
Murchie, R. W., and Chester R. Wasson. *Beltrami Island, Minn.: Resettlement Project.* Minnesota Agricultural Experiment Statement 334 (December 1937).
National Institute of Mental Health. *Mental Health in Appalachia: Problems and Prospects in the Central Highlands.* Washington, DC: Government Printing Office, 1965.
Resettlement Administration. *America's Land.* Washington, DC: Government Printing Office, September 1935.

Roosevelt, Theodore. "Special Message." In *Report of the Country Life Commission*, 3–9.
    Washington, DC: Government Printing Office, 1909.
U.S. Public Health Service and Bureau of Education. *High Schools and Sex Education*.
    Washington, DC: Government Printing Office, 1922.

Newspapers and Periodicals

Capital Times (Madison, Wisconsin; *CT*)
Chicago Daily Tribune (Illinois; *CDT*)
Chicago Defender (Illinois; *CD*)
Des Moines Register (Iowa; *DMR*)
Hancock-Coloma News (Wisconsin; *HCN*)
Janesville Daily Gazette (Wisconsin; *JDG*)
Lincoln Journal Star (Nebraska; *LJS*)
Milwaukee Journal (Wisconsin; *MJ*)
Milwaukee Sentinel (Wisconsin; *MS*)
Minneapolis Tribune (Minnesota; *MT*)
New London Press (Wisconsin; *NLP*)
Omaha World-Herald (Nebraska; *OWH*)
Oshkosh Daily Northwestern (Wisconsin; *ODN*)
Plainfield Sun (Wisconsin; *PS*)
Raleigh Register (West Virginia)
Rocky Mount Evening Telegram (North Carolina; *RMET*)
Spring Hope Enterprise (North Carolina; *SHE*)
Stevens Point Daily Journal (Wisconsin; *SPDJ*)
Syracuse Herald American (New York; *SHA*)
Syracuse Post-Standard (New York; *SPS*)
Wisconsin Rapids Daily Tribune (Wisconsin; *WRDT*)
Wisconsin State Journal (Madison, Wisconsin; *WSJ*)

Film and Television

A Current Affair: Fox Broadcasting Company, 1990.
The Brandon Teena Story: Bless Bless Productions, 1998.
Brother's Keeper: American Playhouse, 1992.
"Burt Reynolds/Anne Murray," *Saturday Night Live*, 1980.
Deliverance: Warner Brothers, 1972.
Face to Face with Connie Chung: CBS, 1991.
Fight for Your Life: Blue Underground, 2004 [1977].
The Hills Have Eyes: Blood Relations Co., 1977.
Redneck Zombies: Full Moon Pictures, 1989.
Sling Blade: Miramax, 1996.
The Texas Chain Saw Massacre: Vortex, 1974.
The Texas Chain Saw Massacre: The Shocking Truth: Blue Underground, 2000.

Personal Collections

Robert Gollmar Personal Collection
Scott Hassett Personal Collection

Other Published Primary Sources

Allen, James Lane. "Through Cumberland Gap on Horseback." *Harper's Magazine* (June 1886): 50–66.
Alsop, Joseph. "Slab Fork." *Victoria (TX) Advocate*, April 17, 1960.
Appalachian Mental Health, ed. Susan Emley Keefe. Lexington: University of Kentucky Press, 1988.
Armour, George. "Science Unable to Explain Gein." *Monroe (LA) Morning World Sun*, November 24, 1957.
Arndt, George W. "Community Reactions to a Horrifying Event." *Bulletin of the Menninger Clinic* 23, no. 3 (May 1959): 106–111.
Arny, Malcolm. "My Nerves Are Busted." *Mountain Life and Work* 31, no. 3 (1955): 24–29.
Atcheson, Dorothy. "Culture Vultures in Nebraska." *Out*, October 1995, 100.
Beale, Lewis. "Craven Changes the Face of Horror." *Daily News of Los Angeles*, February 13, 1988.
Bethea, Charles. "Mountain Men: An Oral History of Deliverance." *Atlanta Magazine*, September 1, 2011. https://www.atlantamagazine.com/great-reads/deliverance/.
Blackmar, Frank. "The Smoky Pilgrims." *American Journal of Sociology* 2, no. 4 (January 1897): 485–500.
Bliss, George. "Tell Gein's Crime Motive." *Chicago Daily Tribune*, November 21, 1957, 1A.
"Brandons: Living with Death Difficult." *Omaha World-Herald*, October 13, 1994.
Burnham, David. "Appalachia." *Newsweek*, February 17, 1964.
Canby, Vincent. "State Says Delbert Killed Bill; Delbert Says Bill Just Plain Died." *New York Times*, September 9, 1992, C15.
Carpenter, Niles. "Feebleminded and Pauper Negroes in Public Institutions." *Annals of the American Academy of Political and Social Science* 140 (November 1928).
Caudill, Harry. *Night Comes to the Cumberlands: A Biography of a Depressed Area*. Boston and Toronto: Little, Brown and Company, 1962.
Cohen, Elias S. "Administration of the Criminal Sexual Psychopath Statute in Indiana." *Indiana Law Journal* 32, no. 4 (1956): 450–467.
Coles, Joanna. "Baby-Sitter, Killer and Cannibal." *Times* (London), July 19, 2001.
The Contributors' Club. "Heritages of the Lord." *Atlantic Monthly*, January 1917.
"Current Literature." *Galaxy: An Illustrated Magazine of Entertaining Reading* 24, no. 4 (October 1877).
Daly, Mary. *Gyn/Ecology: The Metaethics of Radical Feminism*. Boston: Beacon Press, 1990 [1978].
Davenport, Charles. "Laws Against Cousin Marriages." *Eugenics: A Journal of Race Betterment* 2, no. 8 (August 1929).
———. "The Nams: The Feeble-Minded as Country Dwellers." *Survey*, March 2, 1912.
Davenport, Charles B. *The Feebly Inhibited: Violent Temper and Its Inheritance*. Cold Spring Harbor, NY: Eugenics Record Office, 1915.

Dickey, Christopher. *Summer of Deliverance: A Memoir of Father and Son.* New York: Simon & Schuster, 1998.

Dickey, James. *Deliverance.* New York: Delta Publishing, 1970.

Dickey, James, and John Boorman. "Deliverance" [film script], second draft. January 11, 1971. http://www.dailyscript.com/scripts/deliverance.pdf.

Dugdale, Richard. *The Jukes: A Study in Crime, Pauperism, Disease, and Heredity.* New York: Knicker Bocker Press, 1877.

Dunne, John Gregory. "The Humboldt Murders." *New Yorker*, January 13, 1997.

Duscha, Julius. "A Long Trail of Misery Winds the Proud Hills." *Washington Post*, August 7, 1960.

Elkin, Henry. "Aggressive and Erotic Tendencies in Army Life." *American Journal of Sociology* 51, no. 5 (March 1946): 408–413.

Estabrook, Arthur. "Country Slums." *Eugenics: A Journal of Race Betterment* 2, no. 7 (July 1929).

Estabrook, Arthur, and Ivan McDougle. *Mongrel Virginians.* Baltimore: Williams and Wilkins Company, 1926.

Fairbanks, Harold. "'Deliverance'—Rollin' Down the River with Machismo." *The Advocate*, August 2, 1972, 18.

Farber, Stephen. "'Deliverance'—How It Delivers." *New York Times*, August 19, 1972.

Farley, Ellen. "Impresario of Axploitation Movies." *Los Angeles Times*, November 13, 1977.

"Farmers Ask for Help Getting in the Food." *New York Times*, July 7, 1943.

Finger, Anne. "'Welfare Reform' and Us." *Disability Rag*, November/December 1997.

Fiske, George Walter. *Challenge of the Country: A Study of Country Life Opportunity.* New York and London: Association Press, 1916.

Fletcher, S. W. "How to Improve the Texture of Soil." *Country Life in America* 8, no. 5 (September 1905).

Fox, James Alan, and Jack Levin. *Extreme Killing: Understanding Serial and Mass Murder.* Thousand Oaks, CA: Sage Publications, 2005.

Frost, William Goodell. "Our Contemporary Ancestors in the Southern Mountains." *Atlantic Monthly*, 1899.

Garner, Jack. "'Brother's Keeper,' Tells Strange Tale with a Capra-esque Twist." *USA Today*, October 20, 1992.

Gavisk, Francis Henry, and the Indiana Committee on Mental Defectives. *Mental Defectives in Indiana.* Report of the Committee on Mental Defectives Appointed by Governor Samuel M. Ralston. Indianapolis: Indiana Department of Public Welfare, 1916.

Gesell, Arnold Lucius. "Village of a Thousand Souls." *American Magazine*, no. 76 (October 1913).

Ginsberg, Allen. "Gay Sunshine Interview." *College English* 36, no. 3 (November 1974): 392–400.

Goddard, Henry. *The Kallikak Family: A Study in the Heredity of Feeble-Mindedness.* New York: Macmillan, 1912.

Gollmar, Robert H. *Edward Gein: America's Most Bizarre Murderer.* New York: Windsor Publishing Corporation, 1981.

Graham, S. Keith. "Twenty Years After 'Deliverance': Tale a Mixed Blessing for Rabun County." *Atlanta Journal-Constitution*, March 18, 1990, M1.

Greene, Bob. *Once Upon a Town: The Miracle of the North Platte Canteen*. New York: HarperCollins, 2003.

Gregory, John Walter. *The Dead Heart of Australia*. London and Aylesbury, UK: Hazell, Watson and Viney, 1906.

Grimes, William. "Box Office Poison, 'Brother's Keeper,' Turns Out to Be a Hit." *New York Times*, February 16, 1993, C11.

Groves, Ernest R. "The Feeble-Minded in the Country." *Training School Bulletin* 12, no. 5 (September 1915): 118–121.

Gruhlke, Verna King. *Small Town Wisconsin*. Madison: Wisconsin House Ltd., 1971.

Guzetta, Charles. "Book Reviews." *Journal of Education for Social Work* 10, no. 2 (Spring 1974): 122–124.

H. W. H. "Restricted Ambition." *Life*, May 6, 1920.

Hagadone, Zach. "The Boys of Boise: 60 Years Later." *Boise Weekly*, June 17, 2015.

Hansen, Gunnar. *Chain Saw Confidential: How We Made the World's Most Notorious Horror Movie*. San Francisco: Chronicle Books, 2013.

Harrigan, Phillip. "The Problems of Rural New England: A Remote Village." *Atlantic Monthly*, May 1897.

Harrington, Michael. *The Other America*. New York: Scribner, 2012 [1962].

Harris, Priscilla Norwood. "Undoing the Damage of Dew." *Appalachian Journal of Law* 9, no. 1 (Winter 2009): 53–120.

Hartt, Rollin Lynde. "A New England Hill Town. I. Its Condition." *Atlantic Monthly*, April 1899.

———. "A New England Hill Town. II. Its Revival." *Atlantic Monthly*, May 1899.

"Heart." In *Dictionary of Agriculture*, 3rd ed., ed. Heather Bateman, Steve Curtis, and Katy McAdam. London: Bloomsbury Publishing, 2011.

Hodson, William. "What Minnesota Has Done and Should Do for the Feeble-Minded." *Journal of the American Institute of Criminal Law and Criminology* 10, no. 2 (1919): 208–217.

Hofman, Charles. "American Indian Music in Wisconsin, Summer 1946." *Journal of American Folklore* 60, no. 237 (July–September 1947): 289–293.

Holmes, Paul. "15 Horror Victims Found." *Chicago Daily Tribune*, November 20, 1957.

Howe, Desson. "True Crime, Artful Drama." *Washington Post*, February 5, 1993.

Hyde, William DeWitt. "Impending Paganism in New England." *Forum* 13 (June 1892).

Isenberg, Barbara. "Horror Films: Are They Hazardous to Your Health?" *Los Angeles Times*, August 24, 1980.

Johnson, Lady Bird. *A White House Diary*. New York, Chicago, and San Francisco: Holt, Rinehart and Winston, 1970.

Johnson, Patty. "I Was Just Thinking." *Palm Beach Post*, January 12, 1958.

Jolliffe, Norman. "The Pathogenesis of Deficiency Disease." In *Clinical Nutrition*, ed. Norman Jolliffe, F. F. Tisdall, and Paul R. Cannon, 8–38. New York: Paul B. Hoeber, Inc., 1950.

Jones, Aphrodite. *All She Wanted: A True Story of Sexual Deception and Murder in America's Heartland*. New York: Pocket Books, 1996.

Jordan, David Starr. *The Heredity of Richard Roe: A Discussion of the Principles of Eugenics*. Boston: American Unitarian Association, 1913.

Kahn, Kathy. *Hillbilly Women*. New York: Doubleday & Company, 1973.

Kempley, Rita. "Movies: The Mysterious Affair in Munnsville." *Washington Post*, February 6, 1993.

"Kennedy in West Virginia." *New York Times*, April 30, 1964.

Kennedy, Robert. *The Pursuit of Justice*. New York: Harper and Row, 1964.

Kerne, Don. "Front Row: *Brother's Keeper*—An Unforgettably Stunning Documentary." *Gay and Lesbian Times*, February 25, 1993, 30.

Kite, Elizabeth S. "The 'Pineys': Today Morons; Yesterday Colonial Outcasts, 'Disowned' Friends, Land Pirates, Hessians, Tory Refugees, Revellers from Joseph Bonaparte's Court at Bordentown, and Other Sowers of Wild Oats." *Survey*, October 4, 1913.

Knox, Howard. "Tests for Mental Defects." *Journal of Heredity* 5, no. 3 (March 1, 1914): 122–130.

Kolbert, Elizabeth. "A Dairy Town Doubts Brother Killed Brother: A Brother's Arrest, a Town's Doubt." *New York Times*, July 19, 1990.

Konigsberg, Eric. "Death of a Deceiver." *Playboy* 42, no. 1 (1995): 92–94, 193–199.

Krajicek, David J. "His Brother's Keeper." *New York Daily News*, March 25, 2008.

Lane, John. *Chattooga: Descending into the Myth of the* Deliverance *River*. Atlanta and London: University of Georgia Press, 2004.

Lange, Dorothea, Paul Schuster Taylor, and the Oakland Museum. *An American Exodus: A Record of Human Erosion in the Thirties*. New Haven, CT: Yale University Press, 1939.

Laughlin, H. H. "Calculations on the Working out of a Proposed Program of Sterilization." *Proceedings of the First National Conference on Race Betterment* (1914): 478–494.

Lequier, Fred. "Lumber Jacks Appealing to You for Aid." *Minneapolis Labor Review*, January 15, 1937.

Lewis, Oscar. *Five Families: Mexican Case Studies in the Culture of Poverty*. New York: Basic Books, 1959.

———. *La Vida: A Puerto Rican Family in the Culture of Poverty—San Juan and New York*. New York: Random House, 1966.

Loffreda, Beth. *Losing Matt Shepard: Life and Politics in the Aftermath of Anti-Gay Murder*. New York: Columbia University Press, 2000.

Looff, David H. *Appalachia's Children: The Challenge of Mental Health*. Lexington: University of Kentucky Press, 1971.

Lovell, Glenn. "The 'Professor' Who Makes Horror Movies." *Philadelphia Inquirer*, January 21, 1985.

Mabry, John H. "Lay Concepts of Etiology." *Journal of Chronic Disease* 17 (1964): 371–386.

Malloch, Douglas. "The Love of a Man." In *Tote-Road and Trail: Ballads of the Lumberjack*, 12–13. Indianapolis: Bobbs-Merrill Company, 1917.

McClure, Ethel. *More Than a Roof: The Development of Minnesota Poor Farms and Homes for the Aged*. St. Paul: Minnesota Historical Society Press, 1968.

McGarry, T. W. "'Psycho' Sequel Cannot Match Horrible Reality." *Los Angeles Times*, June 26, 1983.

McKenna, Kristine. "The Truth Behind 'Brother's Keeper' Movies: Joe Berlinger and Bruce Sinofsky Made the Film Not to Prove Guilt or Innocence, but 'to Reveal Emotional Truths About the Human Condition.'" *Los Angeles Times*, February 11, 1993.

"Medical Notes." *Boston Medical and Surgical Journal* 92 (January 28, 1875): 112–113.

Merrill, Maud A. "Minnesota's Heritage: From the Mountaineers of the South." *Survey,* August 17, 1918.

Miller, Francis, and Frank Scherschel. "House of Horror Stuns the Nation." *Life,* December 2, 1957.

Miller, Milton H., Peter L. Eichman, and Edward M. Burns. "Sanity Hearing." *Bulletin of the Menninger Clinic* 23, no. 3 (May 1959): 103–105.

Minkowitz, Donna. "How I Broke, and Botched, the Brandon Teena Story." *Village Voice,* June 20, 2018. https://www.villagevoice.com/2018/06/20/how-i-broke-and -botched-the-brandon-teena-story/.

———. "Love Hurts." *Village Voice,* April 19, 1994: 24–30.

Mulder, Arnold. *Bram of the Five Corners.* Chicago: A. C. McClurg, 1915.

Nowell, R. I. "Experience of Resettlement Administration Program in Lake States." *Journal of Farm Economics* 19, no. 1 (February 1, 1937): 206–220.

Noyes, Clara. "The Delano Red Cross Nurses." *American Journal of Nursing* 24, no. 14 (November 1924): 1113–1121.

Olson, Harry. "The Recent History of the Psychopathic Laboratory of the Chicago Municipal Court." *Central Law Journal* 93, no. 8 (August 26, 1921): 132–140.

Park, Robert E., and Ernest W. Burgess. *The City: Suggestions for Investigation of Human Behavior in the Urban Environment.* Chicago and London: University of Chicago Press, 1925.

Parker, Carleton Hubbell. *The Casual Laborer: And Other Essays.* New York: Harcourt, Brace and Howe, 1920.

Popenoe, Paul. "Heredity and Behavior." *Eugenics: A Journal of Race Betterment* 2, no. 9 (September 1929): 2–13.

"Portrait of a Killer." *Time,* December 2, 1957.

"Poverty U.S.A." *Newsweek,* February 17, 1964.

Prince, Morton. "Sexual Perversion or Vice? A Pathological and Therapeutic Inquiry." *Journal of Nervous and Mental Disease* 25, no. 4 (1898): 237–256.

Pym, John. "The Texas Chain Saw Massacre." *Monthly Film Bulletin* 43, no. 504 (December 1976): 258.

Quillen, Robert. "Where the Fence Breaks a Path Is Established." *Washington Post,* September 26, 1928.

Randolph, Julia F. "Canton Kallikaks." *Psychological Clinic* 12, no. 5–9 (May 15, 1919): 279–281.

Raymond, Janice. *Transsexual Empire: The Making of the She-Male.* New York and London: Teachers College Press, 1994 [1979].

Robinson, G. S. "State Supervision and Administration," *Survey,* June 11, 1910.

"A Rockefeller Works with the Poor." *New York Times,* June 27, 1965.

Rogers, A. C., and Maud A. Merrill. *Dwellers in the Vale of Siddem: A True Story of the Social Aspects of Feeble-Mindedness.* Boston: Gorham Press, 1919.

Ronson, Jon. "Marwencol: The Incredible WWII Art Project Created by a Cross-Dresser Who Was Beaten Up by Bigots." *The Guardian,* October 28, 2015.

Roosevelt, Theodore. *The Strenuous Life; Essays and Addresses.* New York: The Century Company, 1900.

Round, William M. F. "Introduction (1884)." In *The Jukes: A Study in Crime, Pauperism, Disease, and Heredity,* 7th ed. New York and London: G. P. Putnam's Sons, 1902.

Russell, Marta. *Beyond Ramps: Disability at the End of the Social Contract*. Monroe, ME: Common Courage Press, 1998.

Ryzick, Melena. "The Outsider Artist as (Imagined) War Hero." *New York Times*, May 14, 2015.

Sadler, William Samuel. *Race Decadence*. Chicago: A. C. McClurg & Company, 1922.

Salamon, Julie. "Film: Aftermath of a Small-Town Murder." *Wall Street Journal*, September 10, 1992, A12.

Sanborn, Alvan F. "The Problems of a Rural New England: A Farming Community." *Atlantic Monthly*, May 1897.

Sandoz, Mari. *Old Jules: Portrait of a Pioneer*, 2nd ed. Winnipeg: Bison Books, 2005 [1935].

Schneider, Karen S. "Blood Secrets." *People Magazine*, November 2, 1992.

Schorr, Alvin L. "The Nonculture of Poverty." *American Journal of Orthopsychiatry* 34, no. 5 (October 1964): 907–912.

Schreiner, David D. "Ed Gein and the Left Hand of God." *Weird Trips* 1, no. 2 (1978).

"The Secrets of the Farm." *Newsweek*, December 2, 1957.

The Southern Appalachian Region: A Survey, ed. Thomas R. Ford. Lexington: University of Kentucky Press, 1962.

Spies, Michael. "Hunters Find Their Pursuers Are Out for Blood." *Houston Chronicle*, June 2, 1987, 2nd ed.

Stack, Peter. "'Brother's Keeper's' True Confessions." *San Francisco Chronicle*, October 16, 1992.

Sullenger, T. Earl. "Female Criminality in Omaha." *Journal of Criminal Law and Criminology* 27, no. 5 (January 1, 1937): 706–711.

Taylor, Barbara, Mary Thomas, and Laurie Bronson. "He Shouted Loud, 'Hosanna, Deliverance Will Come.'" *Foxfire* 7, no. 4 (Winter 1973): 297–312.

Taylor, Paul. "The Thing from Another Swamp: An Interview with Wes Craven." *Monthly Film Bulletin* 49, no. 583 (August 1982): 178–179.

Tharp, Julie. "The Transvestite as Monster: Gender Horror in *The Silence of the Lambs*." *Journal of Popular Film & Television* 19, no. 3 (Fall 1991): 106–113.

Tunley, Roul. "The Strange Case of West Virginia." *Saturday Evening Post*, February 6, 1960.

Underwood, Marsh. *The Log of a Logger*. Portland, OR: Kilham Stationery & Printing Company, 1938.

Vance, J. D. *Hillbilly Elegy: A Memoir of a Family and Culture in Crisis*. New York: Harper-Collins, 2018.

Vance, Kyle. "Confusion in Poverty: He's Too Sick for Work, Too Well for Welfare." *Louisville Courier-Journal*, August 24, 1969, B1.

Verhovek, Sam Howe. "To Village's Disbelief, Farmer Is Indicted in Brother's Death." *New York Times*, August 4, 1990.

Vidich, Arthur J., and Joseph Bensman. *Small Town in Mass Society: Class, Power and Religion in a Rural Community*. Garden City, NY: Doubleday Anchor Books, 1958.

"A Village Psychoanalyzed." *Newsweek*, June 1, 1959.

Vincent, George E. "A Retarded Frontier." *American Journal of Sociology* 4, no. 1 (July 1898): 1–20.

"Violence in America." *NBC News Reports*, transcript, National Broadcasting Company, aired January 5, 1977.

Vitaris, Paula. "X-Files: Behind the Scenes of Morgan and Wong's Controversial Episode." *Cinefantastique*, October 1997.

"War Food Head Says Labor Is Very Essential." *Atlanta Daily World*, September 17, 1943.

Wasson, Chester R. "The Grubstake Plan for the Evacuation and Resettlement of the Inhabitants of Beltrami Island, Minnesota." *Social Service Review* 12, no. 2 (June 1, 1938): 276–297.

Weiss, Phillip. "Brothers Grim." *Vogue*, October 1992.

Weller, Jack E. *Yesterday's People: Life in Contemporary Appalachia*. Lexington: University of Kentucky Press, 1965.

"What Happened to a Family LBJ Visited." *U.S. News and World Report*, September 7, 1964.

"When the Kallikaks Moved to Harrisburg." *Survey* 38 (April 7, 1917): 23–24.

White, Elizabeth. "The Pineys of New Jersey (Conclusion)." *Training School Bulletin* 14, no. 4 (June 1917): 58–62.

Whittles, Thomas David. *Lumberjack Sky Pilot*. Winona, MN: Winona Publishing Company, 1908.

Worland, Rick. "Slaughtering Genre Tradition: *The Texas Chain Saw Massacre* (1974)." In *The Horror Film: An Introduction*, 208–226. Malden, MA: Blackwell Publishing, 2007.

Worsham, C. G. "Farm Development in the Cut-Over Lands of Northern Minnesota." *Minnesota Farmers' Institute Annual* 33 (1920): 15–26.

Worthington, Bill, Lee Smith, and Ed Ryan. "Miners for Democracy." In *Rank and File: Personal Histories by Working-Class Organizers*, ed. Alice Lynd and Staughton Lynd, 285–296. Boston: Beacon Press, 1973.

Wyman, Walker D. *Lumberjack Frontier: The Life of a Logger in the Early Days on the Chippeway, Retold from the Recollections of Louie Blanchard*. Lincoln: University of Nebraska Press, 1969.

SECONDARY SOURCES

Abramowitz, Mimi. "The Family Ethic and the Female Pauper: A New Perspective on Public Aid and Social Security Programs." *Journal of Social Work Education* 21, no. 2 (1985): 15–26.

Aho, Tanja, Liat Ben-Moshe, and Leon J. Hilton. "Mad Futures: Affect/Theory/Violence." *American Quarterly* 69, no. 2 (June 2017): 291–302.

Albrecht, Charlotte Karem. "An Archive of Difference: Syrian Women, the Peddling Economy and US Social Welfare, 1880–1935." *Gender & History* 28, no. 1 (April 2016): 127–149.

Allen, Ruth, and Raymond G. Nairn. "Media Depictions of Mental Illness: An Analysis of the Use of Dangerousness." *Australian and New Zealand Journal of Psychiatry* 31, no. 3 (1997): 375–381.

Allison, Dorothy. *Skin: Talking about Sex, Class and Literature*. Ithaca, NY: Firebrand Books, 1994.

Anderson, Warwick. "Geography, Race and Nation: Remapping 'Tropical' Australia, 1890–1930." *Historical Records of Australian Science* 11, no. 4 (2000): 457–468.

Appalachian Reckoning: A Region Responds to Hillbilly Elegy, ed. Anthony Harkins and Meredith McCarroll. Morgantown: West Virginia University Press, 2019.

Arndt, Grant. *Ho-Chunk Powwows and the Politics of Tradition*. Lincoln and London: University of Nebraska Press, 2016.

Arondekar, Anjali. "Without a Trace: Sexuality and the Colonial Archive." *Journal of the History of Sexuality* 14, no. 1 (2005).

Arthur, Paul. "Let Us Now Praise Famous Yokels: Dadetown and Other Retreats." *Cineaste* 23, no. 1 (July 1997): 30–33.

Awkward-Rich, Cameron. "Trans, Feminism: Or, Reading like a Depressed Transsexual." *Signs: Journal of Women in Culture and Society* 42, no. 4 (June 2017): 819–841.

Back Talk from Appalachia: Confronting Stereotypes, ed. Dwight B. Billings, Gurney Norman, and Katherine Ledford. Lexington: University Press of Kentucky, 2000.

Bailey, Moya, and Izetta Autumn Mobley. "Work in the Intersections: A Black Feminist Disability Framework." *Gender & Society* 20, no. 10 (2018): 1–22.

Barraclough, Laura R. *Making the San Fernando Valley: Rural Landscapes, Urban Development, and White Privilege*. Athens: University of Georgia Press, 2011.

Batteau, Allen. *Invention of Appalachia*. Tucson: University of Arizona Press, 1990.

Baynton, Douglas. *Defectives in the Land: Disability and Immigration in the Age of Eugenics*. Chicago: University of Chicago Press, 2016.

Beck, Bill. "Radicals in the Northwoods: The 1937 Timber Workers Strike." *Journal of the West* 35 (1996): 55–65.

Bederman, Gail. *Manliness and Civilization: A Cultural History of Gender and Race in the United States, 1880–1917*. Chicago: University of Chicago Press, 1995.

Bell, David. "Anti-Idyll: Rural Horror." In *Contested Countryside Cultures: Otherness, Marginalisation and Rurality*, ed. Paul Cloke and Jo Little, 94–108. London and New York: Routledge Press, 1997.

Benshoff, Harry. *Monsters in the Closet: Homosexuality and the Horror Film*. Manchester: Manchester University Press, 1997.

Berger, James. *The Disarticulate: Language, Disability, and the Narratives of Modernity*. New York: New York University Press, 2014.

Berne, Patricia, with Stacey Milbern, Aurora Levins Morales, and David Langsaff. "Disability Justice—A Working Draft." In *Skin, Tooth, and Bone: The Basis of Movement Is Our People*, 9–15. San Francisco: Sins Invalid, 2016.

Bettcher, Talia Mae. "Evil Deceivers and Make-Believers: On Transphobic Violence and the Politics of Illusion." *Hypatia* 22, no. 3 (Summer 2007): 43–65.

Billings, Dwight B., and Katherine M. Blee. *The Road to Poverty: The Making of Wealth and Hardship in Appalachia*. Cambridge: Cambridge University Press, 2000.

Bittles, A. H., and M. L. Black. "The Impact of Consanguinity on Neonatal and Infant Health." *Early Human Development* 86 (2010): 737–741.

Bix, Amy Sue. "Experiences and Voices of Eugenics Field-Workers: 'Women's Work' in Biology." *Social Studies of Science* 27, no. 4 (August 1997): 625–668.

Block, Pamela. "Sexuality, Fertility, and Danger: Twentieth-Century Images of Women with Cognitive Disabilities." *Sexuality and Disability* 18, no. 4 (December 1, 2000): 239–254.

Bluestone, Barry. "Deindustrialization and Unemployment in America." *Review of Black Political Economy* 12, no. 3 (March 11, 1983): 27–42.

Boag, Peter N. *Same-Sex Affairs: Constructing and Controlling Homosexuality in the Pacific Northwest*. Berkeley and Los Angeles: University of California Press, 2003.

Bogdan, Robert. "A 'Simple' Farmer Accused of Murder: Community Acceptance and the Meaning of Deviance." *Disability, Handicap & Society* 7, no. 4 (1992): 303–320.

Boster, Dea H. *African American Slavery and Disability: Bodies, Property, and Power in the Antebellum South, 1800–1860*. New York and London: Routledge Press, 2013.

Bowden, Paul. "Pioneers in Forensic Psychiatry: James Cowles Prichard: Moral Insanity and the Myth of Psychopathic Disorder." *Journal of Forensic Psychiatry* 3, no. 1 (1992): 113–136.

Bowler, Betty Miller. "'That Ribbon of Social Neglect': Appalachia and the Media in 1964." *Appalachian Journal* 12, no. 3 (Spring 1985): 239–247.

Boyd, Nan Alamilla. *Wide-Open Town: A History of Queer San Francisco to 1965*. Berkeley and Los Angeles: University of California Press, 2003.

Breeden, James O. "Disease as a Factor in Southern Distinctiveness." In *Disease and Distinctiveness in the American South*, ed. Todd L. Savitt and James Harvey Young, 1–28. Knoxville: University of Tennessee Press, 1991.

Brekke, John S., Cathy Prindle, Sung Woo Bae, and Jeffrey D. Long. "Risks for Individuals with Schizophrenia Who Are Living in the Community." *Psychiatric Services* 52, no. 10 (October 2001): 1358–1366.

Briggs, Lauren. *Reproducing Empire: Race, Sex, Science, and U.S. Imperialism in Puerto Rico*. Berkeley and Los Angeles: University of California Press, 2002.

Brody, Jennifer DeVere. "Boyz Do Cry: Screening History's White Lies." *Screen* 43, no. 1 (2002): 91–96.

Bronner, Simon J. "'The Shooter Has Asperger's': Autism, Belief, and 'Wild Child' Narratives." *Children's Folklore Review* 36 (2014): 35–54.

Broughton, Chad. "Downsizing Masculinity: Gender, Family, and Fatherhood in Post-Industrial America." *Anthropology of Work Review* 27, no. 1 (2006): 1–12.

Brown, Karida L. *Gone Home: Race and Roots through Appalachia*. Chapel Hill: University of North Carolina Press, 2018.

Bruce, La Marr Jurelle. "Mad Is a Place; or, the Slave Ship Tows the Ship of Fools." *American Quarterly* 69, no. 2 (June 2017): 303–308.

Burch, Susan. "Disorderly Pasts: Kinship, Diagnoses, and Remembering in American Indian-U.S. Histories." *Journal of Social History* 50, no. 2 (December 2016): 362–385.

Burch, Susan, and Hannah Joyner. *Unspeakable: The Story of Junius Wilson*. Chapel Hill: University of North Carolina, 2015.

Burch, Susan, and Lindsay Patterson. "Not Just Any Body: Disability, Gender, and History." *Journal of Women's History* 25, no. 4 (Winter 2013): 122–137.

Cacho, Lisa Marie. "'The People of California Are Suffering': The Ideology of White Injury in Discourses of Immigration." *Cultural Values* 4, no. 4 (October 2000): 389–418.

———. *Social Death: Racialized Rightlessness and the Criminalization of the Unprotected*. New York: New York University Press, 2012.

Caison, Gina. *Red States: Indigeneity, Settler Colonialism, and Southern Studies*. Athens: University of Georgia Press, 2018.

Cameron, Ardis. "Sleuthing Towards America: Visual Detection in Everyday Life." In *Looking for America: The Visual Production of Nation and People*, ed. Cameron, 17–41. Malden, MA: Blackwell Publishing, 2005.

———. "When Strangers Bring Cameras: The Poetics and Politics of Othered Places." *American Quarterly* 54, no. 3 (September 2002): 411–435.

Canaday, Margot. *The Straight State: Sexuality and Citizenship in Twentieth-Century America*. Princeton, NJ, and Oxford: Princeton University Press, 2009.

Caputi, Jane. "New Founding Fathers: The Lore and Lure of the Serial Killer in Contemporary Culture." *Journal of American Culture* 13, no. 3 (1990): 1–12.

Carby, Hazel V. "Policing the Black Woman's Body in an Urban Context." *Critical Inquiry* 18, no. 4 (1992): 738–755.

Carey, Allison. *On the Margins of Citizenship: Intellectual Disability and Civil Rights in Twentieth-Century America.* Philadelphia: Temple University Press, 2009.

Carlson, Elof Axel. *The Unfit: A History of a Bad Idea.* Cold Spring Harbor, NY: Cold Spring Harbor Laboratory Press, 2001.

Carlson, Licia. *Faces of Intellectual Disability: Philosophical Reflections.* Bloomington: Indiana University Press, 2009.

Casey, Janet Galligani. *A New Heartland: Women, Modernity, and the Agrarian Ideal in America.* New York and London: Oxford University Press, 2009.

Catte, Elizabeth. *What You Are Getting Wrong about Appalachia.* Cleveland: Belt Publishing, 2018.

Chauncey, George. *Gay New York: Gender, Urban Culture, and the Making of the Gay Male World, 1890–1940.* New York: Basic Books, 1994.

———. "The Postwar Sex Crime Panic." In *True Stories from the American Past*, ed. William Graebner, 160–178. New York: McGraw-Hill, 1993.

Chen, Mel. *Animacies: Biopolitics, Racial Mattering, and Queer Affect.* Durham, NC, and London: Duke University Press, 2012.

Child, Brenda J. *Holding Our World Together: Ojibwe Women and the Survival of Community.* New York: Viking Publishing, 2012.

———. *My Grandfather's Knocking Sticks: Ojibwe Family Life and Labor on the Reservation.* St. Paul: Minnesota Historical Society Press, 2014.

Chivers, S. "The Horror of Becoming 'One of Us': Tod Browning's Freaks and Disability." In *Screening Disability: Essays on Cinema and Disability*, ed. Christopher R. Smit and Anthony W. Enns, 57–64. Lanham, MD: University Press of America (2001).

Chmielewski, Kristen Elizabeth. "Silver Screen Slashers and Psychopaths: A Content Analysis of Schizophrenia in Recent Film." Master's thesis, University of Iowa, 2013.

Choe, Jeanne Y., Lina A. Teplin, and Karen M. Abram. "Perpetration of Violence, Violent Victimization, and Severe Mental Illness: Balancing Public Health Concerns." *Psychiatric Services* 59, no. 2 (February 2008): 153–164.

Clare, Eli. "Body Shame, Body Pride: Lessons from the Disability Rights Movement." In *Transgender Studies Reader* 2, ed. Susan Stryker and Aren Z. Aizura, 261–265. New York: Routledge Press, 2013.

———. *Brilliant Imperfection: Grappling with Cure.* Durham, NC: Duke University Press, 2017.

———. *Exile and Pride: Disability, Queerness, and Liberation.* Cambridge, MA: South End Press, 2009 [1999].

Clover, Carol J. *Men, Women, and Chain Saws: Gender in the Modern Horror Film.* Princeton, NJ: Princeton University Press, 1992.

———. "Her Body, Himself: Gender in the Slasher Film." *Representations* 20 (Autumn 1987): 187–228.

Cohen, Cathy. "Deviance as Resistance: A New Research Agenda for the Study of Black Politics," *Du Bois Review: Social Science Research on Race* 1, no. 1 (2004): 29.

———. "Punks, Bulldaggers, and Welfare Queens: The Radical Potential of Queer Politics?" *GLQ: Journal of Gay and Lesbian Studies* 3, no. 4 (1997): 437–465.

Conti, Richard P. "The Psychology of False Confessions." *Journal of Credibility Assessment and Witness Psychology* 2, no. 1 (1999): 14–36.

Cooke, Anthony Carlton. *Moral Panics, Mental Illness Stigma, and the Deinstitutionalization Movement in American Popular Culture.* Statesboro, GA: Palgrave Macmillan, 2017.

Costello, Cary Gabriel. "Intersex and Trans* Communities: Commonalities and Tensions." In *Transgender and Intersex: Theoretical, Practical, and Artistic Perspectives,* ed. Stefan Horlacher, 83–113. New York: Palgrave Macmillan, 2016.

Creadick, Anna. "Banjo Boy: Masculinity, Disability, and Difference in *Deliverance*." *Southern Cultures* 23, no. 1 (Spring 2017): 63–78.

Currell, Sue. "You Haven't Seen Their Faces: Eugenic National Housekeeping and Documentary Photography in 1930s America." *Journal of American Studies* 51, no. 2 (2017): 481–511.

Daniel, Pete. *Standing at the Crossroads: Southern Life in the Twentieth Century.* Baltimore and London: Johns Hopkins University Press, 1986.

———. "The Transformation of the Rural South: 1930 to the Present." *Agricultural History* 55, no. 3 (1981): 231–248.

Davis, Angela Y. *Women, Race and Class.* New York: Vintage Books, 1983.

Delany, Samuel. *Times Square Red, Times Square Blue.* New York and London: New York University Press, 1999.

Deloria, Vine. *Custer Died for Your Sins.* Norman: University of Oklahoma Press, 1988 [1969].

Douglas, Lawrence. "The Shrunken Head of Buchenwald: Icons of Atrocity at Nuremberg." *Representations* 63 (Summer 1998): 39–64.

Downs, Jim. *Sick from Freedom: African-American Illness and Suffering during the Civil War and Reconstruction.* Oxford: Oxford University Press, 2012.

Driskill, Qwo-Li. *Asegi Stories: Cherokee Queer and Two-Spirit Memory.* Tucson: University of Arizona Press, 2016.

———. "Stolen from Our Bodies: First Nations Two-Spirits/Queers and the Journey to a Sovereign Erotic." *Studies in American Indian Literatures* 16, no. 2 (Summer 2004): 50–64.

DuBois, W. E. Burghardt. *Black Reconstruction: An Essay Toward a History of the Part Black Folk Played in the Attempt to Reconstruct Democracy in America, 1860–1880.* New York: Harcourt, Brace and Company, 1935.

Duggan, Lisa. *Sapphic Slashers: Sex, Violence, and American Modernity.* Durham, NC, and London: Duke University Press, 2000.

Dwyer, Ellen. "Psychiatry and Race during World War II." *Journal of the History of Medicine and Allied Sciences* 61, no. 2 (April 2006): 117–143.

Eby, Carl. "All Man! Hemingway, 1950s Men's Magazines, and the Masculine Persona (review)." *The Hemingway Review* 29, no. 2 (Spring 2010): 149–152.

Elbogen, E. B., and S. C. Johnson. "The Intricate Link between Violence and Mental Disorder: Results from the National Epidemiologic Survey on Alcohol and Related Conditions." *Archives of General Psychiatry* 66, no. 2 (February 2009): 152–171.

Eller, Ronald. *Uneven Ground: Appalachia Since 1945.* Lexington: University of Kentucky Press, 2008.

English, Daylanne K. *Unnatural Selections: Eugenics in American Modernism and the Harlem Renaissance.* Chapel Hill: University of North Carolina Press, 2004.

Erb, Cynthia. "'Have You Ever Seen the Inside of One of Those Places?' Psycho, Foucault, and the Postwar Context of Madness." *Cinema Journal* 45, no. 4 (Summer 2006): 45–63.

Erevelles, Nirmala. *Disability and Difference in Global Contexts: Enabling a Transformative Body Politic*. New York: Palgrave Macmillan, 2011.

Estroff, Susan. "Identity, Disability, and Schizophrenia: The Problem of Chronicity." In *Knowledge, Power, and Practice: The Anthropology of Medicine and Everyday Life*, ed. Shirley Lindebaugh and Margaret Lock, 247–286. Berkeley and Los Angeles: University of California Press, 1993.

Faderman, Lillian. *Odd Girls and Twilight Lovers: A History of Lesbian Life in Twentieth-Century America*. New York: Penguin Books, 1991.

Farland, Maria. "Modernist Versions of Pastoral: Poetic Inspiration, Scientific Expertise, and the 'Degenerate' Farmer." *American Literary History* 19, no. 4 (Winter 2007): 905–936.

Farrell, Mike, and Mary Carmen Cupito. *Newspapers*. New York: Peter Liang Publishing, 2010.

Fazel, Seena, Gautam Glati, Louise Linsell, John R. Geddes, and Martin Grann. "Schizophrenia and Violence: Systematic Review and Meta-Analysis." *PLOS Medicine* 6, no. 8 (2009): 1–15.

Fazel, Seena, N. Langström, A. Hjern, M. Grann, and P. Lichtenstein. "Schizophrenia, Substance Abuse, and Violent Crime." *Journal of the American Medical Association* 301, no. 19 (2009): 2016–2023.

Ferber, Abby L., and Michael S. Kimmel. "'White Men Are This Nation': Right-Wing Militias and the Restoration of Rural American Masculinity." In *Home-Grown Hate: Gender and Organized Racism*, 137–154. New York and London: Routledge, 2004.

Ferguson, Roderick A. *Aberrations in Black: A Queer of Color Critique*. Minneapolis and London: University of Minnesota Press, 2004.

———. "Sissies at the Picnic: The Subjugated Knowledges of a Black Rural Queer." In *Feminist Waves, Feminist Generations: Life Stories from the Academy*, ed. Hokulani K. Aikau, Karla A. Erickson, and Jennifer L. Pierce, 188–196. Minneapolis and London: University of Minnesota Press, 2007.

Fink, Deborah. *Agrarian Women: Wives and Mothers in Rural Nebraska, 1880–1940*. Chapel Hill and London: University of North Carolina Press, 1992.

Finnegan, Cara. *Picturing Poverty: Print Culture and FSA Photographs*. Washington, DC: Smithsonian Institution Scholarly Press, 2003.

Firkus, Angela. "Agricultural Extension and the Campaign to Assimilate the Native Americans of Wisconsin, 1914–1932." *Journal of the Gilded Age and Progressive Era* 9, no. 4 (October 2010): 473–502.

Fisher, Andrea. *Let Us Now Praise Famous Women: Women Photographers for the U.S. Government, 1935–1944*. London: Pandora Press, 1987.

Fisher, James S., and Ronald L. Mitchelson. "Forces of Change in the American Settlement Pattern." *Geographical Review* 71, no. 3 (July 1981): 298–310.

Foote, Kenneth E. *Shadowed Ground: America's Landscapes of Violence and Tragedy*. Austin: University of Texas Press, 2003.

Forret, Jeff. *Race Relations at the Margins: Slaves and Poor Whites in the Antebellum Countryside*. Baton Rouge: Louisiana State University Press, 2006.

Foss, Chris. "Building a Mystery: *Relative Fear* and the 1990s Autistic Thriller." In *Kidding Around: The Child in Film and Media*, ed. Alexander N. Howe and Wynn Yarbrough, 119–138. New York: Bloomsbury Publishing, 2014.

Fox, James Alan, and Jack Levin. "Multiple Homicide: Patterns of Serial and Mass Murder." *Crime and Justice* 23 (1998): 407–455.

Frank, Richard G., and Sherry A. Glied. "Assessing the Well-Being of People with Mental Illness: An Analysis of the Use of Dangerousness." In *Better but Not Well: Mental Health Policy in the United States Since 1950*, 104–139. Baltimore and London: Johns Hopkins University Press, 2008.

Frank, Russell. "When Bad Things Happen in Good Places: Pastoralism in Big-City Newspaper Coverage of Small-Town Violence." *Rural Sociology* 68, no. 2 (2003): 207–230.

Freedman, Estelle B. "'Uncontrolled Desires': The Response to the Sexual Psychopath, 1920–1960." *Journal of American History* 74, no. 1 (1987): 83–106.

Fry, Katherine. *Constructing the Heartland: Television News and Natural Disaster.* Creskill, NJ: Hampton Press, 2003.

Gabriel, Mary Ellen. "Ne-rucha-ja: The Forgotten Tale of Frost's Woods and Charles E. Brown's Fight to Save It for the Ho-Chunk." *Wisconsin Magazine of History* 95, no. 1 (Autumn 2011): 36–49.

Gambino, Matthew. "'The Savage Heart beneath the Civilized Exterior': Race, Citizenship, and Mental Illness in Washington, D.C., 1900–1940." *Disability Studies Quarterly* 28 (Summer 2008), http://dsq-sds.org/article/view/114.

Gelb, Steven A. "'Not Simply Bad and Incorrigible': Science, Morality, and Intellectual Deficiency." *History of Education Quarterly* 29, no. 3 (Autumn 1989): 359–379.

Genter, Alix. "Appearances Can Be Deceiving: Butch-Femme Fashion and Queer Legibility in New York City, 1945–1969." *Feminist Studies* 42, no. 3 (2016): 604–631.

Genter, Robert. "'We All Go a Little Mad Sometimes': Alfred Hitchcock, American Psychoanalysis, and the Construction of the Cold War Psychopath." *Canadian Review of American Studies* 40, no. 2 (2010): 133–162.

geoff. "Destabilizing Disability: Including Addiction for Cross-Movement Solidarity." *Knots: An Undergraduate Journal of Disability Studies* 1 (2015): 67–74.

Gerasse, John G. *The Boys of Boise: Furor, Vice, and Folly in an American City.* Seattle: University of Washington Press, 2001 [1966].

Gilens, Martin. "How the Poor Became Black: The Racialization of American Poverty in the Mass Media." In *Race and the Politics of Welfare Reform*, ed. Sanford F. Schram, Joe Soss, and Richard C. Fording, 101–130. Ann Arbor: University of Michigan Press, 2003.

Gill, Michael. *Already Doing It: Intellectual Disability and Sexual Agency.* Minneapolis: University of Minnesota Press, 2015.

Gitelman, Lisa. *Paper Knowledge: Toward a Media History of Documents.* Durham, NC: Duke University Press, 2014.

Goldman, Marion S. *Gold Diggers & Silver Miners: Prostitution and Social Life on the Comstock Lode.* Ann Arbor: University of Michigan Press, 1981.

Gonzales, Angela, Judy Kertész, and Gabrielle Tayac. "Eugenics as Indian Removal: Sociohistorical Processes and the De(con)struction of American Indians in the Southeast." *The Public Historian* 29, no. 3 (Summer 2007): 53–67.

Gonzalez, Vernadette Vicuña. "Headhunter Itineraries: The Philippines as America's Dream Jungle." *Global South* 3, no. 2 (Fall 2009): 144–172.

Gopinath, Gayatri. *Impossible Desires: Queer Diasporas and South Asian Public Cultures.* Durham, NC: Duke University Press, 2005.

———. *Unruly Visions: The Aesthetic Practices of Queer Diaspora.* Durham, NC, and London: Duke University Press, 2018.

Gordon, Avery. *Ghostly Matters: Haunting and the Sociological Imagination.* Minneapolis and London: University of Minnesota Press, 1997.

Gordon, Linda. "Dorothea Lange: The Photographer as Agricultural Sociologist." *Journal of American History* 93, no. 3 (December 1, 2006): 698–727.

———. *Pitied but Not Entitled: Single Mothers and the History of Welfare, 1890–1935.* New York: Free Press, 1994.

Gorman, Rachel. "Quagmires of Affect: Madness, Labor, Whiteness, and Ideological Disavowal." *American Quarterly* 69, no. 2 (June 2017): 309–313.

Gould, Stephen Jay. *The Mismeasure of Man.* New York and London: W. W. Norton & Company, 1981.

Gray, Mary L. *Out in the Country: Youth, Media, and Queer Visibility in Rural America.* New York: New York University Press, 2009.

Grey, Michael R. *New Deal Medicine: The Rural Health Programs of the Farm Security Administration.* Baltimore and London: Johns Hopkins University Press, 1999.

Griffin, Larry J., and Ashley B. Thompson. "Appalachia and the South—Collective Memory, Identity, and Representation." *Appalachian Journal* 29, no. 3 (Spring 2002): 296–327.

Groth, Paul Erling. *Living Downtown: The History of Residential Hotels in the United States.* Berkeley and Los Angeles: University of California Press, 1994.

Guha, Ranajit. *Elementary Aspects of Peasant Insurgency in Colonial India.* Delhi: Oxford University Press, 1983.

Halberstam, Jack. *In a Queer Time and Place: Transgender Bodies, Subcultural Lives.* New York and London: New York University Press, 2005.

———. *Skin Shows: Gothic Horror and the Technology of Monsters.* Durham, NC, and London: Duke University Press, 1995.

Hale, C. Jacob. "Tracing a Ghostly Memory in My Throat: Reflections on FTM Feminist Voice and Agency." In *Men Doing Feminism*, ed. Tom Digby, 99–129. New York and London: Routledge Press, 1998.

Hall, Jacquelyn Dowd, James Leloudis, Robert Korstad, Mary Murphy, Lu Ann Jones, and Christopher B. Daly. *Like a Family: The Making of a Southern Cotton Mill World.* Chapel Hill and London: University of North Carolina Press, 1987.

Hamamy, Hanan. "Consanguineous Marriages: Preconception Consultation in Primary Health Settings." *Journal of Community Genetics* 3, no. 3 (July 2012): 185–192.

Hamraie, Aimi. *Building Access: Universal Design and the Politics of Disability.* Minneapolis and London: University of Minnesota Press, 2017.

Hanhardt, Christina. *Safe Space: Gay Neighborhood History and the Politics of Violence.* Durham, NC: Duke University Press, 2013.

Hanna, Stephen P. "Three Decades of Appalshop Films: Representations, Strategies, and Regional Politics." *Appalachian Journal* 25, no. 4 (Summer 1998): 372–413.

Hariman, Robert, and John Louis Lucaites. *No Caption Needed: Iconic Photographs, Public Culture, and Liberal Democracy.* Chicago and London: University of Chicago Press, 2007.

Harkins, Anthony. *Hillbilly: A Cultural History of an American Icon.* Oxford and New York: Oxford University Press, 2005.

Harris, Ben. "Arnold Gesell's Progressive Vision: Child Hygiene, Socialism and Eugenics." *History of Psychology* 14, no. 3 (2011): 311-334.

Harris, Cheryl I. "Whiteness as Property." *Harvard Law Review* 106, no. 8 (1993): 1707-1791.

Hartigan, John Jr. *Odd Tribes: Toward a Cultural Analysis of White People*. Durham, NC, and London: Duke University Press, 2005.

———. "Unpopular Culture: The Case of 'White Trash.'" *Cultural Studies* 11, no. 2 (1997): 316-343.

Hartman, Ian C. *In the Shadow of Boone and Crocket: Race, Culture, and the Politics of Representation in the Upland South*. Knoxville: University of Tennessee Press, 2015.

———. "West Virginia Mountaineers and Kentucky Frontiersman: Race, Manliness, and the Rhetoric of Liberalism in the Early 1960s." *Journal of Southern History* 80, no. 3 (August 2014): 651-678.

Hartman, Saidiya V. *Scenes of Subjection: Terror, Slavery, and Self-Making in Nineteenth-Century America*. New York and London: Oxford University Press, 1997.

Haynes, John E. "Revolt of the 'Timber Beasts': IWW Lumber Strike in Minnesota." *Minnesota History* 42, no. 5 (1971): 162-174.

Hays, Matthew. "*In Cold Blood* (review)." *Cineaste* 41, no. 2 (Spring 2016): 64-65.

Heap, Chad. *Slumming: Sexual and Racial Encounters in American Nightlife, 1885-1940*. Chicago: University of Chicago Press, 2008.

Herring, Scott. *Another Country: Queer Anti-Urbanism*. New York and London: New York University Press, 2010.

———. "Hixploitation Cinema, Regional Drive-Ins, and the Cultural Emergence of a Queer New Right." *GLQ: A Journal of Gay and Lesbian Studies* 20, no. 1-2 (2014): 95-113.

Holmes, Kwame. "What's the Tea: Gossip and the Production of Black Gay Social History." *Radical History Review* 122 (May 2015): 55-56.

Howard, John. *Men Like That: A Southern Queer History*. Chicago and London: University of Chicago Press, 1999.

Hyler, S. E., G. O. Gabbard, and I. Schneider. "Homicidal Maniacs and Narcissistic Parasites: Stigmatization of Mentally Ill Persons in the Movies." *Hospital and Community Psychiatry* 42, no. 10 (1991): 1044-1048.

Im, D. S. "Template to Perpetrate: An Update on Violence in Autism Spectrum Disorder." *Harvard Review of Psychiatry* 24, no. 1 (January-February 2016): 14-25.

Isaac, Allan Punzalan. *American Tropics: Articulating Filipino America*. Minneapolis and London: University of Minnesota Press, 2006.

Jacobson, Matthew Frye. *Whiteness of a Different Color: European Immigrants and the Alchemy of Race*. Cambridge, MA, and London: Harvard University Press, 1998.

Jacoby, Karl. *Crimes Against Nature: Squatters, Poachers, Thieves, and the Hidden History of American Conservation*. Berkeley: University of California Press, 2014.

Jarman, Michelle. "Dismembering the Lynch Mob: Intersecting Narratives of Disability, Race, and Sexual Menace." In *Sex and Disability*, ed. Robert McRuer and Anna Mollow, 89-107. Durham, NC, and London: Duke University Press, 2012.

Jennings, Audra. *Out of the Horrors of War: Disability Politics in World War II America*. Philadelphia: University of Pennsylvania Press, 2016.

Johnson, Colin. *Just Queer Folks: Gender, Sexuality, and Rural America*. Philadelphia: Temple University Press, 2013.

Johnson, Colin R., Brian G. Gilley, and Mary L. Gray. *Queering the Countryside: New Frontiers in Rural Queer Studies*. New York and London: New York University Press, 2016.

Johnson, E. Patrick. *Black. Queer. Southern. Women: An Oral History*. Chapel Hill: University of North Carolina Press, 2019.

———. *Sweet Tea: Black Gay Men of the South*. Chapel Hill: University of North Carolina Press, 2008.

Johnson, Merri Lisa, and Robert McRuer. "Cripistemologies: Introduction." *Journal of Literary and Cultural Disability Studies* 8, no. 2 (2014): 127–147.

Johnson, Victoria E. *Heartland TV: Prime Time Television and the Struggle for U.S. Identity*. New York and London: New York University Press, 2008.

Kafer, Alison. *Feminist Queer Crip*. Bloomington and Indianapolis: Indiana University Press, 2013.

Kandaswamy, Priya. "'You Trade in a Man for The Man': Domestic Violence and the U.S. Welfare State." *American Quarterly* 62, no. 2 (June 2010): 253–277.

Karaminski, Theodore J. *Deep Woods Frontier: A History of Logging in Northern Michigan*. Detroit: Wayne State University Press, 1989.

Katz, Michael B. *In the Shadow of the Poorhouse: A Social History of Welfare in America*. New York: Basic Books, 1996.

———. *The Undeserving Poor: From the War on Poverty to the War on Welfare*. New York: Pantheon Books, 1989.

Kelley, Robin D. G. *Race Rebels: Culture, Politics, and the Black Working Class*. New York: The Free Press, 1996.

Kemple, Thomas M. "Litigating Illiteracy: The Media, the Law, and *The People of the State of New York v. Adelbert Ward*." *Canadian Journal of Law and Society* 10, no. 2 (Fall 1995): 73–97.

Kempton, Winifred, and Emily Khan. "Sexuality and People with Intellectual Disabilities: A Historical Perspective." *Sexuality and Disability* 9, no. 2 (1991): 93–111.

Kennedy, Elizabeth Lapovsky, and Madeline D. Davis. *Boots of Leather, Slippers of Gold: The History of a Lesbian Community*. New York and London: Routledge, 1993.

Kim, Jina B. "Toward a Crip-of-Color Critique: Thinking with Minich's 'Enabling Whom?'" *Lateral* 6, no. 1 (Spring 2017).

Klein, Jennifer, and Eileen Boris. "We Have to Take It to the Top: Workers, State Policy, and the Making of Home Care." *Buffalo Law Review* 61 (2013): 291–321.

Kline, Wendy. *Building a Better Race: Gender, Sexuality, and Eugenics from the Turn of the Century to the Baby Boom*. Minneapolis: University of Minnesota Press, 2001.

Klotter, James C. "The Black South and White Appalachia." *Journal of American History* 66, no. 4 (1980): 832–849.

Knobloch, Frieda. *The Culture of Wilderness: Agriculture as Colonization in the American West*. Chapel Hill and London: University of North Carolina Press, 1996.

Kornbluh, Felicia, and Karen Tani. "Siting the Legal History of Poverty: Below, Above, and Amidst." In *A Companion to American Legal History*, ed. Sally E. Hadden and Alfred L. Brophy, 329–348. Malden, MA: Wiley-Blackwell, 2013.

Kozol, Wendy. "Madonnas of the Fields: Photography, Gender, and 1930s Farm Relief." *Genders* 2, no. 2 (1988): 1–23.

Kudlick, Catherine. *Reflections: The Life and Writings of a Young Blind Woman in Post-Revolutionary France*. New York: New York University Press, 2001.

Kunzel, Regina. *Criminal Intimacy: Prison and the Uneven History of Modern American Sexuality.* Chicago: University of Chicago Press, 2008.

——. "Queer History, Mad History, and the Politics of Health." *American Quarterly* 69, no. 2 (June 2017): 315–319.

Lancaster, Roger N. *Sex Panic and the Punitive State.* Berkeley and Los Angeles: University of California Press, 2011.

Lave, Tamara Rice. "Only Yesterday: The Rise and Fall of Twentieth Century Sexual Psychopath Laws." *Louisiana Law Review* 69 (2009): 549–591.

Lawrence, Jane. "The Indian Health Service and the Sterilization of Native American Women." *American Indian Quarterly* 24, no. 3 (2000): 400–419.

Lawrie, Paul D. "'Salvaging the Negro': Race, Rehabilitation, and the Body Politic in World War I America, 1917–1924." In *Disability Histories,* ed. Susan Burch and Michael Rembis, 321–344. Urbana: University of Illinois Press, 2014.

Levin, Josh. *The Queen: The Forgotten Life Behind an American Myth.* New York: Little, Brown, and Company, 2019.

Levine, Lawrence W. "The Historian and the Icon: Photography and the History of the American People in the 1930s and 1940s." In *Documenting America,* ed. Carl Fleischhauer and Beverly W. Brannan, 15–42. Berkeley and Los Angeles: University of California Press, 1988.

Linker, Beth. *War's Waste: Rehabilitation in World War I America.* Chicago and London: University of Chicago Press, 2011.

Lipsitz, George. *The Possessive Investment in Whiteness: How White People Profit from Identity Politics.* Philadelphia: Temple University Press, 2006.

——. "The Possessive Investment in Whiteness: Racialized Social Democracy and the 'White' Problem in American Studies." *American Quarterly* 47, no. 3 (September 1995): 369–387.

Loew, Patty, and Kelly Mella. "Black Ink and New Red Power: Native American Newspapers and Tribal Sovereignty." *Journalism and Communication Monographs* 7, no. 3 (September 1, 2005): 99–142.

Longmore, Paul K., and David Goldberger. "The League of the Physically Handicapped and the Great Depression: A Case Study in the New Disability History." *Journal of American History* 87, no. 3 (December 2000): 888–922.

Longmore, Paul K., and Lauri Umansky, eds. *The New Disability History: American Perspectives.* New York: New York University Press, 2001.

Love, Heather. *Feeling Backward: Loss and the Politics of Queer History.* Cambridge, MA, and London: Harvard University Press, 2007.

Lovett, Laura L. *Conceiving the Future: Pronatalism, Reproduction, and the Family in the United States, 1890–1938.* Chapel Hill: University of North Carolina Press, 2007.

Luibhéid, Eithne. *Entry Denied: Controlling Sexuality at the Border.* Minneapolis: University of Minnesota Press, 2002.

Lunbeck, Elizabeth. *The Psychiatric Persuasion: Knowledge, Gender, and Power in Modern America.* Princeton, NJ: Princeton University Press, 1994.

Lye, Colleen. *America's Asia: Racial Form and American Literature, 1893–1945.* Princeton, NJ, and Oxford: Princeton University Press, 2005.

Madden, Ed. "The Buggering Hillbilly and the Buddy Movie." In *The Way We Read James Dickey: Critical Approaches for the Twenty-First Century,* ed. William B. Thesing and Theda Wrede, 195–227. Columbia: University of South Carolina Press, 2009.

Madhavan, T., and J. Narayan. "Consanguinity and Mental Retardation." *Journal of Intellectual Disability Research* 35, no. 2 (1991): 133–139.

Manalansan, Martin F. IV, Chantal Nadeau, Richard T. Rodríguez, and Siobhan B. Somerville. "Queering the Middle: Race, Region, and a Queer Midwest." *GLQ: A Journal of Lesbian and Gay Studies* 20, no. 1–2 (2014): 1–12.

Mason, Carol. "The Hillbilly Defense: Culturally Mediating U.S. Terror at Home and Abroad." *NWSA Journal* 17, no. 3 (Fall 2005): 39–63.

Mason, Gail. "Being Hated: Stranger or Familiar?" *Social and Legal Studies* 25, no. 4 (2005): 585–605.

McCarroll, Meredith. *Unwhite: Appalachia, Race, and Film*. Athens: University of Georgia Press, 2018.

McNamara, Jacks Ashley. "On Access Intimacy and Mental Health." *Icarus Project*, August 26, 2013, http://www.theicarusproject.net/article/on-access-intimacy-and -mental-health.

McRuer, Robert. *Crip Theory: Cultural Signs of Queerness and Disability*. New York: New York University Press, 2006.

Meeker, Martin. "The Queerly Disadvantaged and the Making of San Francisco's War on Poverty, 1964–1967." *Pacific Historical Review* 81, no. 1 (February 2012): 21–59.

Melosh, Barbara. *Engendering Culture: Manhood and Womanhood in New Deal Public Art and Theater*. Washington, DC, and London: Smithsonian Institution Press, 1991.

Mental Retardation in America: A Historical Reader, ed. Steven Noll and James W. Trent Jr. New York: New York University Press, 2004.

Metzl, Jonathan. *The Protest Psychosis: How Schizophrenia Became a Black Disease*. Boston: Beacon Press, 2010.

Meyerowitz, Joanne. *How Sex Changed: A History of Transsexuality in the United States*. Cambridge, MA: Harvard University Press, 2002.

Miller, Heather Lee. "Sexologists Examine Lesbians and Prostitutes in the United States, 1840–1940." *NWSA Journal* 12, no. 3 (2000): 67–91.

Miller, Neil. *Sex-Crime Panic: A Journey to the Paranoid Heart of the 1950s*. New York: Alyson Books, 2009.

Mingus, William, and Bradley Zopf. "White Means Never Having to Say You're Sorry: The Racial Project in Explaining Mass Shootings." *Social Thought & Research* 31 (2010): 57–77.

Minich, Julie Avril. "Enabling Whom? Critical Disability Studies Now." *Lateral* 5, no.1 (Spring 2016).

Miranda, Deborah. "Extermination of the *Joyas*: Gendercide in Spanish California." *GLQ: A Journal of Lesbian and Gay Studies* 16, no. 1–2 (2010): 253–284.

Mitchell, David T., and Sharon L. Snyder. *Biopolitics of Disability: Neoliberalism, Ablenationalism, and Peripheral Embodiment*. Ann Arbor: University of Michigan Press, 2015.

Mitchell, Don. *The Lie of the Land: Migrant Workers and the California Landscape*. Minneapolis and London: University of Minnesota Press, 1996.

Mitchell, Roger E. "The Press, Rumor, and Legend Formation." *Midwestern Journal of Language and Folklore* 5, no. 1/2 (Spring/Fall 1979): 5–61.

Mitchell, Stacy. "Union in the North Woods: The Timber Strikes of 1937." *Minnesota History* 56, no. 5 (April 1, 1999): 262–277.

Mitchell, W. J. T. *Landscape and Power*. Chicago: University of Chicago Press, 2002.

Mittelholtz, Erwin F., and Rose Graves. *Historical Review of the Red Lake Indian Reservation: A History of Its People and Progress*. Bemidji, MN: Beltrami County Historical Society, 1957.

Moore, Leroy F. "Krip-Hop Nation, Is Moore than Music." *Wordgathering* 22 (2009).

Morales, Aurora Levins. *Kindling: Writings on the Body*. Cambridge, MA: Palabrera Press, 2013.

———. "Sweet Dark Places: Letter to Gloria Anzaldua on Disability, Creativity, and the Coatlicue State." In *El Mundo Zurdo* 2, ed. Sonia Saldivar-Hull and Norma Alarcon, 75–98. San Francisco: Aunt Lute Books, 2012.

Moreton, Bethany. "Why Is There So Much Sex in Christian Conservatism and Why Do So Few Historians Care Anything about It?" *Journal of Southern History* 75, no. 3 (August 2009): 717–738.

Muir, John K. *Wes Craven: The Art of Horror*. Jefferson, NC: McFarland & Company, Inc., 2004.

Mukherjee, Roopali. *Racial Order of Things: Cultural Imaginaries of the Post-Soul Era*. Minneapolis and London: University of Minnesota Press, 2006.

Mumford, Kevin. *Interzones: Black/White Sex Districts in Chicago and New York in the Early Twentieth Century*. New York: Columbia University Press, 1997.

———. "Untangling Pathology: The Moynihan Report and Homosexual Damage, 1965–1975." *Journal of Policy History* 24, no. 1 (2012): 53–73.

Muncy, Robyn. "Coal-Fired Reforms: Social Citizenship, Dissident Miners, and the Great Society." *Journal of American History* 96, no. 1 (June 2009): 72–98.

Murphy, Mary. "Picture/Story: Representing Gender in Montana Farm Security Administration Photographs." *Frontiers—A Journal of Women's Studies* 22, no. 3 (2001): 93–117.

———. "The Private Lives of Public Women: Prostitution in Butte, Montana, 1878–1917." *Frontiers: A Journal of Women Studies* 7, no. 3 (1984): 30–35.

Murray, Caitlin. "'The Colouring of Psychosis': Interpreting Insanity in the Primitive Mind." *Health and History* 9, no. 2 (2007): 7–21.

Nadasen, Premilla. "Expanding the Boundaries of the Women's Movement: Black Feminism and the Struggle for Welfare Rights." *Feminist Studies* 28, no. 2 (Summer 2002): 270–301.

Nakamura, Karen. *A Disability of the Soul: An Ethnography of Schizophrenia and Mental Illness in Contemporary Japan*. Ithaca, NY, and London: Cornell University Press, 2013.

Natanson, Nicholas. *The Black Image in the New Deal: The Politics of FSA Photography*. Knoxville: University of Tennessee Press, 1992.

Nelson, Jennifer. *Women of Color and the Reproductive Rights Movement*. New York and London: New York University Press, 2003.

Nelson, Joel I., and Jon Lorence. "Industrialization and Income Change: Rural-Urban Comparisons in a Decade of Affluence." *Sociological Perspectives* 28, no. 1 (January 1985): 71–86.

Nestle, Joan. *A Restricted Country*, 3rd ed. San Francisco: Cleis Press, 2003.

Nielsen, Kim. *A Disability History of the United States*. Boston: Beacon Press, 2012.

Noll, Steven. *Feeble-Minded in Our Midst: Institutions for the Mentally Retarded in the South, 1900–1940*. Chapel Hill: University of North Carolina Press, 1995.

Norden, Martin F. *The Cinema of Isolation: A History of Physical Disability in the Movies*. New Brunswick, NJ: Rutgers University Press, 1994.

Novak, Nicole, Natalie Lira, Kate E. O'Connor, Siobán D. Harlow, Sharon L. R. Kardia, and Alexandra Minna Stern. "Disproportionate Sterilization of Latinos under California's Eugenic Sterilization Program, 1920-1946." *American Journal of Public Health* 108, no. 5 (May 2018): 611-613.

Oliver, Michael. *The Politics of Disablement.* London: Macmillan Publishing, 1990.

Ordover, Nancy. *American Eugenics: Race, Queer Anatomy, and the Science of Nationalism.* Minneapolis: University of Minnesota, 2003.

Orleck, Annalise. *Storming Caesar's Palace: How Black Mothers Fought Their Own War on Poverty.* Boston: Beacon Press, 2006.

Patsavas, Alyson. "Recovering a Cripistemology of Pain: Leaky Bodies, Connective Tissue, and Feeling Discourse." *Journal of Literary and Cultural Disability Studies* 8, no. 2 (2014): 203-218.

Patterned Peatlands of Minnesota, ed. H. E. Wright Jr. and Norman E. Aaseng. Minneapolis and London: University of Minnesota Press, 1992.

Patterson, James T. *America's Struggle Against Poverty in the Twentieth Century.* Cambridge, MA: Harvard University Press, 2000.

Paul, Diane B., and Hamish G. Spencer. " 'It's Ok, We're Not Cousins by Blood': The Cousin Marriage Controversy in Historical Perspective." *PLOS Biology* 6, no. 12 (December 2008): 2627-2630.

Pérez, Hiram. *A Taste for Brown Bodies: Gay Modernity and Cosmopolitan Desire.* New York: New York University Press, 2015.

Perske, Robert. "Search for Persons with Intellectual Disabilities Who Confessed to Crimes They Did Not Commit." *Mental Retardation* 43, no. 1 (February 2005): 58-65.

Phillips, John. *Transgender on Screen.* London: Palgrave Macmillan UK, 2006.

Piatote, Beth. *Domestic Subjects: Gender, Citizenship, and Law in Native American Literature.* New Haven, CT: Yale University Press, 2013.

Place, Janey. "Deliverance." In *Magill's Survey of Cinema,* ed. Frank N. Magill, vol. 1. Englewood Cliffs, NJ: Salem Press, n.d.

Prendergast, Catherine. "On the Rhetorics of Mental Disability." In *Embodied Rhetorics: Disability in Language and Culture,* ed. James C. Wilson and Cynthia Lewiecki-Wilson, 45-60. Carbondale and Edwardsville: Southern Illinois University Press, 2001.

Price, Margaret. *Mad at School: Rhetorics of Mental Disability and Academic Life.* Ann Arbor: University of Michigan Press, 2011.

Quadagno, Jill, and Catherine Fobes. "The Welfare State and the Cultural Reproduction of Gender: Making Good Girls and Boys in the Job Corps." *Social Problems* 42, no. 2 (May 1995): 171-190.

Rafter, Nicole Hahn. *White Trash: The Eugenic Family Studies, 1877-1919.* Boston: Northeastern University Press, 1988.

Raz, Mical. *What's Wrong with the Poor? Psychiatry, Race, and the War on Poverty.* Chapel Hill: University of North Carolina Press, 2013.

Razack, Sherene H. "When Place Becomes Race." In *Race, Space, and Law: Unmapping a White Settler Society,* 1-20. Toronto: Between the Lines, 2002.

Reilly, Philip. *The Surgical Solution: A History of Involuntary Sterilization in the United States.* Baltimore: Johns Hopkins University Press, 1991.

Rembis, Michael. *Defining Deviance: Sex, Science, and Delinquent Girls 1890-1960.* Urbana: University of Illinois Press, 2013.

———. "Introduction." In *Disabling Domesticity*, 1–23. New York: Palgrave Macmillan, 2017.

Retman, Sonnet. *Real Folks: Race and Genre in the Great Depression*. Durham, NC: Duke University Press, 2011.

Reynolds, David. "White Trash in Your Face: The Literary Descent of Dorothy Allison." *Appalachian Journal* 20, no. 4 (Summer 1993): 356–366.

Richardson, Matt. *The Queer Limit of Black Memory: Black Lesbian Literature and Irresolution*. Columbus: Ohio State University Press, 2013.

Rifkin, Mark. *When Did Indians Become Straight? Kinship, the History of Sexuality, and Native Sovereignty*. New York: Oxford University Press, 2011.

Roberts, Dorothy. *Fatal Invention: How Science, Politics, and Big Business Re-Create Race in the Twenty-First Century*. New York and London: The New Press, 2011.

———. *Killing the Black Body: Race, Reproduction, and the Meaning of Liberty*. New York: Vintage Books, 1997.

Root, Kenneth. "The Human Response to Plant Closures." *Annals of the American Academy of Political and Social Science* 475 (September 1984): 52–65.

Rose, Sarah. "'Crippled' Hands: Disability in Labor and Working-Class History." *Labor: Studies in the Working-Class History of the Americas* 2, no. 1 (2005): 27–54.

———. *No Right to Be Idle: The Invention of Disability, 1840s–1930s*. Chapel Hill: University of North Carolina Press, 2017.

Rosen, Ruth. *The Lost Sisterhood: Prostitution in America, 1900–1918*. Baltimore: Johns Hopkins University Press, 1982.

Rowland, D. T. "Theories of Urbanization in Australia." *Geographical Review* 67, no. 2 (April 1, 1977): 167–176.

Rubin, Gayle. "Thinking Sex: Notes for a Radical Theory of the Politics of Sexuality." In *The Lesbian and Gay Studies Reader*, ed. Henry Abelove, Michele Aina Barale, and David M. Halpern, 3–44. New York: Routledge Press, 1993.

Ruby, Jay. "Appalachia Portraits." *Appalachian Journal* 23, no. 3 (Spring 1996): 337–341.

Saloutos, Theodore. *The American Farmer and the New Deal*. Ames: Iowa State University Press, 1982.

Sandahl, Carrie. "Queering the Crip, or Cripping the Queer? Intersections of Queer and Crip Identities in Solo Autobiographical Performance." *GLQ: A Journal of Lesbian and Gay Studies* 9, no. 1–2 (2003): 25–56.

Scandura, Jani. *Down in the Dumps: Place, Modernity, American Depression*. Durham, NC: Duke University Press, 2008.

Schalk, Sami. *Bodyminds Reimagined: (Dis)ability, Race, and Gender in Black Women's Speculative Fiction*. Durham, NC: Duke University Press, 2018.

Schmitt, Edward R. "The Appalachian Thread in the Antipoverty Politics of Robert F. Kennedy." *Register of the Kentucky Historical Society* 107, no. 3 (Summer 2009): 371–400.

Schwartz, Joel. *Fighting Poverty with Virtue: Moral Reform and America's Urban Poor, 1825–2000*. Bloomington: Indiana University Press, 2000.

Schweik, Susan M. *The Ugly Laws: Disability in Public*. New York and London: New York University Press, 2009.

Sedgwick, Eve Kosofsky. *Epistemology of the Closet*. Berkeley: University of California Press, 2008 [1990].

———. *Tendencies.* Durham, NC: Duke University Press, 1993.

See, Sarita Echavez. *The Filipino Primitive: Accumulation and Resistance in the American Museum.* New York and London: New York University Press, 2017.

Serlin, David. *Replaceable You: Engineering the Body in Postwar America.* Chicago: University of Chicago Press, 2002.

Shah, Nayan. "Between 'Oriental Depravity' and 'Natural Degenerates': Spatial Borderlands and the Making of Ordinary Americans." *American Quarterly* 57, no. 3 (2005): 703–725.

———. *Contagious Divides: Epidemics and Race in San Francisco's Chinatown.* Berkeley and Los Angeles: University of California Press, 2001.

———. "Policing Privacy, Migrants, and the Limits of Freedom." *Social Text* 23, no. 3–4 (2005): 275–284.

———. *Stranger Intimacy: Contesting Race, Sexuality, and the Law in the North American West.* Berkeley: University of California Press, 2011.

Shapiro, Henry D. *Appalachia on Our Mind: The Southern Mountains and Mountaineers in the American Consciousness, 1870–1920.* Chapel Hill: University of North Carolina Press, 1978.

Sharrett, Christopher. "The Horror Film in Neoconservative Culture." *Journal of Popular Film and Television* 21, no. 3 (1993): 100–110.

Siebers, Tobin. *Disability Aesthetics.* Ann Arbor: University of Michigan Press, 2010.

———. *Disability Theory.* Ann Arbor: University of Michigan Press, 2008.

Simplican, Stacy Clifford. *The Capacity Contract: Intellectual Disability and the Question of Citizenship.* Minneapolis and London: University of Minnesota Press, 2015.

Skidmore, Emily. "Constructing the 'Good Transsexual': Christine Jorgensen, Whiteness, and Heteronormativity in the Mid-Twentieth-Century Press." *Feminist Studies* 37, no. 2 (Summer 2011): 270–300.

———. "Ralph Kerwineo's Queer Body: Narrating the Scales of Social Membership in the Early Twentieth Century." *GLQ: A Journal of Lesbian and Gay Studies* 20, no. 1–2 (2014): 141–166.

Slesinger, Doris P. "The Role and Future of Migrant Farmworkers in Wisconsin Agriculture." *Wisconsin Academy Review* 33, no. 1 (December 1986): 32–35.

Smith, Angela M. *Hideous Progeny: Disability, Eugenics, and Classic Horror Cinema.* New York: Columbia University Press, 2012.

Smith, Barbara. "Toward a Black Feminist Criticism." *Women's Studies International Quarterly* 2, no. 2 (1979): 183–194.

Smith, Barbara Ellen. "De-Gradations of Whiteness: Appalachia and the Complexities of Race." *Journal of Appalachian Studies* 10, no. 1/2 (Spring/Fall 2004): 38–57.

———. *Digging Our Own Graves: Coal Miners and the Struggle over Black Lung Disease.* Philadelphia: Temple University Press, 1987.

Smith, Erin A. *Hard Boiled: Working-Class Readers and Pulp Magazines.* Philadelphia: Temple University Press, 2000.

Smith, J. David. *Minds Made Feeble: The Myth and Legacy of the Kallikaks.* Rockville, MD: Aspen Publication, 1985.

Smith, Terry. *Making the Modern: Industry, Art, and Design in America.* Chicago: University of Chicago Press, 1994.

Snorton, C. Riley. *Black on Both Sides: A Racial History of Trans Identity.* Minneapolis and London: University of Minnesota Press, 2017.

Snyder, Sharon L., and David T. Mitchell. *Cultural Locations of Disability*. Chicago: University of Illinois Press, 2006.

Somerville, Siobhan. *Queering the Color Line: Race and the Invention of Homosexuality in American Culture*. Durham, NC, and London: Duke University Press, 2000.

Spacks, Patricia. *Gossip*. New York: Alfred A. Knopf, 1985.

Spirn, Anne Whiston. *Daring to Look: Dorothea Lange's Photographs and Reports from the Field*. Chicago: University of Chicago Press, 2008.

Stange, Maren. "'The Record Itself': Farm Security Administration Photography and the Transformation of Rural Life." In *Official Images: New Deal Photography*, ed. Pete Daniel, 1–5. Washington, DC, and London: Smithsonian Institution Press, 1987.

Stanley, Amy Dru. *From Bondage to Contract: Wage Labor, Marriage, and the Market in the Age of Slave Emancipation*. Cambridge and New York: Cambridge University Press, 1998.

Stein, Sally. "Peculiar Grace: Dorothea Lange and the Testimony of the Body." In *Dorothea Lange: A Visual Life*, ed. Elizabeth Partridge, 68–73. Washington, DC: Smithsonian Institution Press, 1994.

Stern, Alexandra Minna. *Eugenic Nation: Faults and Frontiers of Better Breeding in Modern America*. Berkeley and Los Angeles: University of California, 2005.

Stiker, Henri-Jacques. *A History of Disability*. Ann Arbor: University of Michigan Press, 1999 [1982].

Stone, Sandy. "The *Empire* Strikes Back: A Posttranssexual Manifesto." In *Body Guards: Cultural Politics of Sexual Ambiguity*, ed. Julia Epstein and Kristina Straub, 280–304. New York: Routledge, 1991.

Stryker, Susan. "*We Who Are Sexy*: Christine Jorgensen's Transsexual Whiteness in the Postcolonial Philippines." *Social Semiotics* 19, no. 1 (March 19, 2009): 79–91.

Sullivan, K. E. "Ed Gein and the Figure of the Transgendered Serial Killer." *Jump Cut: A Review of Contemporary Media* 43 (July 2000): 38–47.

Summers, Martin. "'Suitable Care of the African When Afflicted with Insanity': Race, Madness, and Social Order in Comparative Perspective." *Bulletin of the History of Medicine* 84, no. 1 (Spring 2010): 58–91.

Surdam, Maia A. "Families on Farms: Migrants, Farmers, and the Transformation of Wisconsin's Countryside, 1920s–1960s." PhD dissertation, University of Wisconsin-Madison, 2012.

Taylor, Brenda J. "The Farm Security Administration and Rural Families in the South: Home Economists, Nurses, and Farmers, 1933–1946." In *The New Deal and Beyond: Social Welfare in the South Since 1930*, ed. Elna C. Green, 34–40. Athens and London: University of Georgia Press, 2003.

Taylor, Sunaura. *Beasts of Burden: Animal and Disability Liberation*. New York and London: The New Press, 2017.

Terry, Jennifer. *An American Obsession: Science, Medicine, and Homosexuality in Modern Society*. Chicago: University of Chicago Press, 1999.

Titchkosky, Tanya. *The Question of Access: Disability, Space, and Meaning*. Toronto: University of Toronto Press, 2011.

Tomczik, Adam. "'He-Men Could Talk to He-Men in He-Man Language': Lumberjack Work Culture in Maine and Minnesota, 1840–1940." *Historian* 70, no. 4 (December 2008): 697–715.

Tongson, Karen. *Relocations: Queer Suburban Imaginaries*. New York: New York University Press, 2011.

Transgender Studies Reader, ed. Susan Stryker and Stephen Whittle. New York: Routledge Press, 2006.

Trent, James W. Jr. *Inventing the Feeble Mind: A History of Mental Retardation in the United States*. Berkeley and Los Angeles: University of California, 1995.

Tuck, Eve, and C. Ree. "A Glossary of Haunting." In *Handbook of Autoethnography*, ed. Stacey Holman Jones, Tony E. Adams, and Carolyn Ellis, 639–658. Walnut Creek, CA: Left Coast Press, 2013.

Tuck, Eve, and K. Wayne Yang. "Decolonization Is Not a Metaphor." *Decolonization: Indigeneity, Education, & Society* 1, no. 1 (2012): 1–40.

Tullos, Allen. *Habits of Industry: White Culture and the Transformation of the Carolina Piedmont*. Chapel Hill: University of North Carolina Press, 1989.

Virdi, Jaipreet. "Prevention and Conservation: Historicizing the Stigma of Hearing Loss," 1910–1940." *Journal of Law, Medicine & Ethics* 45 (2017): 531–544.

Wahl, Otto F. *Media Madness: Public Images of Mental Illness*. New Brunswick, NJ: Rutgers University Press, 1997.

———. "Stop the Presses: Journalistic Treatment of Mental Illness." In *Cultural Sutures: Medicine and Media*, ed. L. D. Friedman, 55–69. Durham, NC, and London: Duke University Press, 2004.

Wald, Sarah D. *The Nature of California: Race, Citizenship, and Farming Since the Dust Bowl*. Seattle: University of Washington Press, 2016.

Walker, William. "John C. Ewers and the Problem of Cultural History: Displaying American Indians at the Smithsonian in the Fifties." *Museum History Journal* 1, no. 1 (2008): 51–74.

Wang, Esmé Weijun. *The Collected Schizophrenias: Essays*. Minneapolis: Graywolf Press, 2019.

Watson, Elwood, and Darcy Martin. "The Miss America Pageant: Pluralism, Femininity, and Cinderella All in One." *Journal of Popular Culture* 34, no. 1 (2000): 105–126.

Weston, Kath. "Get Thee to a Big City: Sexual Imaginary and the Great Gay Migration." *GLQ: A Journal of Lesbian and Gay Studies* 2, no. 3 (1995): 253–277.

Wiegman, Robyn. "Whiteness Studies and the Paradox of Particularity." *boundary 2* 26, no. 3 (Autumn 1999): 115–150.

Wilkerson, Abby L. "Disability, Sex Radicalism, and Political Agency." *NWSA Journal* 14, no. 3 (2003): 33–57.

Wilkerson, Jessica. *To Live Here, You Have to Fight: How Women Led Appalachian Movements for Social Justice*. Urbana, Chicago, and Springfield: University of Illinois Press, 2019.

Williams, Patricia J. *The Alchemy of Race and Rights*. Cambridge, MA, and London: Harvard University Press, 1991.

Williams, Raymond. *The Country and the City*. New York: Oxford University Press, 1973.

Williams, Tony. *Hearths of Darkness: The Family in the American Horror Film*. Cranbury, NJ: Associated University Presses, 1996.

Williamson, J. W. *Hillbillyland: What the Movies Did to the Mountains & What the Mountains Did to the Movies*. Chapel Hill: University of North Carolina Press, 1995.

Willoughby-Herard, Tiffany. *Waste of a White Skin: The Carnegie Corporation and the Racial Logic of White Vulnerability*. Oakland: University of California Press, 2015.

Wolfe, Patrick. "Settler Colonialism and the Elimination of the Native." *Journal of Genocide Research* 8, no. 4 (2006): 387–409.

Wood, Robin. *Hollywood from Vietnam to Reagan . . . and Beyond*. New York: Columbia University Press, 2003.

Wray, Matt. *Not Quite White: White Trash and the Boundaries of Whiteness*. Durham, NC, and London: Duke University Press, 2006.

Wyman, Marilyn. "Affirming Whiteness: Visualizing California Agriculture." *Steinbeck Studies* 16, no. 1 (2007): 32–55.

Yar, Majid, and Nicole Rafter. "Justice for the Disabled: Crime Films on Punishment and the Human Rights of People with Learning Disabilities." In *Law, Culture and Visual Studies*, ed. Anne Wagner and Richard K. Sherwin, 791–804. Dordrecht: Springer Netherlands, 2014.

Yergeau, Melanie. *Authoring Autism: On Rhetoric and Neurological Queerness*. Durham, NC, and London: Duke University Press, 2018.

Yu, Henry. *Thinking Orientals: Migration, Contact, and Exoticism in Modern America*. Oxford: Oxford University Press, 2002.

Zenderland, Leila. *Measuring Minds: Henry Herbert Goddard and the Origins of American Intelligence Testing*. Cambridge: Cambridge University Press, 2001.

INDEX

Page numbers in italics refer to figures.

Mexican, 105, 109, 168, 211n172; "Migrant Mother" photograph, 53
Miller, Milton, 208n84
Milwaukee Journal, 93, 100, 109
Miners of Democracy, 141
Mingus, Mia, 173-74
Minneapolis Tribune, 93, 95, 102
Minnesota, 32, 42, 102, 119, 202n37; Faribault, 6; Lake of the Woods County, 61, 75, 203n60; northern, 52, 61-77, 203nn78-79; Spooner, 64-65, 69, 74. *See also* Northern Minnesota Pioneers' Home; North Woods; Red Lake Indian Reservation
Minnesota Rural Rehabilitation Corporation (MRRC), 201n32. *See also* Beltrami Island Project
Minnesota State School for the Feeble-Minded, 6, 35
Missouri, 58, 189
Mitchell, Roger, 101
Mitchell, W. J. T., 163
Mobilization for Youth, 121
momism, 96-97
Mongrel Virginians, 46
moral disability/moral imbecility/moral insanity/moronism, 31, 116
moral panics, 90, 163, 168
Moyers, Bill, 127
Moynihan, Daniel Patrick, 121, 123, 125
Mrs. America figure, 52-54, 61-62, 77-79
Mulder, Arnold: *Bram of the Five Corners*, 35, 45
Mumford, Kevin, 123
Muska, Susan, 167, 185. See also *Brandon Teena Story, The*
mutual aid, 3, 16, 74, 84, 168

Nakamura, Karen, 92
National Geographic, 106
Nazis, 107, 170
Nebraska, 12, 167, 184; Falls City, 169, 182-83, 185-86, 222n59; Humboldt, 23, 169-70, 181-85; Lincoln, 169, 185-86, 222n66; North Platte, 78-80, 82-83, 204n93; Omaha, 78-79, 82, 185
Nelson Allotment Act, 76

nerves, 14, 122, 125, 129, 136-37, 139, 177
Nestle, Joan, 82
neuroqueers, 188
Nevada, 204n109
New Deal, 52, 62, 66, 76, 84
New England, 18, 30-32. *See also individual states*
New Jersey, 25
New London Press, 113
Newsweek, 95, 139
New Yorker, 12, 23, 181, 183
New York State, 1, 82, 170, 189, 220n25; Kingston, 187; Munnsville, 2-3, 168-69, 171, 176, 178-80; New York City, 83, 121, 165, 167, 185, 187-88, 193n22; Syracuse, 178
New York Times, 5, 142, 153, 175, 179
Nissen, Marvin "Tom," 181-86
noble poor, 54
nonce taxonomy, 19
nonheteronormativity, 4, 10-11, 59, 62, 72, 119, 122-23, 125, 168
North Carolina, 19, 56, 59, 128, 136; Rocky Mount, 127-29, 133-34, 216n78
Northern Minnesota Pioneers' Home, 52, 59, 62-77, 84
North Woods, 64-65, 73-74

Očhéthi Šakówiŋ, 184. *See also* Sioux
oedipal complex, 93, 95, 207n70
Office of Juvenile Delinquency (OJD), 136, 216n82
Office of War Information, 200n3. *See also* Farm Security Administration (FSA)
Ojibwe, 114, 203n79; Red Lake Ojibwe, 63-64, 75-77, 202nn37-38
Okie figure, 12
Ólafsdottir, Gréta, 167, 185. See also *Brandon Teena Story, The*
Old Age Assistance (OAA), 62, 74, 201n31
Old Age Insurance (OAI), 201n31
Omaha World-Herald, 82, 183
orientalism, 46, 107
"other America," 119, 121, 123
O'Toole, Corbett, 188
Ott, Katherine, 13